Visitor's
NORTHER

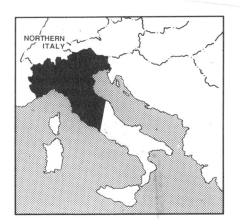

VISITOR'S GUIDE
Northern Italy

Amanda Hinton

MPC
HUNTER

Published by:
Moorland Publishing Co Ltd,
Moor Farm Road West,
Ashbourne,
Derbyshire DE6 1HD
England

ISBN 0 86190 432 X

Published in the USA by:
Hunter Publishing Inc,
300 Raritan Center Parkway,
CN 94, Edison, NJ 08818
ISBN 1 55650 533 7 (USA)

British Library Cataloguing in
Publication Data:
A catalogue record for this book is
available from the British Library.

Colour origination by:
P. & W. Graphics Pte Ltd, Singapore

Printed in the UK by:
Richard Clay Ltd, Bungay, Suffolk

Cover photograph: *Gondolas, Venice*
(International Photobank)

The illustrations have been
supplied by:

Amanda Hinton: pp 15, 30 (top), 42
(bottom), 47, 55, 63, 70 (top), 79, 83
(both), 95 (both), 107, 114, 123, 126,
127 (top), 130, 134, 143, 146, 150,
159 (both), 162 (both), 166, 170, 179,
183, 198 (both), 203, 206, 215 (both),
218, 230, 231; MPC Picture Library:
87; Italian National Tourist Office:
18, 22, 23, 42 (top), 46, 67, 70
(bottom), 103, 127 (bottom), 147,
219.

MPC Production Team:
Editorial: Tonya Monk
Design: Dan Clarke
Cartography: Alastair Morrison
Typesetting: Christine Haines

CONTENTS

Key to Symbols Used in Text Margin and on Maps

🚶 Recommended walk

🐐 Nature reserve/Animal interest

🌼 Garden

🐦 Birdlife

♣ Parks

❋ Other place of interest

⛪ Church/Ecclesiastical site

🏛 Building of interest

⊓ Archaeological site

🏛 Museum/Art gallery

🌲 Beautiful view/Scenery, Natural phenomenon

🎿 Skiing facilities

⛵ Watersport facilities

Key to Maps

▨ • City/Town

▬▬▬ Main road

═══ Motorway

– – – – Country Boundry

—·—·— Provincial Boundry

〜〜 Rivers/Lakes

How To Use This Guide

This MPC Visitor's Guide has been designed to be as easy to use as possible. Each chapter covers a region or itinerary in a natural progression which gives all the background information to help you enjoy your visit. MPC's distinctive margin symbols, the important places printed in bold, and a comprehensive index enable the reader to find the most interesting places to visit with ease. At the end of each chapter an Additional Information section gives specific details such as addresses and opening times, making this guide a complete sightseeing companion. At the back of the guide the Fact File, arranged in alphabetical order, gives practical information and useful tips to help you plan your holiday — before you go and while you are there. The maps of each region show the main towns, villages, roads and places of interest, but are not designed as route maps and motorists should always use a good recommended road atlas.

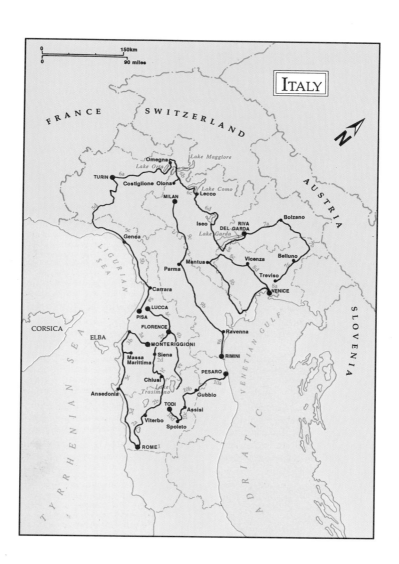

ITALY

150km

90 miles

FRANCE
SWITZERLAND
AUSTRIA
SLOVENIA

Lake Maggiore
Omegna
Lake Orta
6a
TURIN
Costiglione Olona
6d
MILAN
Lake Como
Lecco
Iseo
Lake Garda
RIVA DEL GARDA
7a
Bolzano
6c
Genoa
Parma
Mantua
Vicenza
Belluno
Treviso
8a
VENICE
Carrara
LUCCA
PISA
FLORENCE
MONTERIGGIONI
Siena
2d
Massa Marittima
Ravenna
RIMINI
PESARO
Chiusi
Lake Trasimeno
Gubbio
10a
10b
Ansedonia
TODI
Assisi
Viterbo
Spoleto
ROME

CORSICA
ELBA
L I G U R I A N   S E A
T Y R R H E N I A N   S E A
A D R I A T I C
V E N E T I A N   G U L F

INTRODUCTION

Northern Italy has many facets, like a gem stone, and at least one of its delightful aspects is sure to appeal to any visitor. Its towns and cities are packed with fine architecture, and its numerous museums are filled, almost to overflowing, with collections of some of the greatest works of art in Europe. The landscape has great natural beauty, whether it is the rugged Alps or the more homely, rolling hills of Tuscany. It produces an enormous variety of quality wines, cheeses and other delicacies, while restaurants offer exquisite food and often specialise in the regional cuisine.

The area has attracted foreign visitors since travel became popular in the eighteenth century so do not expect to venture off into the unknown. The Victorians came to sojourn here by the sparkling blue waters of the northern lakes, while Britain's young dandies came to complete their education, on what was known as the Grand Tour.

The ten interconnecting routes in this book cover most of Northern Italy, taking in all the major places of interest as well as many of the lesser-known. Each chapter is carefully planned so as to follow the most picturesque route from one place to the next, although more direct routes are often suggested for those in a hurry. Only where there is little of interest, or where the roads are particularly congested, are visitors recommended to take motorways, as the smaller roads are generally quite good and pass through much more interesting terrain. Each route is divided into sections, which are well-packed with sights, and can be generally regarded as about two days worth of travelling.

THE REGIONS

Northern Italy is largely contained within natural borders, the Alps and Dolomites forming the northern boundary between France, Switzerland and Austria. Its western shores are washed by the Ligurian and Tyrrhenian seas, while the Adriatic sea laps the east coast. At the base of the northern mountain ranges lay a series of lakes, and below them the flat expanse of the Po river plain. The southern edge of the plain is bounded by the Apennine Mountains, which run southwards down the length of the peninsula like a rocky backbone, dividing east from west. The ten regions of Northern Italy covered in this book include: Liguria, Piedmont, Lombardy, Trentino-Alto Adige, Venetia, Emilia-Romagna, Tuscany and Umbria, plus a corner each of the Marches and Lazio. The major cities visited are spread across these regions and include Genoa, Turin, Milan, Venice, Florence, and of course Rome.

THE SEASONS

The best time to travel in Italy is during the milder seasons, spring and early autumn. The summer, hot and busy, reaches a frantic peak in August, when the entire Italian nation takes a month's holiday. This, rather oddly, often includes hotels and restaurants although it is the time of year when the resorts are at their liveliest and every town and city stages its summer festivals, fairs and other such local events. The winter months, as in other parts of Europe, are generally cold. The mountains offer excellent winter sport facilities, but the coastal resorts and inland towns tend to be rather dead, and museums and galleries have restricted opening hours.

HISTORY

Vulnerable to sea attack along its long coastlines and to land attack across its northern mountains, it is not surprising that Italy's history is peppered with foreign invasions. It would be wrong to assume though that Italy's position was always a disadvantage, for many of the invaders did not just bring havoc and destruction, but often assimilated into Italian society, enriching and diversifying it, and of course its location at the centre of the Mediterranean also gave the Italian maritime cities a head start in early European trade.

The earliest waves of migrants, dating from the second millennium BC, brought Alpine people from the north who then integrated with the indigenous neolithic peoples. At the same time as this, groups of highly cultured people were infiltrating from Greece and Asia Minor, some of whom might have been the ancestors of the Etruscans, the most powerful of Italy's early civilisations. Their culture bears more than a passing resemblance to that of the Lycians in Asia Minor, but whether indigenous or migrant, much of their cultural identity was passed on to the Romans, who succeeded them. The Roman Republic ruled from 509BC up until 31BC, after which the Roman Empire, ruled by an emperor, expanded its dominion over most of the known world.

The dissolution of the Roman Empire, around AD476, gradually lead to the break up of Italy into numerous small states. The Byzantine emperors clung to remnants of the Empire for as long as they could, but invasions by the Lombards and Franks, which started around AD500, wrested Northern Italy from their control. The medieval era saw a succession of wars between foreign kings, greedy popes and local dukes alike, so that Northern Italy was by and large a patchwork of petty states. By the fourteenth century it was the most divided and invaded country in Europe although, surprisingly, this turbulent climate not only produced a mass of excellent medieval art and architecture, but also spawned the Renaissance. This, perhaps the greatest period in Italian history, reached its peak during the sixteenth century.

The sack of Rome by Charles V in 1527 signalled, like the tolling of a bell, the symbolic end of the Renaissance. In the centuries that followed, Northern Italy was continually fought over by the French, Austrian and Spanish, and by the eighteenth century power was concentrated in the north in the hands of the Hapsburg dynasty in Lombardy, and King Carlo Alberto in Piedmont. Their rule offered security and brought about a period of intellectual enlightenment which gradually fuelled a movement towards Italian unity. The rule of the next king of Piedmont, Vittorio Emanuele II, was extended, after Garibaldi, who had won control over the southern part of the peninsula, handed it to him in 1861. Vittorio Emanuele II was then proclaimed King of Italy, although complete unification was not achieved until 1870, when Italian troops captured Rome.

The nineteenth century found Italy somewhat behind other countries in Europe in terms of living standards and industrial development and although improvements were attempted, the instability of the government and breakdowns in law and order, meant that little ground was gained. During the turbulent period after World War I the Italian Fascist party, headed by Mussolini, was born. Quickly rising to power Mussolini ruled Italy from 1922 up until 1943, entering it into World War II on the side of the Germans. Italy was liberated again after allied troops, who had landed at Anzio in 1944, gradually fought their way up through the peninsula. In 1946, a government mainly formed of Christian Democrats, took control of the Italian Republic and large companies, first established under Mussolini, such as Fiat and Olivetti, put Italy back on the road to economic prosperity. In 1956 it joined the European Economic Community and from 1959 to 1962 experienced an 'economic mir-acle', thanks mainly to the large reserves of cheap labour available in Southern Italy. Labour conditions and the social changes in the 1960s led to revolutions, strikes and student protests in the 70s, although in the last decade many of Italy's problems seem to have been smoothed out, and at the start of the 90s it was rated as the fifth leading industrial country in the developed world.

1

ROME

This chapter the most southerly in the book, is devoted entirely to Italy's capital, Rome. The first impression one gets of the city is one of noise and incessant movement, but gradually one becomes aware that beneath the bustle and the traffic there is a clear sense of order and of permanence. Ancient structures poke through Rome's modern exterior in great profusion, like the bones of a skeleton, and in parts the city resembles an architectural dig where all the layers and strata are exposed to view. The site was settled as early as the tenth century BC, although according to the ancient historian Varro, Rome itself was founded in 753BC. The true origins of its early rulers are unclear; myth has Romulus and Remus as the founders and a series of legendary kings as their successors, but what is known for sure is that the city was ruled by three Etruscan kings from 616BC to 509BC. The deposition of the last Etruscan king, Tarquinius Superbus, in 509BC marked the beginning of the Roman Republic and was quickly followed by the introduction of the Senate as the city's ruling body. Over the following centuries the city expanded rapidly as Rome conquered great tracts of land in and around the Mediterranean basin. After the murder of Julius Caesar in 44BC, the appointment 17 years later of his nephew Octavian (later to be named Augustus) as the first Emperor of Rome, heralded the Golden Age of the city. By the end of the first century Rome had already conquered half the known world and was unequalled in its wealth and power. Its pre-eminence, however, was not to last forever, a point made very forcibly by Constantine I, who chose Constantinople as his capital in AD330 and divided the Empire in two, east and west. In AD410 the city was humiliated at the hands of the Visigoths, under Alaric, and again in AD455 by the Vandals, under Genseric. It never really made much of a recovery during the following centuries, and it was only in AD800, when Charlemagne was crowned here and the Holy Roman Empire established, that things began to look a bit brighter. The next 600 years saw the city periodically afflicted by both plague and civil strife, but the presence of the papacy ensured the city's place at the centre of western Christianity. During the exile of the papal court to Avignon between 1305 and

1376 Rome degenerated, and it was not until 1420, with the return of papal authority under Martin V, that the city recovered some of its former glory. By the time Julius II came to the papacy in 1503, Rome had resumed its place as one of the world's foremost cities, and became a major centre of the Renaissance. Italy's general decline in the seventeenth century also took its toll on Rome, and the city was under foreign domination for almost two centuries before being made the capital of united Italy in 1871.

Today, Rome possesses an astounding wealth of art and architecture, with 7km (4 miles) of galleries in the Vatican alone, many ancient monuments and grand churches, numerous well-endowed museums, as well as major works by names such as Michelangelo and Raphael. So much in fact that the visitor can expect to see but a fraction of what is on offer before their appetite is sated. Added to this, the city has a great many attractive squares, over a thousand fountains as well as obelisks and statues left, right and centre.

Visitors should be cautioned that traffic is a real problem in Rome. It roars through the city from daybreak to the early hours of the morning, creating a considerable amount of noise and fumes. August, when the Romans are on holiday, is the city's quietest month, but it is also when the museums are busiest with tourists. The large number of tourists has unfortunately attracted a growing number of thieves. The culprits are usually seemingly-innocent children, who hang around the major tourist sights, namely the Colosseum, the Forums, the Pantheon, the Vatican and usually around the railway station too. They approach tourists in groups and proceed to search through pockets and bags for likely valuables at lightening speed. If you are attacked in this way, grab the children, who are often only 'pint-sized', and search their clothing, by which time the police will have probably arrived on the scene. Mopeds are another danger, their tactic is to whisk past removing a handbag as they go. It is obviously safest to leave all your valuables in the hotel safe, carrying sufficient money for the day in a zipped bag or pocket. Remember to take extra caution around tourist sights, and avert confrontation by clutching your pocket or bag whenever anyone suspicious approaches, letting them know that you are aware of their game.

The chapter is divided into four itineraries, each of which covers a different district of Rome. The first three itineraries start from Piazza Venezia, the city centre, while the fourth, itinerary 1D, is devoted to the Vatican. Itinerary 1A takes in the sights of ancient Rome and the east of the city, itinerary 1B concentrates on the historic centre which is contained within a bend of the River Tiber, and itinerary 1C explores the north of the city and the beautiful Villa Borghese park. Each route could easily take 2 or 3 days, so those in a hurry are recommended to pick and choose rather than try to visit everything on the itinerary. It should be noted that to cover all four of the itineraries on foot, involves a walk of some 50km (31 miles), and that therefore using public transport is advisable. The bus service is good, the main terminus is next to the Termini rail station and tickets are available from *tabacchi*, kiosks and at main bus-stops. There is a metro too, which although the stops are quite widely spaced, is useful for getting about the city. Visitors in cars are advised to leave them outside the city and take public transport in, as parking is either difficult or expensive, and thieving, particularly of car stereos is commonplace.

Route 1A

Piazza Venezia, the centre of Rome, is towered over by the colossal, white marble monument, the Vittoriano, which was built to commemorate the founder of modern Italy, King Vittorio Emanuele II. It was constructed between 1885 and 1911 as an attempt to recreate the pomp and grandeur of ancient Rome. It fails perhaps, not because it isn't immensely impressive and monumental, but because its sheer size completely dwarfs everything around it, unlike Greek and Roman architecture which was essentially articulated on a more human scale. The top of the monument is crowned with a pair of bronze chariots, which can be seen from most parts of the city, however, the focal point is the 16m (52ft) equestrian statue of the king.

The opposite side of the *piazza* is filled by the early-Renaissance **Palazzo Venezia**. Built in 1455, it was the residence of various popes, as well as Napoleon, before becoming Mussolini's headquarters. The balcony from where Mussolini made many of his speeches looks over the *piazza*, while the interior of the building, complete with its original Renaissance decoration, is used as an exhibition space and has a collection of the applied arts, dating from medieval to Renaissance times.

Leave Piazza Venezia, passing to the right of the Vittoriano, and climb up the first flight of steps on the left to **Santa Maria in Aracoeli**. The church was built in 1250 and lies at the summit of the ancient Capitoline hill on the site of a former Roman shrine to Juno. Its interior is covered by a magnificent, coffered ceiling which was added in 1575 to commemorate the victory at Lepanto over the Turks. The wide central aisle, which has remnants of its original, thirteenth-century Cosmati paving, is lined along either side with chapels. The first chapel on the right contains a beautiful fresco cycle, depicting the *Life of San Bernardino* by Pinturicchio (around 1485), while in the third chapel on the left there is a fine fresco of *Sant'Antonio da Padova* by B. Gozzoli (around 1449). The door at the back of the church on the right leads out to Michelangelo's Piazza di Campidoglio and saves the effort of descending the church steps only to climb the next flight, the Cordonata, back up again. This monumental stairway starts at the foot of the church steps, a little way to the south.

Piazza di Campidoglio is the site of the ancient Capitol, and

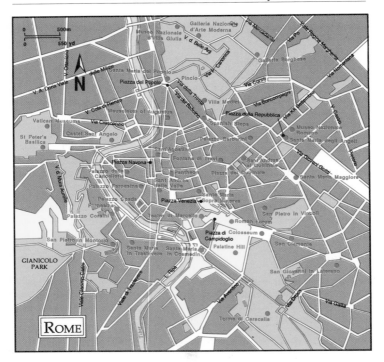

Palazzo Senatorio, along its eastern side, stands on the foundations of the Roman Senator's Palace. Ancient remains from the site are housed in the **Musei Capitolini** which fill the twin palaces lining either side of the *piazza*. Palazzo Nuovo, along the left side, has a colossal antique statue decorating a fountain by G. della Porta in its courtyard. To the right of the fountain is a second-century, bronze, equestrian statue of Marcus Aurelius which once stood at the centre of Piazza di Campidoglio and was the prototype for many of the equestrian statues made during the Renaissance. Stairs lead up from the right side of the courtyard to the main part of the collection, which is on the first floor. Unfortunately, none of the statues are labelled, but it is fairly easy to identify the most famous, including the *Dying Gaul* in the first room, the *Old and Young Centaurs* sculpted from grey marble in the third room, the *Capitoline Venus* in the small octagonal room off the main corridor, and the statue of *Elena*, Constantine's mother, in the fifth room, along with some sixty-four busts of Roman emperors.

Palazzo dei Conservatori on the right side of the *piazza* also contains a fine collection of ancient sculpture. Its courtyard holds some impressive fragments of a colossal statue of Constantine, but pass through the door on the right into the museum shop and upstairs to the museum itself. On the first floor, numerous statues, including important bronzes such as the Etruscan *Capitoline She-Wolf* in Room 4 and the *Boy Removing Thorn* in Room 3, are displayed in a grand suite of rooms, complete with their sixteenth-century frescoes and friezes depicting the *History of Rome*. Other antiquities are housed in the series of rooms at the back of the palace, including the Galleria degli Orti Lamiani which has sculptures found on the Esquiline hill, the Sala dei Bronzi which contains an impressive first-century bronze bed and the Museo Nuovo which holds a good collection of pottery, funerary urns and sculptures, dating from both Hellenistic and Roman eras. Continue up to the Pinacoteca on the second floor, where there is a fine collection of paintings dating from the fourteenth to seventeenth centuries, including the *Rape of the Sabine Women* by P. da Cortona, the *Gypsy* by Caravaggio and other well-known works by Bellini, Veronese, Lotto and Tintoretto.

Before leaving Piazza di Campidoglio it is worth walking along the right side of Palazzo Senatorio, down Via del Campidoglio, from where there is a panoramic view of the **Roman Forum** with the wooded hill of the Palatine to the right, and the Colosseum in the distance to the left. Return to Piazza di Campidoglio and head along the left side of Palazzo Senatorio, passing a short column sur-

Roman Forum and San Luca Church

mounted by a replica of the *Capitoline She-Wolf*, and take the steps down, passing alongside the church of San Pietro in Carcere, which was built on the site of the Roman prison where St Peter is believed to have converted the guards. Next to it is the Baroque church of San Luca, which was designed by P. da Cortona. On the right, opposite the church, is the beautifully-carved Arch of Septimus Severus which marks the westernmost end of the Foro Romano, the Roman Forum. The entrance to the Forum is a little further on the right, along Largo Romolo e Remo.

A ramp leads down from the ticket office onto Via Sacra, the main ancient road through the Forum. Turn right and follow the road to the Arch of Septimus Severus. It was built in AD205 to celebrate the tenth anniversary of Severus' reign and is richly-carved with reliefs depicting the Emperor's campaigns. The large brick building to the right, the Curia, was constructed in AD303 as the seat of the Senate, but was converted to a church in the seventh century. The interior is comprised of a large hall, 27m (88ft) long and 18m (59ft) wide, and has fragments of its original marble paving as well as good reliefs depicting the life of Trajan (AD117-38).

To the left of the Arch of Septimus Severus, is Colonna di Foca, a solitary column, 14m (46ft) high, which was reconstructed with the original Roman stones in AD608. Heading past the column, the Temple of Saturn with its eight Ionic columns is on the right, and there is a good view of the ancient Tabularium upon which Palazzo Senatorio stands. The remains of Basilica Giulia, which was founded in 54BC by Julius Caesar, lie just south of the Temple of Saturn. Follow along the steps of the Basilica, past the circular Temple of Vesta, before turning right into the Casa di Vestali, the house of the Vestal Virgins, where statues on pedestals surround a large court-yard which has two pools at its centre.

Return to Via Sacra, heading north of the Casa di Vestali towards the impressive, second-century portico of the Temple of Anthony and Faustina which is incorporated into the façade of a Baroque church. Turn right, following Via Sacra past the Temple of Romulus on the left, to the massive brick-built walls of the Basilica di Massenzio. The entrance to the Basilica, which is 80m (262ft) long and 60m (197ft) wide, is just before the seventeenth-century façade of San Francesco Romano. The Basilica was started by Maxentius in AD306, but completed by Constantine in AD330. The north aisle with its three vast, coffered vaults is the best-preserved part of the structure.

The Arch of Titus, to the right of the church, San Francesco Romano, marks the easternmost end of the Forum. It was erected after the death of Titus by the Emperor Domitian in AD81, and is decorated on the inside with reliefs depicting the capture of Jerusalem. Head towards the Palatine Hill, past the arch, and climb the steps to the ruined, sixteenth-century Farnese palace, which is surrounded by a formal Italian garden. During the Republican Era (509-

31BC), the Palatine was a wealthy residential area, but by medieval times the once-fine buildings had either tumbled down or had been exploited for their stone. The Renaissance interest in Classicism, once more made the Palatine a popular residential area, although little was done to preserve the ruins, and Palazzo Farnese with its extensive gardens was laid out by the cardinal, Alessandro Farnese, on top of the ruins of Tiberius' palace.

The best ruins are on the southern side of the hill and are reached by heading through the Farnese gardens and descending the steps at the end to the scant remains of Casa di Livia. From here the Cripto Portico, a 122m (400ft) long tunnel, leads to the former imperial palace. Follow the tunnel, taking the first passage on the right, which emerges amongst the scattered foundations of the Palazzo dei Flavi, built by Domitian between AD81 and AD96. Head east of these ruins, past the Antiquarium, the excavation headquarters, to the stadium of Domitian. This sunken arena, littered with column fragments, is an impressive 160m (525ft) long and 80m (262ft) wide. The ruined brick walls of the Baths of Septimus Severus lie on the other side of the stadium, where steps lead down to the exit on Via di San Gregorio.

From Via di San Gregorio there are three options: the first is to end the tour by heading north to the Colosseum and returning to Piazza Venezia along Via dei Fori Imperiali; the second, best attempted by bus or car as the roads are busy and unpleasant, is south to the Roman Circo Massimo, continuing along Via dei Terme di Caracalla to the massive, crumbling, brick walls of the thermal baths, built by Caracalla in AD217; the third is to spend some time exploring the less-frequented spots in the eastern part of the city. To do the latter, cross over Via di San Gregorio and take the first steps up from the main road, passing the Baroque church of San Gregorio Magno, before continuing up the Celio hill along Clivo di Scauro. After 100m (110yd) the walls of **Santissimi Giovanni e Paolo**, a twelfth-century church built on top of a Roman house, are passed to the left. The façade, with its attractive portico made up of eight ancient columns, looks onto a small *piazza* at the right side of which, is the prettily-decorated, Romanesque, *campanile*, built on the site of the Roman Temple of Claudius. From the interior of the church, stairs lead down to the remains of the Roman house where St Paul and St John are believed to have been executed. The house dates from the second century and a number of its original frescoes remain intact.

An entrance to the park of **Villa Celimontana** lies opposite the church, at the top of the *piazza* on the right. Follow the path through this charming public gardens, which contains a children's play-ground as well as the graceful, sixteenth-century Villa Celimontana, to the east gate. Cross over Via Claudia and head east along Via di San Stefano Rotondo. After 90m (96yd) turn off right to visit the church of **San Stefano Rotondo**. This small, circular building dates back to the fifth century and contains good seventh-century mosaics as well as later seventeenth-century frescoes. After continuing along Via di San Stefano Rotondo for some 500m (547yd) the road opens out into the busy **Piazza San Giovanni in Laterano**, at the centre of which is the tallest of Rome's Egyptian obelisks (31m/102ft). Along the south and east sides of the *piazza* is **San Giovanni in Laterano**, the cathedral church of Rome and the papal residence up until their exile to Avignon in 1309. The baptistery, on the south side of the *piazza*, dates back to the founding of the church by Constantine in the fourth century, and contains fine mosaics. Both the baptistery and the church were, however, remodelled between 1646 and 1649 at the request of Pope Innocenzo X by one of the greatest architects of the Baroque era, Borromini. The portal to the left of the baptistery, which is flanked by two small towers, leads into the right transept of the church. The vast interior, divided into five aisles, is covered by a highly decorative, coffered ceiling, studded with rosettes and coats of arms, while the domed ceiling in the apse holds a mosaic in the style of the thirteenth century on a gold ground. The ornate Gothic tabernacle in front of the apse dates from 1367 and holds relics of St Paul and St Peter. A door in the left aisle leads through to a charming,

The Colosseum

thirteenth-century cloister which is surrounded by double columns and stone-carved remnants of the earlier church. A room in the left corner contains a tapestry of 1599 which depicts the *Life of St John the Evangelist*, as well as a collection of chalices and papal garments. It is worth going out of the church through the main entrance to see the grand façade, which is adorned with massive Corinthian columns and monumental statues. It faces onto a large, busy *piazza*, on the left side of which is the Scala Santa, a flight of twenty-eight marble steps transported by Elena, Constantine's mother, to Rome from Pilate's house in Jerusalem.

Return to Piazza San Giovanni in Laterano and leave from its north-west corner along Via San Giovanni in Laterano, continuing along it to the small church of **San Clemente** on the right. Although this church is not very remarkable from the outside, the interior is of considerable interest. It has three aisles divided by ancient columns with an attractive choir made from sixth-century stone originating from the former basilica. The dome of the apse holds a splendid, thirteenth-century mosaic depicting the *Triumph of the Cross* with fourteenth-century frescoes on the lower walls of *Jesus, Mary and the Apostles*. In the left aisle, the Cappella di San Caterina d'Alessandria, holds some fine Renaissance frescoes of scenes depicting the *Life of Saint Catherine*, the *Crucifixion*, and an *Annunciation*. Other frescoes, dating from the sixth to twelfth centuries can be seen in the Chiesa Inferiore, the remains of the former basilica, which is reached by descending the stairs from the sacristy. It is also possible to visit the Roman remains of a Temple of Mithras behind the apse of the church.

The **Colosseum** is a further 300m (328yd) west of San Clemente along Via San Giovanni in Laterano. This magnificent building dates from AD72 when Vespasian, the first of the Flavian emperors, commissioned its construction on the former site of Nero's pleasure palace. It was used for public spectacles, mostly bloody in nature, although dramatic and athletic performances were also staged here, and could hold up to 50,000 spectators. It remained in use up until the sixth century, after which it was transformed into a fortress, later to be plundered for stone. In 1740, Pope Benedict XIV consecrated the Colosseum in memory of the Christians who were martyred here during gladiatorial spectacles and the monument was given the respect it deserved. A large section of the outer walls, clad in the original travertine marble, remain standing to a height of 57m (187ft) and are made up of three arcaded tiers, the first in the Doric order, the second in the Ionic and the third in the Corinthian. The wall making up a fourth tier was added by Titus in AD80. The entrance is on the west side and although visitors are admitted free of charge into the eliptical arena, which is 76m (250ft) long and 46m (151ft) wide, a ticket must be bought in order to climb to the upper levels.

Constantine's Arch, just to the left of the Colosseum entrance, is one of the best-preserved, ancient buildings in Rome. It was erected between AD313 and AD315 to celebrate Constantine's conquest over his rival Maxentius. It has three monumental arches and is richly decorated with carved reliefs. The panels on the column bases depict Constantine's good deeds, while in the circular medallions above the arches, the Emperor is shown hunting. The frieze along the top was removed from an earlier building, dating from the second century, and is carved with scenes from the *Life of Marcus Aurelius*.

Those who wish to return to the city centre can follow Via dei Fori Imperiali from the west side of the Colosseum to Piazza Venezia. The itinerary, however, continues by heading north from the Colosseum, up a flight of steps to Via Nicola Salvi. Take the first left, Via delle Terme di Tito, where, after 150m (164yd) visitors can choose either to continue right along Viale dei Monti Opio to visit the Terme Traiano, the scant remains of Trajan's Baths, or turn left, passing through Largo delle Polveriera, to Via Eudossiana which, shortly after passing the Engineering University, opens out into **Piazza di San Pietro in Vincoli**. The main attraction of the church in the north-east corner of this *piazza*, is Michelangelo's Memorial to Julius II, which stands inside, at the back of the right aisle. It is a far cry from the original project which was designed to stand in splendour at the centre of the Pantheon, but it is nonetheless impressive. The central figure, Moses, was just one of the numerous large statues designed for the original monument and gives some idea of the scale upon which it was envisaged. In the niches either side of Moses (1514-16) are statues of Leah and Rachel (1542), the rest of the monument is the work of Michelangelo's pupils. The church also contains the chains which are believed to have held St Peter prisoner in Palestine. They are on display in a glass casket beneath the fine bronze tabernacle (1477) in the main apse. The apse itself is decorated with frescoes and the central aisle, which is lined with antique Doric columns along either side, is covered by a fine ceiling painted by F. Fontana. Also of interest is the small, Byzantine mosaic of St Sebastian, dating from the seventh century, in the second chapel along the left aisle.

Leave the *piazza* following Via delle Sette Salle along the left side of the church and descend the first steps on the left to Largo Viscevelosta. Turn right and follow Via Cavour for 450m (492yd) to Piazza dell'Esquilino where a monumental flight of steps skirts the apse of **Santa Maria Maggiore**. Enter the church from the top of the steps and head for the dome of the apse, which contains a beautiful thirteenth-century mosaic depicting the *Coronation of the Virgin*, while the triumphal arch in front is covered by a cycle of mosaic scenes of the *Childhood of Christ*, dating from the church's foundation in the early fifth century. The main part of the church is comprised of a very wide central nave with aisles at either side divided by antique columns. The high walls supported above the columns are also decorated with fifth-century mosaics, arranged in panels depicting scenes in the lives of Abraham, Moses and Joseph. The grand, coffered ceiling covering the nave was designed by G. da Sangallo (1493-8), while the Cosmati paving on the floor dates from the twelfth century. The ornate, eighteenth-century baldachin in front of the altar is built over relics from the crib at Bethlehem. To its right, a large domed chapel contains the decorative tombs of Popes Sixtus V and Pius V, while to its left another chapel holds a small, thirteenth-century painting of the *Madonna*.

From Piazza dell'Esquilino, which has an ancient obelisk from the Mausoleum of Augustus at its centre, it is possible to continue for a further 250m (273yd) to Piazza dei Cinquecento where the Termini rail station is on the right, and the **Museo Nazionale Romano** on the left. The museum stands on the site of the Terme di Diocleziano which was built by Diocletian in AD298. Its collection of ancient art is contained in one of the vast rooms of the baths and in the cloister of a convent that was built amongst the ruins in the sixteenth century. It is one of the most important collections of ancient art in the world and includes numerous mosaics, statues and frescoes dating from Roman times. On the west side of the baths complex, looking onto Piazza della Repubblica, is the church of **Santa Maria degli Angeli**, designed by Michelangelo in 1566 on the site of the ancient tepidarium. A large domed hall leads into a very wide but short nave with seventeenth- and eighteenth-century paintings decorating the walls.

The curved porticoes (1896-1902) surrounding Piazza della Repubblica stand over the former exedra, a semi-circular recess, of the Diocletian baths. There are no antique remains visible, but the *piazza* has an attractive fountain at its centre, decorated with bronze statues dating from 1901. Take a bus if possible along Via Nazionale which heads south from the *piazza* towards the city centre. Those who wish to visit the **Mercati Traianei** (Trajan's Market), should stop at Largo Magnanapoli. Designed by the architect Apollodoro di Damasco (AD107-12), the market, was originally five-storeys high, and has a fine curved façade looking over Trajan's forum (closed to the public). Next to it stands the Torre Milizia, a stout, thirteenth-century tower which can be ascended and offers good views of the city. From **Torre Milizia** head down the first steps on the left to Trajan's Column, which is 38m (125ft) high and is covered by a spiral of carved scenes depicting Trajan's victory over the Dacians. Piazza Venezia, the starting point for Route 1B, is a short distance to the west of the column.

Route 1B

Itinerary 1B leaves Piazza Venezia from its north side, and follows Via del Corso for 150m (164yd) before turning left to Piazza del Collegio Romano. **Galleria Doria-Pamphili** is housed in the grand, eighteenth-century *palazzo* in the north-east corner of the *piazza*, and contains an important collection of paintings dating from the fif-teenth to eighteenth centuries. Amongst the most famous works in the collection are: *Portrait of Two People* by Raphael; *Flight into Egypt* by Caravaggio; and *Innocent X* by Velazquez.

Head west from the *piazza* for 200m (218yd) to Piazza della Minerva, at the centre of which is Bernini's rather whimsical elephant (1667), supporting a small Egyptian obelisk on its back. The simple, Renaissance façade of **Santa Maria Sopra Minerva**, along the east side of the *piazza*, belies its finely decorated interior, which has three vast aisles lined with chapels along either side. There are also chapels in the transepts, the one in the right transept is decorated with frescoes by F. Lippi (1489-93), that in the left contains the tomb of the great Florentine painter, Fra Angelico. Also of importance is the small statue by Michelangelo of *Christ Bearing the Cross* (1519-21) which is to the left of the main altar.

One of Rome's most outstanding monuments, the **Pantheon**, is within easy striking distance as it lies just a short distance to the

Hall of Mirrors in the Doria-Pamphili Palace

north-west of Piazza della Minerva. This circular building is crowned by a large dome and fronted by a massive portico, eight columns wide, which is surmounted by a high pediment. The inscription on the portico states that the Pantheon was built by Marcus Agrippa in 27BC, although the present structure was erected between AD120 and AD125, by Hadrian. It was an extraordinary feat of engineering for the dome, the largest in the history of architecture, was supported, without the aid of buttresses, by the immense walls which were up to 6m (20ft) thick. Its period of glory, however, was relatively short-lived, for being a pagan temple, it was closed in AD399 in accordance with Christian law. The building was plundered and generally neglected up until AD608, when Pope Boniface IV consecrated it as a church. It is, nonetheless, remarkably well-preserved. The interior is still complete with its splendid, coffered dome, the diameter of which is equal to the overall height of the building. The pilasters and columns lining the lower walls are made of the original *giallo antico*, a very rare, yellow, Numidian marble, while the alternately curved and oblong recesses which once held

Italian works of art can be viewed not only in museums but also on street corners

statues, now contain tombs and altars. The first recess on the right has a fresco of an *Annunciation* by M. Da Forli, while the second, next to it, contains the revered tomb of King Vittorio Emanuele II (died 1878). Another famous tomb, that of Raphael, is on the left, between the second and third recesses.

Head across the *piazza* in front of the Pantheon, past its fountain, and follow the street from the left corner to the impressive façade of **San Luigi dei Francesi**. This church was built for the French community in 1518, although the richly decorated interior with its variegated marbles, stucco and gilt work, dates from the eighteenth century. It contains a fine fresco depicting the *Life of St Cecilia* in the second chapel on the right, and three important paintings by Caravaggio of the *Story of Matthew* (1598-1601) in the fifth chapel on the left.

Follow Via della Scrofa north of San Luigi dei Francesi and take the second turning on the left to the church of **Sant'Agostino**. Constructed between 1479 and 1483, this was one of the first Renaissance churches to be built in Rome. Its interior is divided into three aisles by square pillars which are decorated with statues and frescoes of saints and prophets. The third pillar on the left has a painting of Isiah by Raphael (1512). The most important statue in the church, the *Madonna del Parto*, is set in a niche to the right of the main door and is by J. Sansovino (1521).

Take Via Sant'Agostino south of the church, passing under an arch into Piazza delle Cinque Lune from where a passage, Passetto delle Cinque Lune, leads through to **Piazza Navona**. This elongated *piazza* stands on the site of Domitian's stadium which was built in AD86. There are no ancient remains, but the absence of traffic, and the richly coloured façades of the fine surrounding buildings, make this one of the most charming spots in Rome. At the centre of the *piazza* are four elaborate Baroque fountains designed by Bernini, the largest of which, the *Fountain of the Four Rivers*, is surmounted by an obelisk and dates from 1651.

Leave the *piazza* from its east side and follow Corsia Agonale to the high walls of the sixteenth-century Palazzo Madama. Turn right and continue along Corso del Rinascimento, passing Palazzo Sapienza (number 33) which contains Borromini's quaint Chapel of St Ivo (1660) inside its courtyard. Continue to the end of Corso del Rinascimento and cross over the busy street, Corso Vittorio Emanuele, to the grand Baroque façade of **Sant'Andrea delle Valle**. The church was started in 1591 by G. della Porta, but it was not finished until 1625 when Maderno designed its distinctive dome, the second highest in Rome. The interior, with its richly decorated ceiling, is lit by the number of windows that pierce the high drum of the dome. The ceiling of the dome holds a fine fresco of the *Glory of Paradise* by Lanfranco (1625) while the pendentives below the drum are decorated with the *Evangelists* by Domenichini (1628).

On the opposite side of Corso Vittorio Emanuele at number 141 is the sadly neglected **Palazzo Massimo**. The building was commissioned by the descendant of an ancient Roman family, Prince Pietro Massimo, who wanted a house in the style of his patrician forefathers. The project was undertaken by B. Peruzzi (1532-6), one of the most important architects of the High Renaissance. Given the awkward shape and size of the site, Peruzzi did well to create a townhouse that in many ways resembles one of Augustan Rome. The columned portico has a finely moulded ceiling and niches at either end. A long passage leads to the first courtyard, modelled on the ancient atrium, and continues to a second courtyard, the peristylium, private quarters.

Continue for a short distance along Corso Vittorio Emanuele to the **Museo di Roma**, a museum of the life and history of Rome, which is on the right, and the **Museo Barracco**, which occupies a fine, Renaissance *palazzo* designed by A. da Sangallo and contains a collection of ancient statues, on the left. Take the next left turn to **Palazzo della Cancelleria**, another fine Renaissance building. It was constructed between 1483 and 1517 and is the seat of the apostolic chancellery. It is possible to peek into the courtyard, which was designed in the style of the great architect, Bramante, and is surrounded by elegant arches on two storeys.

Head south through the colourful market on Piazza Campo di Fiore to **Palazzo Farnese**. This grand *palazzo*, set on a quiet *piazza*, was started by A. da Sangallo in 1514 and completed by Michelangelo in 1546. It was built for Alessandro Farnese, later Pope Paul III, and is now the seat of the French Embassy. The two fountains in the *piazza* contain ancient granite basins removed from the Caracalla baths. **Palazzo Spada**, a short distance east of Palazzo Farnese, along Via Capo di Ferro, is also very impressive. Built in 1540, it surrounds a charming courtyard decorated with ancient statues. On the left side of the courtyard there is a short corridor which Borromini, through the use of *trompe-l'oeil*, made appear quite long.

From here the itinerary crosses the River Tiber to the west bank and the district of Trastevere. It is a delightful part of Rome, the narrow streets are filled with small restaurants and the absence of traffic in them is a welcome change from the busy main roads in the city centre. Head south of Palazzo Spada, along Via Polverini and cross over Ponte Sisto, a pedestrianised bridge, to Piazza Trilussa. Follow Via di Ponte Sisto to the crenellated gate, Porta Settimana, and turn right, through the gate, following Via della Lungara to **Palazzo Corsini** on the left. This large Baroque *palazzo*, built in 1736, houses the Galleria Nazionale d'Arte Antica which contains a notable collection of paintings dating from the sixteenth to eighteenth centuries. The Farnesina, on the opposite side of the road, houses a collection of fifteenth to nineteenth-century prints, but the building itself is perhaps of more interest. Set in fine gardens on the bank of the Tiber, the villa was designed by B. Peruzzi between 1508 and 1511 and is a good example of Roman High Renaissance architecture.

Raphael frescoed the *Galatea* on the ground floor, and the *Marriage of Alessandro and Roxana* by Sodoma is on the first floor.

Return to Porta Settimana and head south along Via della Scala to the lovely twelfth-century church of **Santa Maria in Trastevere**. Its façade, which looks onto a peaceful *piazza*, is decorated with bands of mosaics, dating from the twelfth and thirteenth centuries. The interior also contains fine mosaics, both in the dome of its apse and on the lower walls. Those in the dome depict the *Redeemer, Virgin and Saints* and date from 1140, while the six mosaic panels on the lower walls showing the *Life of Mary* date from the end of the thirteenth century. The church also has fine Cosmati paving on its floor and a rich, gilt, coffered ceiling which was added in 1617 by Domenichino.

Visitors may wish to head uphill from here, visiting the small Renaissance church of **San Pietro in Montorio**, which is famous for the circular Tempietto del Bramante in its courtyard. Just beyond it is the Gianicolo, a park which covers the top of the ancient Janiculum Hill. Shaded by lofty umbrella pine trees it offers fine views over the city and contains an equestrian statue of Garibaldi, commemorating his valiant defense here in 1849 against the French. Those who do not wish to climb up to these sights should head east from Santa Maria in Trastavere along Via della Lungaretta, to the Tiber. Continue in an easterly direction following the river bank, past the small island, Isola Tiberina, which was the site of the ancient Aesclepion, a medical centre, and is now a hospital. The bridge crossing the Tiber to the island, Ponte Fabricio, is one of the oldest in Rome and dates back to 62BC. Take the next bridge, Ponte Palatino, across the river to **Piazza Bocca della Verita** which holds the remains of two small temples. The rectangular temple on the left, Tempio di Portuno, is well-preserved and stands complete with its Ionic columns. It dates from 100BC. The Augustan circular temple to the right, Tempio d'Ercole, is also in good condition and is surrounded by attractive columns of the Corinthian Order. At the southern end of the *piazza*, looking onto a fine Baroque fountain (1715), is the façade of the Greek basilica, **Santa Maria in Cosmedin**, with its pretty, Lombardic *campanile*. The basilica dates from the eighth century, although it was largely reconstructed in 1123 and is typical of Romanesque architecture. Inside its portico, against the wall on the left, is the Bocca della Verita, a marble stone, carved into a face, which was used in Roman times as a drain cover. During the medieval period the superstition began that anyone who put their hand into the gaping hole of the mouth and told a lie would have it bitten off. The interior of the church is well-restored and has a traditional, flat ceiling which is painted with stars in the section over the central nave. The excellent Cosmati paved floor dates from 1123, while the choir, which is complete with its original marble walls, pulpits and seats, as well as the iconastasis, a screen that divides the nave and choir from the sanctuary, dates from the medieval period.

Return to the city centre by heading north of Santa Maria in

Cosmedin along Via Teatro di Marcello. The church of **San Nicola in Carcere**, passed on the left, has numerous ancient columns built into its walls, while the remains of an Augustan gate lie nearby. **Teatro di Marcello**, with its impressive ancient curved walls, is passed a short distance further on. The theatre was built by Julius Caesar between 13 and 11BC, and was later dedicated by Augustus to his nephew Marcellus. The three columns just to the right of the theatre are all that remain of the Tempio di Apollo Sosiano, an Augustan temple. Piazza Venezia, the starting point for itinerary 1C, is 400m (437yd) further north.

Route 1C

Itinerary 1C starts at the north-east corner of Piazza Venezia and heads up Via IV Novembre. At the top of the hill turn left and follow Via Pilotta, a small street beneath a series of four arches, to Galleria Colonna, which is at number 17 on the left. The gallery is housed in part of the vast **Palazzo Colonna** and contains a good collection of paintings dating from the fifteenth to eighteenth centuries, with works by well-known artists such as Tintoretto, Poussin, Van Dyck and Rubens. Continue along Via Pilotta and keep straight on along Via Lucchese to **Fontana di Trevi**. This splendid Rococo fountain, created in 1762, is the most impressive of all Rome's many fountains. It was designed by Bernini in the seventeenth century, but the project was abandoned and only came to fruition over 100 years later, when Pope Clement XII commissioned the little-known architect, N. Salvi, to build it. A colossal statue of Neptune stands at the centre of a Roman triumphal arch, being drawn on a cockle-shell by winged sea-horses, which are led by tritons, across a foaming sea. Water cascades from the sea, over sculpted rocks, before spilling into the vast basin below.

Return back along Via Lucchese and turn left up Via della Dataria just before the small church of Santa Croce. At the top of the hill, which is the highest of Rome's Seven Hills, is Piazza del Quirinale. **Palazzo Quirinale**, along the left side of the *piazza*, was the residence of numerous popes and kings from the sixteenth century up until 1946 when it became the presidential palace. The grand, white marble building along the east side of the *piazza* is Palazzo della Consulta (1734), while set in the gardens at the centre of the square is an Egyptian obelisk, flanked on either side by the antique statues of Castor, Pollux and their horses. These statues originally stood in the Roman Baths of Constantine. There is a good view from the *piazza* across the city's roof tops to the dome of St Peter's.

Follow Via del Quirinale out of the east corner of the *piazza*, between the two palaces, to the little church of **Sant'Andrea al Quirinale** which is on the right. Designed by the papal architect, Bernini, in 1658, it has a large, curved portico with Corinthian pilasters at either side, surmounted by a classical pediment. The oval-shaped interior, sumptuously decorated with rare marbles, porphyry and gilded stucco, is covered by a shallow dome with a high lantern.

Continue down Via del Quirinale to another small, Baroque church, **San Carlo alle Quattro Fontane**, designed by Bernini's contemporary, Borromini. It was built exactly 20 years before Bernini's Sant'Andrea, in 1638, and has all the sinuous curves and elaborate decoration typical of the Baroque style. The interior, which is long and narrow, has an eliptical ground plan and is decorated with ornate stucco work. The church stands at a really remarkable crossroads, there being a Rococo fountain on each corner and long views down each of the four roads. Looking back down Via del Quirinale it is possible to see the obelisk on Piazza Quirinale. Obelisks are also visible at either end of Via del Quattro Fontane, while at the end of Via XX Settembre is Michelangelo's gate, Porta Pia. Those interested in the work of Bernini should make the excursion along Via XX Settembre to the church of **Santa Maria della Vittoria** which contains one of his greatest sculptural works, the *Ecstasy of St Teresa*. It stands in the fourth chapel on the left. The church, also notable for its rich marble decoration, was designed by Maderno, the papal architect before Bernini, in 1605.

The itinerary, however, heads down Via del Quattro Fontane, in a north-westerly direction, to **Palazzo Barberini**, on the right. This grand Baroque *palazzo*, surrounded by pleasant gardens, was started by Maderno in 1625 with the help of Borromini, and finished by Bernini in 1633. It houses the Galleria Nazionale d'Arte Antica, the other part of which is visited on itinerary 1B (Palazzo Corsini). The paintings the gallery contains, date from the thirteenth to eighteenth centuries and include notable works such as: the *Madonna and Child* and *Annunciation* by F. Lippi in Room 2; *La Fornarina* by Raphael in Room 6; *Judith and Holofernes* by Caravaggio in Room 13; and *Henry VIII* by Holbein in Room 19. It is also possible to visit the Rococo apartments on the second floor which contain seventeenth-century paintings, as well as furniture, porcelain and costumes of the period.

Piazza Barberini is a short distance further down the hill beyond the *palazzo*. It contains a fountain designed by Bernini which is decorated with the three bees of the Barberini coat of arms. From the *piazza* continue in a north-westerly direction along Via Sistina, to the massive obelisk which stands in front of the Baroque, Santa Trinita dei Monti. The church was built for the French King Louis XII in 1502, but the façade, which has bell-towers at either side, dates from 1585 and was designed by Maderno. From the top of the steps which lead up to the portal there is a fine view across the city and of Villa Medici to the right. The interior, made up of a single aisle, has deeply recessed chapels along either side. The frescoes in the second chapel on the left of the *Descent from the Cross*, and also in the third chapel on the right of the *Ascension of Mary*, are by the sixteenth-century painter, D. da Volterra.

Just below the church are the famous **Spanish Steps**, the Scalinata ❋ della Trinita dei Monti, designed in 1723 by F. de Sanctis. They take their name from the Spanish Embassy which was established here in the same year. The *piazza* at the foot of the steps, which contains a fountain by Bernini (1629), has been the popular abode of numerous foreign writers and musicians over the years including George Eliot, James Joyce, Stendahl, Balzac, Wagner, Henry James and Byron. The house where Keats died in 1821 is on the right of the steps and is now a museum, the **Keats and Shelley Memorial House**, and contains an ⌂ assortment of memorabilia. The Babington Tea Rooms, which is as popular today as it was when it was established in 1896, are on the left side of the steps.

Climb back up the steps to Trinita dei Monti and turn left, following Via Trinita dei Monti past Villa Medici, designed by A. Lippi in 1544. The first ramp on the right after the Villa leads up to the Pincio, a formal gardens dotted with the busts of Roman patriots. At the end of the garden there is a vast terrace, above Piazza Popolo, with a ♣ magnificent panorama. Rome's largest park, Villa Borghese, stretches over an area of 6sq km (2sq miles) behind the Pincio. Take the Magnolia-lined, Via dei Magnoli, one of the principal roadways through the park, to Piazzale Canestre, and continue up Viale Pietro Canonica, passing Piazza Siena, a horse-riding centre, to **Museo** ⌂ **Canonica**. The museum, a low crenellated building, resembling a fortress, is built round a courtyard and contains the work of the sculptor Pietro Canonica (1869-1959) as well as a number of antique statues.

Continue up to the four columns at the top of Viale Pietro Canonica and follow Viale Antonino e Faustina to Viale delle Due Piramide. Turn left up Viale delle Due Piramide and at the top of the hill turn right, following Viale dell'Uccelliera for 200m (218yd) to **Galleria** ⌂ **Borghese**. The gallery is arranged in the seventeenth-century villa of Cardinal Scipione Borghese, who founded the park between 1613 and 1616, and contains a good collection of paintings and sculpture. The sculpture collection ranges from antique to Baroque, and includes Canova's famous statue of *Pauline Borghese* (1805), who was Napoleon's sister. There are also numerous famous paintings by well-known masters such as Raphael, Caravaggio, Correggio and Titian.

Return back along Viale dell'Uccelliera and continue past the **Zoo**, which is the best in Italy and covers some 12 hectares (30 acres), to Viale delle Belle Arti. The **Galleria Nazionale d'Arte Moderna** is a ⌂ short distance along this road on the right. It was built in 1911 as an exhibition centre and houses Italy's largest collection of modern art, which dates from the nineteenth and twentieth centuries. Continue along Viale delle Belle Arti for a further 400m (437yd) to **Museo** ⌂ **Nazionale di Villa Giulia**. This is a museum not to be missed: it contains the best collection of Etruscan finds in the world, and is arranged in a magnificent, Late Renaissance villa, which was built

St Peter's Basilica, the largest and most important in the Catholic world

The Villa Borghese provides an escape from the metropolis of Rome

for Pope Julius III in 1551. The collection, which is displayed according-ing to the geographical locations of the sites, fills the thirty-two rooms around the large central courtyard. The courtyard contains formal gardens and has a large *nymphaeum*, or fountain, at its centre. To the left of the *nymphaeum* there is an impressive reconstruction of an Etruscan temple from *Alatri*, which is just to the south of Rome.

Return to Galleria Nazionale d'Arte Moderna and head south to Viale Washington. The gate at the bottom of Viale Washington leads into Piazzale Flaminio, at the left side of which another gate, the large sixteenth-century Porta del Popolo, leads through to **Piazza del Popolo**. This large oval *piazza* took on its symmetrical appearance in 1816 when it was re-arranged by G. Valadier. Just inside the gate on the left is the church of Santa Maria del Popolo, with its mirror-image on the right, which was commissioned by the Renaissance pope, Sixtus IV in 1477. Its interior, divided by attractively carved pillars into three aisles, is lined with chapels along either side. The first chapel on the right contains a fine fresco by Pinturicchio dating from 1485, the second chapel on the left was designed by Raphael for the Chigi family. Also of interest is the thirteenth-century, Byzantine *Madonna* on the main altar.

Cross to the far side of Piazza del Popolo, passing the Egyptian obelisk at its centre, and follow Via di Ripetta to the **Ara Pacis** monument, which is enclosed within a glass show room on the right. The monument was built between 13 and 9BC in celebration of the peace that ensued during the Augustan era. It is very finely carved and has beautiful reliefs depicting the imperial procession of Augustus and his family, as well as scenes of sacrifice and of fertility rites. The large, grassy tumulus on the opposite side of the road is the Mausoleum of Augustus, which was built in the Etruscan style in 28BC. Converted to a fortress in medieval times, it now stands in a state of neglect, and is best viewed from a distance.

To join the start of itinerary 1D, head south along the banks of the Tiber to Ponte Sant'Angelo. Otherwise return to the city centre along Via del Corso, from where a great many pleasant pedestrian shop-ping streets lead off from either side. On the way it passes through **Piazza Colonna**, where there is the beautifully-carved column of Marcus Aurelius.

Route 1D

Itinerary 1D begins at Ponte Sant'Angelo, one of the many fine bridges spanning the River Tiber. Cross over the bridge, which is lined with statues by Bernini (1669-71), to **Castel Sant'Angelo**. This circular edifice was built first as a mausoleum for Hadrian in AD135, but was later surrounded by a wall and converted to a fortress to defend the Vatican. Today it contains a collection of arms and armour, as well as the papal apartments complete with their Renais-sance decor and furnishings.

From Castel Sant'Angelo head west along the monumental road, Via della Conciliazione, which was built in 1937 to celebrate the reconciliation of Mussolini and Pope Pius XI, to **St Peter's Basilica**. The basilica, the largest and most important in the Catholic world, stands majestically above Bernini's circular, colonnaded *piazza* which can hold a crowd of 400,000 and has an Egyptian obelisk at its centre. The original basilica was built by Constantine in AD324 on the site of Nero's Circus where St Peter was martyred. Plans for the present building were, however, drawn up in 1452, although it was not until more than 50 years later that building actually commenced. Over ten of Rome's leading architects, including Michelangelo, Bramante, Bernini and Maderno, were involved in its construction and it was not completed until 1667. The façade, which was designed by Maderno (1606), has eight gigantic Corinthian columns and four pilasters. It is surmounted by a balustrade which is adorned with statues of Christ and the Apostles. Of the five massive bronze doors which lead into the building, that in the centre is the oldest. It was cast between 1433 and 1445.

The interior, overwhelming both in size and decoration, was designed by Bernini who embellished every facet with polished marble, gilded stucco or rich fresco. The vast pillars that divide the interior into three immense aisles are clad with umpteen statues. However, the most important statue in the basilica is that in the first chapel on the right, the *Pieta* by Michelangelo, which was carved in 1499, when the sculptor was still in his early twenties. A magnificent gold coffered ceiling leads up to the famous dome which was started by Bramante in 1506, then taken over by Michelangelo, and finally completed in 1593 by G. della Porta. The bronze baldachin, under the dome, was designed by Bernini (1633), and stands above the tomb of St Peter. Other works in bronze can be seen in the treasury, the entrance of which is in the left aisle. The collection is well-displayed and includes the bronze sepulchre designed by Pollaiolo (1489-93) for Sixtus IV. To visit the crypt, descend the steps from the right transept. A circular passage, beautifully-decorated with frescoes, leads to St Peter's tomb, while a wide corridor, lined along either side with the tombs of many Popes, leads out of the basilica, emerging near the entrance to the dome, which can be ascended by lift.

The **Vatican** is a tiny state, covering little more than 40 hectares (100 acres), but it has its own army of Swiss Guards, its own stamps and coins, a duty-free supermarket and one of the richest collections of art in the world. The Vatican museums can either be reached by taking the service bus through the Vatican gardens from St Peter's Square, or by walking around the Vatican walls to the entrance at its north side. To do the latter, turn left out of St Peter's Square, passing the barracks of the Swiss Guards and follow Via di Porta Angelica to Piazza del Risorgimento, from where Via Leone IV heads uphill to the museum's entrance. Either take the lift or walk up the massive circular staircase to the ticket office on the upper floor.

There are four colour-coded itineraries around the museum, each of varying length. The fourth, the yellow itinerary, is the longest and most comprehensive. With some 7km (4 miles) of galleries it is impossible to visit all of the Vatican's collection and hope to appreciate it, so it is best to select a few of the most important things and concentrate on them. The museums are arranged around two massive courtyards. In the left corner of the first courtyard, Cortile della Pigna, is the Museo Gregoriano Egizio, which houses a well-displayed collection of ancient Egyptian statues, mummies, carved reliefs and artefacts. Along the west side of the courtyard is Museo Pio Clementino which contains an outstanding collection of Greek and Roman statues, including the Hellenistic *Laocoon Group*, and the first-century BC *Belvedere Torso* which was greatly admired by Michelangelo. The Braccio Nuovo (New Wing) along the south side of the courtyard also houses classical statues.

The **Sistine Chapel**, probably the most famous feature of the Vatican, is at the southernmost end of the second courtyard, joined, in actual fact, to the right aisle of St Peter's Basilica. The chapel was built between 1475 and 1481 by Pope Sixtus IV. In 1508 Pope Julius II commissioned Michelangelo to paint the ceiling, which having been restored, can now be seen in all its former splendour. Michelangelo worked single-handed for 4 years to complete the massive project. The scenes depicting the *Creation* and the *Flood*, amongst others, and the sculpturally painted figures are composed on an architectural grid and demonstrate Michelangelo's astounding ability to use light and dark, and vivid colour to maximum effect. The fresco of the *Last Judgement* filling the apse is also by Michelangelo, although it is a later work and dates from 1534. The walls of the chapel are frescoed by other artists, including Botticelli, Perugino and Pinturicchio.

Pinturicchio also decorated the Borgia Apartments which are next to the Sistine Chapel, while the Cappella di Niccolo V, also nearby, contains beautiful frescoes by Fra Angelico, depicting scenes from the lives of San Stefano and San Lorenzo (1448-50). On the upper floor, directly above the Borgia Apartments are the **Stanze di Raffaello**. These four rooms were frescoed by Raphael at the same time as Michelangelo was working in the Sistine Chapel. From here, one of the most impressive of the Vatican's galleries extends along the entire length of both courtyards, back to the entrance. The first section of the gallery, the **Galleria delle Carte Geographiche**, has maps of the Roman provinces frescoed on the walls along either side. It continues into the **Galleria degli Arazzi** which contains an extraordinary collection of vast tapestries, and includes numerous sixteenth-century Brussels tapestries designed by Raphael. The last section of the gallery, the **Galleria dei Candelabri**, is divided into six parts and is filled with antique statues.

The **Pinacoteca**, which looks out onto the Vatican gardens, in the small courtyard at the entrance, is well worth visiting. It contains many fine altarpieces dating from the thirteenth to fifteenth centuries, and religious paintings by well-known artists such as Giotto, Fra Angelico, F. Lippi, Pinturicchio and Perugino. The largest room, Room 8, is devoted to the work of Raphael and includes ten tapestries made to his designs, as well as a *Transfiguration* and the small panels of a predella depicting the *Coronation of the Virgin*.

SHOPPING IN ROME

The main shopping area is the historic centre of Rome in the network of streets around Piazza di Spagna. High fashion shops are in Via Sistina and Via Gregoriana, other boutiques fill the area around Via Condotti, Via Frattina and Via del Corso. For antiques and art objects, Via del Babuino has the best reputation, but lower prices are found on Via dei Coronari, between Piazza Navona and Tor di Nona and on Via Gulia and Via Giubbonari.

La Rinascente is Rome's most prestigious department store, and has branches on Piazza Colonna and Piazza Fiume. Otherwise, the only chain department stores are Upim and Standa, both of which have branches throughout the city.

A lively flea market is held in Trastevere, every Sunday, in the streets around Porta Portese. In Via Sannio, near Porta San Giovanni there is a daily market of new and second-hand clothes. Every morning, except Sunday, prints and reproductions are sold in a street market on Piazza Fontanella Borghese. For general food markets, the most interesting are on Piazza Vittorio, Via Andrea Doria and Campo dei Fiori. There is also a colourful flower market held every Tuesday morning in Via Trionfale.

Additional Information

Places of Interest in Rome

ROUTE 1A
Museo di Palazzo Venezia
118 Via del Plebiscito
00100 Roma
☎ (06) 6798865
Open: Monday to Saturday 9am-1.30pm, Sunday 9am-12.30pm.

Musei Capitolini
Piazza del Campidoglio
00100 Roma
☎ (06) 6782862 or 67102771
Open: winter Tuesday to Saturday 9am-1.30pm, Tuesday and Saturday also 5-8pm, Sunday 9am-1pm. Summer Tuesday to Saturday 9am-1.30pm, Tuesday also 5-8pm, Saturday also 8-11pm, Sunday 9am-1pm.

Foro Romano e Palatino
Via dei Fori Imperiali
00100 Roma
☎ (06) 6790333
Open: winter Tuesday to Sunday 9am-3pm. Summer daily 9am-6pm except Sunday and Tuesday 9am–1pm.

Terme di Caracalla
Via delle Terme di Caracalla
00100 Roma
☎ (06) 5758626
Open: winter daily 9am-3pm. Summer Tuesday to Saturday 9am-6pm, Sunday and Monday 9am-1pm.

San Clemente Scavi
Via San Giovanni in Laterano
00100 Roma
Open: daily 9am-12noon and 3.30-6.30pm.

Colosseum
00100 Roma
☎ (06) 735227
Open: winter daily 9am-3pm.
Summer daily 9am-7pm, except
Sunday and Wednesday 9am-1pm.

San Pietro in Vincoli
Piazza di San Pietro in Vincoli
00100 Roma
Open: daily 7am-12.30pm and 3.30-6pm.

Museo Nazionale Romano
79 Viale E. De Nicola
00100 Roma
☎ (06) 460530
Open: Tuesday to Saturday 9am-
2pm, Sunday 9am-1pm.

Mercati Traianei
94 Via IV Novembre
00100 Roma
☎ (06) 67102070
Open: winter Tuesday to Saturday
9am-1.30pm, Sunday 9am-1pm.
Summer Tuesday to Saturday 9am-
1.30pm, Tuesday, Thursday and
Saturday also 4-7pm, Sunday 9am-
1pm.

ROUTE 1B
Galleria Doria-Pamphili
1A Piazza del Collegio Romano
00100 Roma
☎ (06) 6794365
Open: Tuesday, Friday, Saturday
and Sunday 10am-1pm.

Pantheon
Piazza della Rotonda
00100 Roma
☎ (06) 369831
Open: Monday to Saturday 9am-
2pm, Sunday 9am-1pm.

Museo di Roma
Palazzo Braschi
Piazza San Pantaleo
00100 Roma
☎ (06) 6875880

Museo Barracco
168 Corso Vittorio Emanuele
00100 Roma
☎ (06) 6540848
Open: Tuesday to Saturday 9am-
2pm, Sunday 9am-1pm.

Galleria Spada
3 Piazza Capodiferro
00100 Roma
☎ (06) 6861158
Open: Monday to Saturday 9am-
2pm, Sunday 9am-1pm.

Galleria Nazionale di Palazzo Corsini
10 Via della Lungara
00100 Roma
☎ (06) 6542323
Open: Monday to Saturday 9am-
2pm, Sunday 9am-1pm.

ROUTE 1C
Galleria Colonna
17 Via della Pilotta
00100 Roma
☎ (06) 6794362
Open: Saturday 9am-1pm; closed
in August.

Galleria Nazionale d'Arte Antica a Palazzo Barberini
13 Via Quattro Fontane
00100 Roma
☎ (06) 4814591
Open: Monday to Saturday 9am-
2pm, Sunday 9am-1pm.

Keats and Shelley Memorial House
26 Piazza di Spagna
00100 Roma
☎ (06) 6784235
Open: winter Monday to Friday
9am-1pm and 2.30-5.30pm.
Summer Monday to Friday 9am-
1pm and 3-6pm.

Museo Canonica
Viale Pietro Canonica
Villa Borghese
00100 Roma
☎ (06) 8842279
Open: Tuesday to Sunday 9am-
2pm, Tuesday and Thursday also
4-7.30pm.

Galleria Borghese
Villa Borghese
00100 Roma
☎ (06) 8548577
Open: Tuesday to Saturday 9am-
7pm, Sunday 9am-1pm.

Giardino Zoologico
Villa Borghese
00100 Roma
Open: daily 8am-5pm.

Galleria Nazionale d'Arte Moderna
131 Viale delle Belle Arti
00100 Roma
☎ (06) 8082751
Open: Tuesday to Saturday 9am-2pm, Sunday 9am-1pm.

Museo Nazionale di Villa Giulia
9 Piazzale di Villa Giulia
00100 Roma
☎ (06) 3201951
Open: Tuesday to Saturday 9am-7pm, Sunday 9am-1pm.

Ara Pacis Augustae
Via Ripetta
00100 Roma
Open: winter Tuesday to Saturday 9am-1.30pm, Sunday 9am-1pm. Summer Tuesday to Saturday 9am-1.30pm, Tuesday, Thursday and Saturday also 4-7pm, Sunday 9am-1pm.

ROUTE 1D
Museo Nazionale di Castel Sant'Angelo
Lungotevere Castello
00100 Roma
☎ (06) 6544572
Open: Tuesday to Saturday 9am-2pm, Monday 2-6pm, Sunday 9am-1pm.

Musei Vaticani
Viale Vaticano 00100 Roma
☎ (06) 6983333
Open: Monday to Saturday 9am-2pm, and last Sunday of every month (admission free) 9am-2pm.

Useful Information
Tourist Information Centre
Ente Provinciale per il Turismo
5 Via Parigi
00100 Roma
☎ (06) 463748

Emergency Telephone Numbers
Emergencies (Soccorso Pubblico di Emergenza) 113

Police (Carabinieri Pronto Intervento) 112
Fire (Vigili del Fuoco) 115
Ambulance (Ambulanza) 118
Car Breakdown (Soccorso Stradale) 116

Leisure and Entertainment
Listings for coming events in Rome can be found in the local Saturday supplement, *Trovaroma*, of the daily newspaper *La Repubblica*. Local editions of other daily national newspapers, such as *Il Messaggero*, also have listings. Otherwise, Ente Provinciale per il Turisimo, the local tourist board, produce a monthly listings called *Carnet di Roma*.
Concert and opera venues are as follows:
Teatro dell' Opera
Piazza Beniamino Gigli
☎ (06) 461 755
Open: December to June.

Terme di Caracalla
Via delle Terme di Caracalla
☎ (06) 5758302
Open: July and August.

Saint Cecilia Conservatory of Music
Via dei Greci 18
☎ (06) 6784552
Open: October to May.

Medical
Red Cross Ambulance (Croce Rossa Italiana)
☎ (06) 5100

Municipality Medical Service
Via del Colosseo 20
☎ (06) 4756741

Ospedale San Camillo
Circonvallazione Gianicolense 87
☎ (06) 58701

Ospedale San Giovanni
Via Amba Aradam
☎ (06) 77051

Ospedale Nuova Regina Margherita
Viale Trastevere 72
☎ (06) 58441

Telephone 1921 to find out which pharmacies are open. Daily newspapers also publish lists of pharmacies on rotation duty, as well as the 24 hour pharmacies.

Postal Services
Main Post Office
Piazza San Silvestro
☎ (06) 6771
Open: Monday to Friday 8.30am 9pm, Saturday 8.30am-12noon.
Services: current accounts, telegraphic money orders, postal, poste restante, telegrams. 24 hour telegram service ☎ 6795530

Central Post Office
Via della Mercede 96
☎ (06) 6795167
Open: Monday to Saturday 8.30am-12noon.
Services: information, current accounts, money orders, emergency services.

Parcel Post Office
Piazza dei Caprettari
☎ (06) 6545901
Open: Monday to Friday 8.30am-3.30pm. Saturday 8.30am-12noon
Services: parcels, packages.

Disabled
Organisations which can provide information for disabled travellers are as follows:
A.I.A.S. (Italian Association to Spastics)
Via Cipro 4/H
☎ (06) 316312

Associazione per la Terapia e la Riabilitazione degli Handicappati Psicofisici (Association for the therapy and Rehabilitation of the Pyscho-Physically Handicapped)
Opera Sante de Sanctis
Via Conte Verde 47
☎ (06) 7008311

Lost Property Offices
Ufficio Oggetti Smarriti (General Lost Property Office)
Via Niccolo Bettoni 1
☎ (06) 5810583
Open: 9am-12noon.

ATAC (City Bus Lost Property Office)
Via Volturno 65
Open: 9am-12noon

Ufficio Oggeti Rinvenuti (Railway Lost Property Office)
Via Marsala 53
☎ (06) 473 06682
Open: 7am-12midnight.

Travel
ATAC (City Bus)
Information Office
Piazza Cinquecento
☎ (06) 46954444

Ferrovie dello Stato (Railway)
Information Office
Stazione Termini
☎ (06) 4775

A.CO.TRA.L (Underground and Provincial Transport)
Information Office
☎ (06) 5915551

Car Hire
Hertz (Car Hire)
Via Sallustiana 28
☎ (06) 463334

Avis (Car Hire)
Piazza Esquilino 1
☎ (06) 47011

Maggiore (Car Hire)
Via Po 8
☎ (06) 858698

Budget (Car Hire)
Via Sistina 37
☎ (06) 4755726

Automobile Club d'Italia
Via Marsala 8
☎ (06) 49981

2

NORTHERN LAZIO AND CENTRAL TUSCANY

The routes covered in this chapter head from Rome to Florence, northwards from the region of Lazio and up through central Tuscany. Three lakes are passed on the way: Lake Bracciano, Lake Vico and Lake Bolsena, as well as several fine towns such at Viterbo and Orvieto. Siena, the only major city on the route, has a wealth of art and architecture, surpassed only by Florence. The rolling landscape with its numerous vineyards, produces some of Italy's best wines. The route passes through the wine-making regions of Montefiascone, Orvieto, Montepulciano, Montalcino and last but not least, Chianti.

At Siena, instead of continuing north to Florence, visitors have the option of joining chapter 3 and following the coast back down to Rome.

Route 2A — Rome to Viterbo

One of the first places of interest after leaving Rome on the Via Claudia Braccianese is the small town of **Bracciano** on the shores of Lake Bracciano. The main attraction in the town is the Castello Orsini-Odescalchi. Originally built as a fortress in 1419, but re-built in 1470 as the Orsini family residence, it dominates the town from the hill overlooking the lake. It owes its double-barrelled name to the fact that in 1696 it passed into the hands of the Odescalchi family, however, most that is seen today dates from the Orsini period. Guided tours of the interior leave at regular intervals (every 20 minutes in season) from the ticket office. The entrance is in the corner of the small car park in Piazza Mazzini. It takes one hour to visit the fifteen rooms with their decorated ceilings and fine frescoes by T. Zuccari and A. Romano (1490s). In the Great Hall there is a collection of armour and weapons while from the parapets at the top of the castle there are good views of the lake. The tour ends with a visit to the kitchens.

The quarter to the east of the castle, at the foot of its walls, is very picturesque and has a pleasant promenade, the Belvedere Sentiniere, which overlooks the lake. A long, steep track, the Strada della

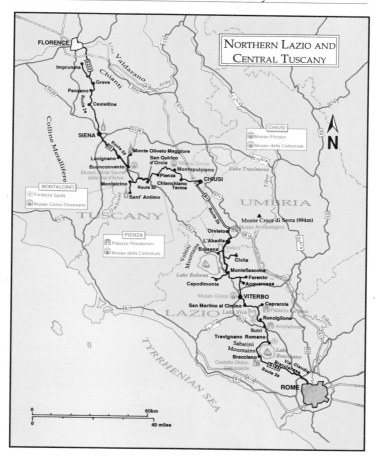

Sentinella, descends from here through olive groves to the lake edge. The lake can also be reached by following the road out of the town to **Porticciolo**, a small resort about 1km ($^1/_2$ mile) away, where there are facilities for wind-surfing, water-sports and boat hire.

Lake Bracciano, which is 9.3km (5.7 miles) long and 8.7km (5.4 miles) wide, is completely encircled by a road following the lake edge for $31^1/_2$km ($19^1/_2$ miles). The lake, 165m (541ft) deep in places, is screened from the road by tall bamboos and trees through which tracks lead to the water's edge. From Bracciano follow signs to Trevignano Romano along the north-western shore of the lake. There are good views back to the *castello*, and the forested hills and olive groves that slope down to the lake.

Trevignano Romano, 12km (7 miles) from Bracciano, has a scenic position on the lake edge. Overlooked by a ruined castle, also built by the Orsini family, the small town is centred around the *piazza* and a tree-lined promenade along the water's edge. The *municipio* on the *piazza* has a small museum containing Etruscan finds from the nearby site, *Sabatia*. At the top of the town the parish church of Assunta is decorated with Raphael school frescoes and there are good views of the lake from its terrace.

From Trevignano Romano retrace the road along the lake shore for 2km (1 mile) before taking the right turn to Sutri and Viterbo. There are scenic views back to the lake as the road climbs up into the hills to a height of 630m (2,066ft). After 5km (3 miles) the road enters the province of Viterbo and passes through 20km (12 miles) of pleasant landscape before reaching Via Cassia. Turn left on the road to Sutri, which passes the rock-cut tombs of an Etruscan necropolis before reaching the Roman amphitheatre on the outskirts of the town.

Sutri was settled by Etruscans as early as the eighth century BC, but most of the ancient remains seen today derive from the Roman settlement of *Sutrium*. The amphitheatre, which dates from the first century BC, is unusual as it was formed by cutting into the soft tufa rock rather than being built with blocks of stone. The softness of the rock means that much of the seating is badly eroded, although the underground passages and entrance ways are well-preserved. During the summer it is used for theatrical performances, and on the 15 to17 September the arena is lit by candles for the religious festival of Santa Dolcissima.

The town of Sutri, built on the hill overlooking the amphitheatre, is entered through a Roman gate, also built of tufa. The main square, the Piazza del Comune is surrounded by medieval buildings and has an attractive Baroque fountain at its centre. Via Vittorio Veneto leads from the *piazza* to the Cattedrale Santa Maria Sutrina, which dates from the thirteenth century, although, apart from the *campanile* (1207), it was largely rebuilt during the sixteenth and eighteenth centuries. Inside the cathedral there are remains of the original Cosmati paving and a thirteenth-century, Byzantine-style painting of the *Saviour* in the second chapel on the left.

While there are no other major monuments in Sutri the town itself is quite attractive and shops selling imitation Etruscan pottery (*ciotola Sutrina*), the local cheese (*caciotte*) and wine can be found. *Fagiolo della Regine*, a local dish made from beans is one of the specialities of the traditional cuisine.

Just outside the town walls in the direction of Viterbo a small track on the left leads to the tiny church of Madonna del Parto. It is built around an Etruscan rock tomb which was used as a Roman shrine before being converted to a church in the sixth to seventh centuries. Continuing towards Viterbo along Via Cassia the road forks right to Ronciglione. After 6km (4 miles) the road climbs up through an avenue of trees to the walls of Ronciglione where there are parking spaces inside the gate and on the main *piazza*.

Ronciglione with its old medieval quarter, known as the Borgo, stands above two deep ravines. A footpath leads right from inside the lower town gate, down into one of the ravines and up to a small loggia at one end of the Borgo. The narrow, cobbled streets and overhanging houses wind uphill to the Baroque Duomo on Piazza Principe di Napoli which was built in the seventeenth century to a design by Rainaldi. The fountain in the centre of the *piazza*, decorated with unicorns, dates from the sixteenth century. The remains of the medieval Castello della Rovere, and the *campanile* of Sant'Andrea, which was built in 1436, are further uphill on the right.

Lake Vico, a pleasant excursion, 2km (1 mile) north-west of Ronciglione, fills the crater of the ancient volcano, Cimino. It is small, having an area of 12sq km (7sq miles) and is surrounded by low mountains with the peak of Mount Venere on the north side, 838m (2,749ft) high. The lake is surrounded by a nature reserve which covers 3,000 hectares (7,410 acres) and offers good opportunities for hiking, cycling, canoeing and horse-riding. **Punte di Lago**, the main resort also has facilities for water-sports.

The small country road to Caprarola, 7km (4 miles) north of Ronciglione, leaves the town to the left of the Duomo. **Caprarola** lies either side of a main street which leads up to the massive Palazzo Farnese above. Built between 1559 and 1575 on the foundations of a pentagonal fortress, this vast edifice was designed in the Mannerist style by Vignola, for Cardinal Alessandro Farnese. Grand staircases climb up a series of terraces in front of the symmetrical façade, to the ticket office in the Salone delle Garde (Guard's Room). Guided tours are obligatory, leaving every 15 to 30 minutes in season. A magnificent circular staircase, the Scala Regina (1580), designed by Vignola and adorned with frescoes leads to the Piano Nobile. Grand apartments with fine frescoes and terracotta floors surround a circular courtyard, which is one of the few remnants of A. da Sangallo's former castle. The frescoes in the first room, the Fatiche di Ercole, and in the chapel, are by Federico Zuccari (1566-9). Those in the Sala dei Fasti Farnesiani are by Taddeo Zuccari (1560-66) and depict the history of the Farnese family. The Sala del Mappamondo is decorated with a curious map of the world, painted in 1574. The tour ends with a visit to the extensive gardens behind the palace.

Follow the Viterbo road from Caprarola for 7km (4 miles), up through the Lake Vico nature reserve, before turning left to **San Martino al Cimino**. From the carpark on Piazza Nazionale, just inside the medieval walls, pass under the arch into Piazza dell'Oratorio. The square is dominated by the grey church of San Martino, which was built in the thirteenth century as a Cistercian abbey. The façade, with its Gothic windows, has two great towers, dating from the seventeenth century, on either side. The well-proportioned interior is divided into three aisles by stone pilasters.

An aerial view of
Bracciano and its
castle which
dominates the town

An idyllic setting for
fishermen on Lake
Bracciano

Leave San Martino al Cimino from the lower end of town and follow the road across the plain for 7km (4 miles) to Viterbo. Parking is available in the city centre on Piazza Martiri d'Ungheria which is within easy walking distance of all the main sights.

Viterbo was an important Etruscan town, but the city today is ✳ predominantly medieval in character. Allied with the church from as early as the eighth century it gradually increased in importance, becoming a papal seat during the thirteenth century. The medieval Rocca, in the public gardens north of the town centre, is part of the excellent defensive walls built during this period. It was constructed, as were the numerous medieval towers and fountains in the city, between the eleventh and thirteenth centuries.

Piazza del Plebiscito is the centre of the city. The Palazzo del Podesta on the north side has a tall tower built in 1487. The fifteenth-to sixteenth-century Palazzo Comunale on the north-west side has a charming courtyard with good views across to Santissimi Trinita on the far side of the valley. From the far corner of the *piazza*, head up the narrow winding street, Via San Lorenzo, for 200m (656ft), turning off left to the small, twelfth-century church of Santa Maria Nuova. The simple façade has an ancient head of Jupiter set in the wall above the main door. The exterior pulpit on the right was added in the fifteenth century. Continue along Via San Lorenzo for a short distance before bearing right to Gesu, a small twelfth-century church, with the lions of the city emblem on its façade. It is located on a picturesque square that was once the business centre of the medieval city. Return to Via San Lorenzo and continue up to Piazza della Morte, where a cluster of medieval buildings surround a thirteenth-century fountain. Palazzetto di San Tommaso, which houses a small museum devoted to local medieval freemason guilds, is passed on the left. Via San Lorenzo continues across a bridge, past Palazzo Farnese with its rows of mullioned windows on the right, before reaching Piazza San Lorenzo.

Cattedrale San Lorenzo, originally built in the twelfth century, dominates the *piazza*. The fine black and white striped *campanile* was added in the fourteenth century and the façade in 1570. The interior, restored to its simple Romanesque form, retains sections of the original Cosmati paving and there is a twelfth-century painting of the *Madonna della Carbonara* in the chapel on the left.

The Palazzo Papale (1255-66) was built as the papal residence. The grand hall, the Sala dei Papi, reached by a flight of stone steps, is open to the public in the afternoons, while the rest of the building is used to show exhibitions. Along with the elegant loggia, at one end, the *palazzo* is considered the most characteristic of Viterbo's Gothic architecture.

San Pellegrino, the excellently-preserved medieval quarter, lies to the east of Piazza della Morte. Via San Pellegrino, paved with old flag-stones, starts at Piazza San Carluccio, and winds along between overhanging houses and through arches, to a delightful little square,

Piazzetta San Pellegrino. The medieval quarter has numerous small antique shops and quiet restaurants, and being pedestrianised is a pleasant escape from the otherwise busy city.

A pleasant excursion can be made to Villa Lante, a fine sixteenth-century palace, which is located in the medieval village of **Bagnaia**, 5km (3 miles) to the east of Viterbo. The road to Bagnaia passes Santa Maria della Quercia 2km (1 mile) from Viterbo, an attractive Renaissance church built between 1470 and 1525, where it is worth pausing briefly to see the Della Robbian, blue and white terracotta reliefs. They show a pair of lions guarding a miraculous image in an oak tree. At Bagnaia cross over the bridge and head up the hill to the right to the entrance to the palace. This, one of the finest palaces in Italy, was designed by Vignola, and was the residence of several popes. It is surrounded by beautifully landscaped grounds with numerous fountains and looks onto a fine Italian garden arranged on a series of terraces. The interior of the palace is not generally open to the public, but the hunting lodge can be visited during the summer.

Route 2B — Viterbo to Chiusi

Leave Viterbo from the north end of town, following signposts to Ferento. The road passes the sparse Etruscan remains at **Acquarossa** after 8km (5 miles), before turning right to **Ferento**. The road ends at a carpark next to the theatre, which although it is over-restored, is the most impressive remains of Roman *Ferentium*. Built on Etruscan foundations, it was expanded during the Augustan period and is still in use today, with concerts held here during the summer months. A Roman road leads beyond the theatre to a baths where the remains of the hypocaust are visible. Other ruins around the site date from the medieval settlement which was destroyed by Viterbo in 1172.

Return to the turning to Ferento and follow signs to Montefiascone down a small road on the left. After 11km (7 miles) the road joins the main road, Via Cassia, and heads uphill to **Montefiascone**. The large dome of the Duomo dominates the skyline. Designed in the seventeenth century by C. Fontana, it was not completed until the nineteenth century.

Montefiascone is a wine-making centre, best known for its white wine 'Est Est Est'. Legend has it that the German prelate, Johannes Fuger, ordered his servant to travel ahead to indicate the places where good wine was to be found. His mark, 'Est', meaning 'there's some here' was placed on the town's gates. At Montefiascone his enthusiasm for the wine was so great that he repeated it three times. A procession in honour of the wine is held during the local wine festival in the first half of August.

At the summit of the town there are excellent panoramic views of Lake Bolsena from the ruined castle. Built between the fourteenth and sixteenth centuries, the ruins are surrounded by pleasant public gardens. The fine church of San Flaviano lies just below the town on the road to Orvieto. The lower church was built in 1032 and has a wide but shallow interior, filled with columns surmounted by fine capitals. The walls are decorated with frescoes, dating from the fourteenth to sixteenth centuries, and a gallery opens up to the upper church which was added in the twelfth century.

An excursion can be made to **Capodimonte**, a village built on a promontory on the shores of Lake Bolsena, 7km (4 miles) from Montefiascone. The village is overlooked by the Palazzo Farnese which was designed by A. da Sangallo in the sixteenth century. It is not open to the public, however there are facilities at the lake-edge for water-skiing, sailing and boating.

From Montefiascone follow the SS71 for about 9km (6 miles), then turn right to Bagnoregio and the village of Civita. The road passes the church of San Nicolo, at the centre of **Bagnoregio**, which was designated as the *duomo* in 1699 when Civita was abandoned. Further on, in front of the fourteenth-century Gothic church of Sant'Agostino, there is a monument to St Bonaventura, who was born in Bagnoregio in 1221. Continue on to the carpark from where steps lead to the footbridge which crosses the ravine to **Civita**. The isolated spur of tufa upon which it is built, has over the centuries been so seriously eroded that the village was largely abandoned after the seventeenth century, the inhabitants moving to Bagnoregio. Recently however, people have started moving back to Civita for the first time in centuries and many of its buildings are being restored. The footbridge, which crosses high above the ravine, climbs up to the Porta San Maria, a fine gateway, carved of tufa with lions either side of the arch. Most of the houses in the village are also built of tufa, apart from around the windows and doorways where stronger, grey basalt is used. On the small *piazza* at the centre of the village is the former Duomo of San Donato with its large *campanile*. It was originally built in the eighth century on the site of an earlier temple. It was reconstructed in the eleventh century although the façade dates from the seventeenth century.

Those who do not wish to visit Bolsena can take the picturesque country road from Bagnoregio to Orvieto. Others should return to the SS71, and head towards Orvieto before taking a left fork to Bolsena.

The popular resort of **Bolsena** is picturesquely located above the lake. The Basilica San Cristina at the centre of the town is famous for the Bolsena miracle, when drops of blood fell from the host onto the altar linen. Named after the saint who is buried in the crypt, the basilica was built in the eleventh century. The façade, however, is Renaissance and was added between 1492 and 1494. The Cappella dei Miracoli, where the miracle took place, is off the left aisle.

The castle on the hilltop above Bolsena, Rocca Monaldeschi della Cervara, was built between the twelfth and fifteenth centuries. It houses a small museum of archaeological finds dating from Etruscan and Roman times. The remains of ancient Bolsena, *Volsini*, are 50m (55yd) from the castle carpark. *Volsini* was established by Etruscans who had fled from their settlement at Orvieto after it was sacked by the Romans in 280BC. The ruins are scant and only the outlines of an amphitheatre, baths and some tombs remain. There are sections of an Etruscan wall further up the road.

Continuing up the hill above Bolsena the road joins the SS71 to Orvieto. After a further 22km (14 miles), the former twelfth-century abbey of Santissimi Severo e Martirio, known as L'Abadia, comes into view on a hillside on the left. Surrounded by olive groves, the abbey is built in the Romanesque-Gothic style, and has fine views of Orvieto. It is now a popular hotel, but visitors are free to wander about the grounds and the church which has an impressive twelve-sided *Campanile*. Inside the church there are remains of recently-restored Cosmati paving.

Orvieto stands on the top of a long tufa crag, encompassed by fine city walls. Parking can be difficult, and as traffic is restricted in the city centre, it is best to park outside the walls. Founded in the eighth century BC as Etruscan *Volsini*, the city was destroyed by Romans in 280BC. It rose to prominence again during the medieval period so that many of the city's fine monuments, built of tufa and basalt, date from the twelfth and thirteenth centuries. Orvieto also boasts a fine local white wine, sold, along with hand-made ceramics, in souvenir shops throughout the city.

The Duomo in Orvieto towers above a large *piazza* on the south

The crowning glory of Orvieto is the Duomo

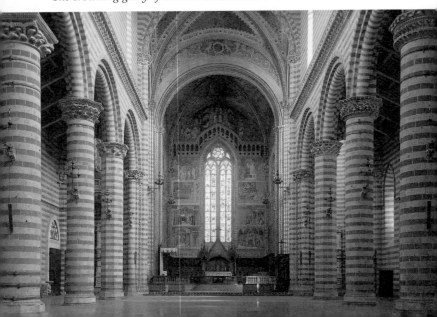

side of the city. Started in 1290 in the Romanesque form, it was continued in 1310 in the Gothic style, under the direction of the Pisano brothers. Additions were made by M. Sammicheli from 1509 to 1525. The magnificent façade is adorned with golden mosaics of the seventeenth and eighteenth centuries. The large rose window in the centre is the work of Orcagna and dates from the fourteenth century. The lower walls are carved with intricate reliefs by L. Maitani, depicting scenes from the Testaments. The main portal, flanked by smaller side entrances, has vast bronze doors cast by E. Greco during 1964 to 1967. The sides of the building are decorated with bands of black and white stone interwoven with strips of tiny mosaics.

The splendid, vast interior is also decorated with black and white stone work and there are numerous excellent frescoes. The Cappella Nuova o della Madonna di Brizio has a major fresco cycle, considered one of the most important of the Renaissance period. It was begun by Fra Angelico in 1447, but completed by L. Signorelli in 1504. In the Cappella del Corporale there is another important fresco

A delicatessen in Orvieto

cycle painted between 1357 and 1364 by Ugolino.

Other art works are housed in the Palazzo dell'Opera del Duomo. The *palazzo* (1297-1304) contains a collection of ecclesiastical paintings and sculptures, including a fine *Madonna and Child* by Andrea Pisano (1347). In the vaults of the adjoining Palazzo Papale, built in the thirteenth century, is the Museo Archeologico. The museum contains a well-displayed collection of Etruscan and Roman finds from the region, and Etruscan frescoes removed from nearby fourth-century BC tombs.

From the Duomo, follow Via Duomo past the medieval clock tower, Torre del Moro, to the busy thoroughfare, Corso Cavour. The street, lined with medieval houses and sixteenth-century *palazzi*, is a busy pedestrianised shopping area. The Piazza del Popolo, on the north side of Corso Cavour, has a lively vegetable market every morning and is overlooked by the Romanesque-Gothic Palazzo del Popolo. Built during the twelfth and thirteenth centuries, the façade of soft tufa is decorated with attractively carved window surrounds. A grand stone staircase leads to a terrace overlooking the *piazza*.

The Piazza della Repubblica, at the west end of Corso Cavour, is the administrative centre of the city. The sixteenth-century Palazzo Comunale, built of a sombre, grey stone forms one side of the square. On the east side is the small Romanesque church of Sant'Andrea which was built during the eleventh and twelfth centuries.

Chiusi is 41^1/$_2$ km (26 miles) north of Orvieto on the *autostrada* (A1) to Firenze. Leave the motorway at the Chiusi-Chianciano exit and follow the road for 3km (2 miles) up the gentle hill to Chiusi. The centre of town is pedestrianised, but parking spaces are provided on the outskirts. The history of Chiusi dates back to the Villanovan period in the first millennium BC. It was settled by Etruscans in the seventh century BC, when it was known as *Clevsin* or *Camars*. The Etruscans were defeated by the Romans in the fifth century BC but only became fully Romanised in 90BC, when it was renamed *Clusium*. Etruscan remains are scattered through the town which is surrounded by an extensive Etruscan necropolis. Two of the major tombs outside the town, Tomba Pelerine and Tomba Lione, can be visited with a guide from the local museum, the Museo Nazionale Etrusco, which is in the centre of town on Via Porsenna. It houses a good collection of Etruscan funerary urns, as well as bronze and pottery from the necropolis.

On the small *piazza* opposite the museum stands the Cattedrale San Secondiano. It was built in the twelfth century on sixth-century foundations using Etruscan and Roman masonry. The simple Romanesque façade is flanked by a twelfth-century *campanile*, built over an ancient cistern. Inside, the walls are decorated with painted, imitation mosaics, while original, fifth-century mosaics can be seen on the floor at the altar. The columns dividing the nave into three sections are mostly Roman and are topped with attractive capitals, some of them antique. In the chapel on the left, Cappella del

Sacramento, there is a notable painting by B. Fungai of the *Nativity*.

The Museo della Cattedrale to the right of the cathedral, has a well-displayed and interesting collection of ecclesiastical artefacts and paintings, including twenty-one illuminated manuscripts from the fifteenth century, as well as stone-carved fragments dating from Roman and medieval times. The catacombs of San Caterina and San Mustiola can be visited with a guide by asking the museum attendant.

Route 2C — Chiusi to Siena

Follow the signposts to Firenze out of Chiusi as far as the left turn onto the SS146 to Montepulciano. The road passes through attractive vine-covered hills to the modern thermal spa of **Chianchiano Terme**, 13km (8 miles) from Chiusi. The spa is famous for its liver cures, and the 'acquasanta' drinking water which rises from natural springs in the Parco di Fucoli, at the northern end of the resort. Six kilometres (4 miles) beyond Chianchiano Terme, there is another spa, **Terme di Montepulciano**. It specialises in the treatment of hearing problems and has thermal waters rich in sulphur and salts of bromine. Montepulciano lies a further 4km (2 miles) north, on a hilltop surrounded by cypress trees. Traffic is not allowed into the town, but parking areas are available outside the walls.

Montepulciano, known as the 'pearl of the sixteenth century', is exceptional for both its Renaissance architecture and its good wine. Montepulciano Nobile, the town's best wine, as well as many others, can be tasted in any of the numerous *enoteca* to be found around the town. Pecorino cheese is also produced locally, and Panforte or Cantucci, types of fruit-cake, dipped in the local sweet wine Vinsanto is one of Montepulciano's specialities.

The principal square, Piazza Grande, is at the highest point of the town, just north of the Fortezza. It is surrounded by fine, sixteenth-century buildings, including the Duomo. It has an unimposing brick façade (1592-1630), but a vast interior which is divided into three aisles by enormous piers. At the main altar there is a fine triptych by the Sienese painter, Taddeo di Bartolo (1401). The chapel on the left contains a stone-carved, fourteenth-century font and on the wall behind, a blue and white terracotta by Della Robbia and a relief attributed to Benedetto da Maiano. Palazzo Tarugi, opposite the Duomo, was designed by A. da Sangallo (1518-34). The elegant well next to the *palazzo*, with its griffins and lions, was erected in 1520. To the left of Palazzo Tarugi is the Gothic style Palazzo del Capitano del Popolo. The crenellated Palazzo Comunale with its high clock tower, on the west side of the *piazza*, was started in the fourteenth century, and finished by Michelozzo in 1465. It still serves as the *comune* but the clock tower is open to the public on weekday mornings. The entrance to the tower is on the first floor, at the end of the corridor on the right. Narrow stairs climb to the top, from where there are good views to the domed church of San Biagio and the Val d'Orcia.

Via Ricci leads downhill from Piazza Grande past the Museo Civico which is housed in the fourteenth-century, Sienese-Gothic style Palazzo Neri Orselli. Most of the collection of religious work, which dates from the thirteenth to seventeenth centuries, was donated by Francesco Crociani in 1859. There is also a small collection of local archaeological finds.

Via di Voltaia and Via di Gracciano, are excellently preserved examples of sixteenth-century architecture. Continuing past the museum, take the first alley on the right, down to Via di Voltaia, and continue downhill past Palazzo Cervini. It was designed around a U-shaped courtyard by A. da Sangallo (1518-34) and is now a bank. Slightly further on, on the left, a road leads up past the Loggia di Mercato, designed by Vignola, to San Lucia. This small Baroque church was built in 1653 and has an attractive stone façade with garlands of fruit carved either side of the door. Return back to the loggia and pass under the arch into Via di Gracciano. Sant'Agostino with its façade, designed in 1440 by Michelozzo, stands opposite the sixteenth-century clock tower, Torre di Pulcinella. The endearing figure of Pulcinella is poised on top of the tower, ready to strike the bell on the hour. Via di Gracciano is lined with particularly fine Renaissance buildings. On the left at number seventy-three, the seventeenth-century Palazzo Bucelli has a number of Etruscan funerary urns and Roman inscription stone set in its lower walls. Opposite is the Palazzo Coccioni with its rusticated stone façade. It was designed in the sixteenth century by A. da Sangallo. Further downhill, on the left, at number ninety-three, is Palazzo Avignonese, also sixteenth-century, but designed by Vignola. The fine gateway, Porta al Prato, at the end of Via di Gracciano is part of the town fortifications designed by A. da Sangallo in the second half of the sixteenth century. The guard house, now converted to a restaurant, can be entered through a narrow passage from outside the gate. Below the walls on the south-west side of the town is the fine Renaissance church of San Biagio, considered to be A. da Sangallo's best work. Built of a warm-coloured travertine stone, it is designed in the form of a Greek cross with a high dome at the centre. Started in 1518, the church was not completed until 1545, and one of the two bell towers which stands at the corner was never completed at all. The interior is symmetrical with attractive carvings on the walls. The nearby canon's house with its fine stone loggia was also designed by A. da Sangallo.

From Montepulciano follow signs to Pienza on the SS146, past numerous producers of the local wine and cheese. The fortified Palazzo Masaini, 9km (6 miles) from Montepulciano, is one of the more interesting wineries. Pienza, a further 3km (2 miles), sits on a flat hilltop above the Val d'Orcia. Visitors should park around the walls of the town as the centre is pedestrianised.

Pienza was the creation of Aeneas Silvius Piccolomini, who was born here in 1405. When in 1458 he became Pope Pius II, he had his birthplace, formerly known as Corsignano, rebuilt to a design by B. Rossellino, and renamed it Pienza. The project was started in 1459 and finished in 1462, just 2 years before Pope Pius II died. Palazzo Piccolomini (1460-62), in the centre of the town, is open as a museum with a collection of arms and art objects on the first floor. It is built around a large colonnaded courtyard and has a three-tier loggia, overlooking the Sienese hills.

The Cattedrale, in Piazza Pio II next to the *palazzo*, has an attractive Renaissance façade. The simple, well-lit interior is lined with fine paintings and retains the original inlaid choir stalls (1462) in the apse. The cathedral treasury, and a collection of paintings, mostly by the Sienese School, are housed in the Museo della Cattedrale, at the back of the building on the left. The Palazzo Comunale on the opposite side of the *piazza* has a fine crenellated tower. Built in 1463, the *palazzo* has attractive sgraffito decoration above an elegant arcaded basement. Palazzo Vescovile, built for Pope Alexander IV, is on the left side of the *piazza*. The small road between the *palazzo* and the cathedral leads to the town walls where a sentry walk offers fine views over the countryside.

Take the SS146 from Pienza to San Quirico d'Orcia, $9^1/_2$km (6 miles) to the west. After 2km (1 mile) the road passes the turning to Sant'Anna in Caprena, where there are fine frescoes by Sodoma (1502-3) in the refectory. **San Quirico d'Orcia**, like nearby Castiglion d'Orcia, is built on a fortified hill. Inside its fifteenth-century walls the major attraction is the Collegiata. Built during the twelfth century of travertine and sandstone in the Romanesque style, it is decorated with fine carvings of caryatids and animals. Of the three richly carved portals, the one in the façade is the oldest, dating from 1080. The side portal supported by two figures is thought to be the work of G. Pisano and dates from the thirteenth century. The attractive choir stalls inside date from 1655 and the altarpiece in the left chapel is by Sano di Pietro (around 1470).

Take the SS2 from San Quirico d'Orcia in the direction of Siena for 6 km (4 miles) before turning left to **Montalcino**. Nine kilometres (6 miles) from the main road, Montalcino is dominated by a large Sienese fortress which guards the Ombrone and Asso valleys. Built in 1361, the fortress now houses a well-stocked *enoteca* from where it is possible to ascend the walls and visit a small museum. Montalcino is well-known for its good quality wine, the Brunello di Montalcino. As well as the numerous other *enoteca* in the town, the Palazzo Comunale on the main *piazza* has a permanent exhibition of Montalcino wines. There is also a wine festival, the Sagra del Tordo (Festival of the Thrush) on the last Sunday in October. The only other monument in the town of any note is the Romanesque-Gothic church of Sant'Agostino which, built in the fourteenth century, has a striking black and white striped façade and a good rose window. The

Museo Civico Diocesano, uphill from Sant'Agostino, has a collection of fourteenth- and fifteenth-century Sienese school paintings. There are fine views of the surrounding countryside from the promenade along the west wall that leads to the church of Madonna del Soccorso.

The abbey of **Sant'Antimo**, 8km (5 miles) south-east of Montalcino, makes a pleasant excursion. Surrounded by olive groves Sant'Antimo dates from 1118, although the original Benedictine abbey was founded by Charlemagne in AD 781. Towards the end of the twelfth century the abbey fell into disuse and only the church and refectory have survived. There are several interesting carved animals and figures set into the outside walls of the church and the portal is very finely decorated. The interior of the church is very beautiful due to the abundant use of alabaster. An ambulatory, with alabaster columns, passes behind the altar and around the apse in which there are three attractive chapels. The capitals in the nave are decorated with animals and foliage, and there is an inscription on one side of the alabaster plinth which supports the altar. Steps lead down to a tiny chapel underneath the altar where there is a simple fresco on one wall.

From Montalcino, the SP45 winds down towards Buonconvento and Siena, joining the SS2 after 14km (9 miles). **Buonconvento**, surrounded by thirteenth-century walls, is a small town with a historic centre and a good museum of religious art, the Museo d'Arte Sacra della Val d'Arbia. The town is also a convenient base from which to visit the abbey of **Monte Oliveto Maggiore**.

The abbey is 9km (6 miles) north-east of Buonconvento on the SS451. A small track leads right to a carpark by the gate-house, from where visitors must walk down through cypresses to the abbey entrance. Visitors are permitted to wander about freely, but are requested to be silent and to wear appropriate clothing. It was founded as a Benedictine hermitage in 1313 by Tolomei of Siena and during the fifteenth and sixteenth centuries became an important centre of Renaissance art and culture. Today it is the headquarters of the Benedictine Order and only a fraction of the extensive buildings are open to the public.

Of the three cloisters in the abbey, the first is the largest. It is closed in by glass and decorated with an important Renaissance fresco cycle which depicts the life of St Benedict. There are thirty-six panels; nine by Signorelli (1497-8), and twenty-seven by Sodoma (1505-8). In one corner of the cloister, a short hall, also frescoed by Sodoma, leads into the church. The Baroque decoration in most of the church dates from 1772, but the beautiful choir stalls, finely inlaid with street scenes and landscapes, are older and were the work of Giovanni da Verona (1505). From the second cloister, where there is a refectory decorated with fifteenth-century frescoes, a stairway leads up to the library.

Visitors should rejoin the SS2 for the remaining $27^1/_2$km (17 miles) to Siena, passing through **Lucignano** with its tower on the way.

Route 2D — Siena

Siena is an elegant city, although it is generally busy and crowded. The limited amount of parking spaces in the centre are soon snapped up so it is best to head for one of the carparks near the stadium to the west of the city. The carparks are all signposted off the *tangenziale* which skirts the city, but it should be noted that the carpark on La Lizza is used as a market place on Wednesday mornings.

The city has been an important centre of art and culture through-out its history and has a wealth of fine buildings and works of art. The feud between Florence and Siena, which lasted from 1125 until 1555, meant that Sienese art and architecture developed its own idiom and style independent of developments in Florence. The Sienese arch, a pointed arch above a Romanesque one, typifies the architecture of the city. Not only are the major monuments well-preserved, Siena's streets are lined with attractive medieval buildings, the Siena-brown of their brick in harmony with their terracotta roofs.

The city's most important monuments are centred around the **Piazza del Campo**, a vast fan-shaped *piazza* at the foot of three hills. Built on the site of the ancient forum of the Roman city, *Sena Juli*, it is divided into nine sections in honour of the nine Signoria who ruled Siena from 1280 to 1355. The stone fountain, the Fonte Gaia, was carved by Jacopo della Quercia (1374-1438) although the relief panels seen today are reproductions. The back of the *piazza* is lined with attractive medieval buildings, housing elegant shops and cafés. It is around this perimeter that on the 2 July and the 16 August the *palio* race takes place. It is one of the most famous *palio* in Italy and dates back to 1659. Competitors from seventeen of the city's districts, the *contrada*, dress up in Renaissance costume and race on horseback for three laps around the Campo.

At the front of the Campo stands the large, crenellated Palazzo Pubblico, and the Torre del Mangia, which is 102m (335ft) tall. The small chapel, the Cappella di Piazza (1352-76), at the foot of the tower was built to commemorate the end of the 1348 plague. The tower itself was built between 1325 and 1344 to a design by M. and F. Rinaldi. A staircase leads up from the courtyard, the Cortile del Podesta, just inside the *palazzo*. The 409 narrow steps lead up to the great bell which was cast in 1666 and weighs 6,724kg (14,826lb). The fine views across the city and surrounding hills are well worth the climb. The *palazzo* which was built between 1297 and 1342 now houses the **Museo Civico**. The entrance is on the right side of the Cortile del Podesta. The museum has a collection of paintings in the Sala della Quadreria and several attractively frescoed apartments. The frescoes in the first apartment, the Sala dei Risorgimento, painted between 1886 and 1891, depict the part played by Vittorio Emanuele II in the unification of Italy. The frescoes in the Sala di Balia (1407) are by Spinello; while Domenico Beccafumi (1486-1551), painted the ceiling in the Sala dei Concistoro. The frescoes in the chapel are by Taddeo di Bartolo (1407-1417) and the beautiful altar piece is by Sodoma (1536). The Sala del Mappamondo contains the *Maesta* (1315), an important work by Simone Martini. In the Sala della Pace there is a famous cycle of allegorical frescoes by A. Lorenzetti, painted between 1338 and 1340. The loggia at the top of the *palazzo* has the original reliefs (1419) from the Fonte Gaia, as well as fine views of the city.

Follow Via di Citta uphill from the Campo, passing the curved façade of the fourteenth-century Palazzo Chigi Saracini on the left, and the rusticated façade with mullioned windows of Palazzo Piccolomini (1495), on the right, before turning right into Piazza del Duomo. **Duomo Santa Maria** is a grand edifice of black and white striped stone, with a richly decorated façade. The statues and carvings on the lower part of the façade, designed by Giovanni Pisano (1284-99), are mostly replaced with reproductions, the originals being in the baptistery and the nearby museum. The upper part of the façade, with its carved pinnacles, was added in 1376, and is reminiscent of the *duomo* at Orvieto. The high gables contain Venetian, gold mosaics of the nineteenth century. The tall black and white *campanile* was built in 1313. The vast interior, also striped in black and white stone, has an outstanding floor paved with fifty-six large, inlaid marble panels. Thirty-five of the panels are the work of D. Beccafumi who spent the 30 years between 1517 and 1547 working on them. Other less important Sienese artists produced the rest. The sgraffitti black and white outlines of the early fourteenth-century panels give way to areas of inlaid red, black and white, especially in the panels executed after 1547. High above the columns of the central nave, lined with 170 terracotta busts of popes, is the great hexagonal dome which was built between 1259 and 1264. The finely carved marble pulpit (1265-8), supported on columns and swathed in beautifully sculpted reliefs, is Nicolo Pisano's masterpiece. The high altar, by B. Peruzzi (1506) has a fifteenth-century, bronze ciborium by Vecchietta, while the striking stained-glass windows in the apse behind were designed in the style of Duccio di Buoninsegna (1288). A door from the left aisle leads to the **Libreria Piccolomini**, a small, Renaissance library, built for Pope Pius III in 1492. It has a collection of illuminated manuscripts, and finely frescoed walls. The cycle, in ten panels, depicts the life of the Pope and was painted by Pinturicchio between 1502 and 1509. In the centre of the room there is a third-century Roman statue of the *Three Graces*.

The **Museo dell'Opera Metropolitana**, opposite the *campanile*, houses other works from the Duomo. The museum building is an incomplete transept, built in 1339 as part of a grand project to increase the size of the Duomo. However, the Plague of 1348 lead to financial problems and the eventual abandonment of the project. The museum contains an excellent collection of Sienese art. On the ground floor are the original carvings and statues by G. Pisano from the Duomo. The second floor has an important collection of ecclesiastical Sienese paintings, including the outstanding altarpiece painted by Duccio (1308-11) for the Duomo. The cathedral treasury is displayed on the third floor, while bishop's vestments and other objects are on the fourth. A stairway, the Scala del Falciatore, leads up from the fourth floor, inside the partly-built transept wall to the top from where there are excellent panoramas across the city.

From Piazza del Duomo follow Via del Capitano which is lined with medieval buildings, to the **Pinacoteca Nazionale** on Via San Pietro. The gallery, housed in the fourteenth-century Palazzo Buonsignori, has an outstanding collection of Sienese art. The paintings are displayed chronologically from the twelfth to the sixteenth centuries. The earliest paintings are on the second floor and range from works by Duccio and Lorenzetti, to later fifteenth-century painters, such as San Pietro (1406-81). Later paintings are on the first floor, there is also a collection of seventeenth-century European paintings on the third floor, the Collezione Spannochi, including a small portrait by A. Dürer.

The church of Sant'Agostino is a further 150m (164yd) up Via San Pietro. Built as an Augustan church in the thirteenth century, it was reconstructed by L. Van Vitelli in 1775. Amongst the numerous fine works of art inside, is the *Crucifix and Saints* by Perugino (1506) in the second niche on the right and an *Epiphany* by Sodoma at the altar. The

A view of the Duomo and campanile, *Siena*

Cappella Piccolomini is decorated with frescoes by A. Lorenzetti.

Other churches in the city are less easily accessible and involve a fair bit of walking up and down hill. The large Gothic church of San Domenico, lies on a hilltop to the west of the city, near the stadium, overlooking the Fonte Brande (1080-1264) a large fountain and loggia in the steep valley below. The church was built by the Domenican Order between 1226 and 1465. The tall *campanile* was added in 1490. Inside, the vast single nave is sparsely decorated, but the Cappella di Santa Caterina, which contains the saint's head, has fine frescoes by Sodoma. Born in Siena, Santa Caterina is the patron saint of Italy. The second chapel to the right of the main apse also has frescoes by Sodoma.

The church of San Francesco lies about a kilometre ($^1/_2$ mile) north-east of San Domenico. The church dates from 1326, although it was enlarged in 1475 and contains good frescoes by P. Lorenzetti (1331). The Oratorio San Bernardino is next door to the church and has seventeenth-century frescoes depicting San Bernardino's life in the lower chapel and frescoes by Sodoma and D. Beccafumi in the upper.

Route 2E — Chianti Route from Siena to Florence

The SS222 Chiantigiana, known as the Chianti route, passes through the heart of the Chianti wine growing region. From the northern suburbs of Siena follow signs to Castellina. Once out of the city the road is lined with *fattoria* and *cantina* which, as well as selling their own wine (look out for signs saying *vendita diretta*), often have accommodation, restaurants and even swimming pools too. With over 7,000 registered vineyards and hundreds of producers, there are enormous variations from one wine to another. The route passes through the best known of the seven Chianti zones, Chianti Classico.

The small town of **Castellina**, 21km (13 miles) north of Siena, is important for its wine production. It stands in the shadow of a ruined fifteenth-century castle and has a pleasant pedestrian centre. The SS222 continues over picturesque hills dotted with vineyards, before crossing a steep valley up through the sprawling village of **Panzano**. The centre of the village is on the hill, below the twelfth-century Oratorio Santissimi Annunziata, to the left of the main road. As it is another important Chianti village, there are several *entoteca* which offer tastings of the local wines along the main street.

Greve, the centre of Chianti wine production, is 6km (4 miles) north of Panzano. Although it is a small town it has a large *piazza*, surrounded by porticoed restaurants, cafés and wine shops, which is the venue for an important wine fair held in September. The road beyond Greve has the greatest concentration of wine producers on the Chianti route. After the left fork to **Impruneta**, which has a large church containing terracottas by Della Robbia, the remaining 10km (6 miles) to Florence become increasingly built-up, eventually becoming the suburbs of the city itself.

Additional Information

Places of Interest

ROUTE 2A
Bracciano
Castello Orsini-Odescalchi
14 Piazza Mazzini
00062 Bracciano (ROMA)
☎ (06) 9024003
Open: winter Tuesday to Sunday
10am-12noon and 3-5pm. Summer
Tuesday to Sunday 9am-12noon and
3-6pm (also open Mondays in
August).

Sutri
Amphitheatre
01015 Sutri (VT)
Open: Tuesday to Sunday 8.30am-
1.30pm.

Caprarola
Palazzo Farnese
01032 Caprarola (VT)
☎ (0761) 64052
Open: winter Tuesday to Sunday
9am-4.30pm. Summer Tuesday to
Sunday 9am-6pm.

Viterbo
Museo Civico
Santa Maria della Verita
01100 Viterbo (VT)
☎ (0761) 340810
Open: summer Monday to Saturday
8.30am-1.30pm and 3.30-6pm. Winter
and holidays 9am-1.30pm.

Bagnaia
Villa Lante
01100 Bagnaia (VT)
☎ (0761) 288200
Open: September and October
Tuesday to Sunday 9am-5.30pm.
November to February Tuesday to
Sunday 9am-4pm. March to May
Tuesday to Sunday 9am-5.30pm.
May to August Tuesday to Sunday
9am-7.30pm.

ROUTE 2B
Bolsena
San Cristina Catacomb
Basilica San Cristina
01023 Bolsena (VT)
☎ (0761) 799067
Open: winter daily 7am-12.30pm
and 3-6pm. Summer daily 7am-
12.30pm and 4-8pm.

Museo Territorale del Lago di Bolsena
Rocca Monaldeschi della Cervara
01023 Bolsena (VT)
Open: Tuesday to Sunday 9.30am-
1pm and 3.30-8pm.

Scavi dei Volsini
01023 Bolsena (VT)
Open: Tuesday to Sunday 8am-1pm.

Orvieto
Museo Archeologico
Palazzo Papale
Piazza del Duomo
05018 Orvieto (TR)
☎ (0763) 41039
Open: Monday to Saturday 9am-
1.30pm and 3-7pm, Sunday 9am-1pm.

Palazzo dell'Opera del Duomo
Piazza del Duomo
05018 Orvieto (TR)
Open: winter Tuesday to Sunday
9am-1pm and 2.30-5pm. Summer
Tuesday to Sunday 9am-1pm and
2.30-6pm.

Chiusi
Museo Nazionale Etrusco
Via Porsenna
53043 Chiusi (SI)
Open: Tuesday to Saturday 9am-
1.45pm Sunday 9am-12.45pm.

Museo della Cattedrale
Piazza Duomo
53034 Chiusi (SI)
☎ (0578) 226490
Open: summer, daily 9.30am-
12.45pm
4.30-7.30pm. Winter, Monday-
Saturday 9.30am-12.45pm, Sunday
9.30-12.45pm, 4-7pm

ROUTE 2C
Montepulciano
Museo Civico
10 Via Ricci
53045 Montepulciano (SI)
☎ (0578) 616935
Open: Wednesday to Sunday 9am-
12.30pm and 3-6pm.

Pienza
Palazzo Piccolomini
53026 Pienza (SI)
Open: winter Tuesday to Sunday
10am-12.30pm and 3-6pm. Summer
Tuesday to Sunday 10am-12.30pm
and 4-7pm.

Museo della Cattedrale
Casa dei Canonici
53026 Pienza (SI)
Open: winter, daily 10am-1pm, 2-4pm
Summer, daily 10am-1pm, 3-6pm.

Montalcino
Museo Civico Diocesano
Palazzo Vescovile
Via Spagni
53024 Montalcino (SI)
☎ (0577) 848135
Open: October to April Tuesday to
Sunday 10am-1pm and 3-5pm.
May to September Tuesday to
Sunday 9.30am-1pm and 3.30-7pm.

Fortezza Spalti
53024 Montalcino (SI)
☎ (0577) 849211
Open: winter Tuesday to Sunday
9am-1pm and 2-6pm. Summer
daily 9am-1pm and 2-8pm.
Wine bar, shop and museum.

Buonconvento
Museo d' Arte Sacra della Val d' Arbia
53022 Buonconvento (SI)
Open: Tuesday and Thursday
10am-12noon.
Saturday 10am-12noon, 4-6pm
Sunday 9am-1pm

Abbazia di Monte Oliveto Maggiore
53041 Asciano (SI)
☎ (0577) 707022
Open: winter daily 9am-12noon
and 3-6.30pm. Summer daily 9am-
12noon and 3-5pm.
Restaurant, souvenir shop.

ROUTE 2D
Siena
Enoteca Italiana di Siena
Fortezza Medicea
53100 Siena (SI)
☎ (0577) 288497
Open: daily 3pm-midnight.

Museo Civico
Palazzo Pubblico
Piazza del Campo
53100 Siena (SI)
Open: winter Monday to Saturday
9.30am-12.45pm, holidays 9am-
1pm. Summer Monday to Saturday
9.30am-6.45pm, holidays 9am-1pm.

Torre del Mangia
Palazzo Comunale
Piazza del Campo
53100 Siena (SI)
Open: winter daily 10am-1.30pm.
Summer daily 10am-5 or 7pm.

Duomo
Piazza del Duomo
53100 Siena (SI)
Open: winter daily 7.30am-1.30pm
and 2.30pm-sunset, summer daily
7.30am-7.30pm.
Book and postcard shop.

Libreria Piccolomini
Duomo
Piazza del Duomo
53100 Siena (SI)
Open: winter daily 10am-1pm and
2.30-5pm. Summer daily 9am-
7.30pm.

Museo dell'Opera Metropolitana
Piazza del Duomo
53100 Siena (SI)
Open: winter daily 9am-1.30pm.
Summer daily 9am-7.30pm.

Cripta delle Statue
Duomo
53100 Siena (SI)
Open: summer daily 10am-1pm
and 2.30-6pm.

Battistero
Duomo
53100 Siena (SI)

Open: winter daily 9am-12.55pm and 3-5pm. Summer daily 9am-12.55pm and 3-6pm.

Pinacoteca Nazionale
Palazzo Buonsignori
29 Via San Pietro
53100 Siena (SI)
Open: Tuesday to Saturday
8.30am-7pm, holidays 8.30am-1.30pm.

Tourist Information Centres

Route 2A
Bracciano
Azienda Autonoma di Soggiorno e Turismo
58 Via Claudia
00062 Bracciano (ROMA)
☎ (06) 9023664

Sutri
Pro Loco
Palazzo Comunale
31 Piazza del Comune
01015 Sutri (VT)
☎ (0761) 68330

Ronciglione
Pro Loco
22 Corso Umberto
01037 Ronciglione (VT)
☎ (0761) 625460

Viterbo
Ente Provinciale per il Turismo
16 Piazza dei Caduti
01100 Viterbo (VT)
☎ (0761) 340810
Open: summer Monday to Saturday 8.30am-1.30pm and 3.30-6pm. Winter and holidays 9am-1.30pm.

Route 2B
Orvieto
Azienda di Promozione Turistica dell'Orvietano
24 Piazza del Duomo
05018 Orvieto (TR)
☎ (0763) 41772

Route 2C
Montepulciano
Ufficio Turistico Comunale
9 Via Ricci
53045 Montepulciano (SI)
☎ (0578) 757442

Pienza
Pro Loco
1 Vicolo della Canonica
53026 Pienza (SI)
☎ (0578) 748502

Montalcino
Ufficio Turistico
8 Costa del Municipio
53024 Montalcino (SI)
☎ (0577) 849331

Route 2D
Siena
Azienda di Turismo
56 Piazza del Campo
53100 Siena (SI)
☎ (0577) 280551

3

THE ETRUSCAN COAST

C hapter 3 crosses Tuscany, west to the coast from Siena and follows the Etruscan Riviera south to Rome, taking in a wealth of excellent Etruscan sites. The origin of the Etruscans is unknown, but there is clear archaeological evidence of their existence at least as far back as the eighth century BC. The oldest settlements appear to be along the western coast of Italy, but by the sixth century BC they ruled the whole of Central Italy through a series of autonomous states. Twelve of the major Etruscan cities formed an alliance, known as the Etruscan League. However, they were never united enough to stand up to the growing power of Rome, and were gradually all conquered, the last Etruscan city falling to the Romans in 265BC.

Among the most interesting Etruscan remains are the remarkably preserved cities of the dead, the necropoli. They have provided the museums of the region with a wealth of artefacts which range from fine bronzes to attractively decorated pottery, as well as frescoes and sarcophagi.

The Etruscan Riviera is a well-developed coast, and the numerous resorts usually have a wide selection of water-sports and other leisure activities on offer, as well as long, sandy beaches. There are also some nature reserves where it is possible to walk or ride amid beautiful, unspoilt scenery.

Those who do not wish to return to Rome can instead head north along the coast from Cecina to join chapter 5 at Pisa.

Route 3A — Siena to Volterra

Monteriggioni, 12^1/$_2$km (7 miles) north-west of Siena, can be reached either by the SS2 or the toll-free *autostrada* to Firenze. The impressive walls of the village, complete with fourteen towers, stand on a low hill overlooking the surrounding countryside. Built in the thirteenth century as part of the Sienese defences against Florence the walls dwarf the present day village inside. A pleasant walk can be made around the outside of the walls, and there is an *enoteca* in the village where local wine is available.

Follow the SS68 in a north-westerly direction for 8km (5 miles) to

Colle di Val d'Elsa. Pass through the modern suburbs in the plain, up to the old town, built along the ridge above. Predominantly Renaissance in character, the attractive main street, Via di Campana, has two small museums. The Museo Archeologico is housed in the Palazzo Pretorio, also known as Palazzo Campana, which was built in 1539. It has a small collection of artefacts from the ancient necropolis of Monteriggioni, and in the basement the old jail is preserved complete with prisoner's graffiti. The Museo Civico, in the Palazzo dei Priori, has a collection of religious paintings. Also of interest is the house of the architect Arnolfo di Cambio (1232-1302) who drew the first designs for the Duomo in Florence, and the cut-crystal workshops where craftsmen keep alive the tradition that has been passed down since the fourteenth century.

The road leaves the town past a fine defensive gate, the Porta Nuova, which was designed by A. da Sangallo in the fifteenth century. Shortly after passing the gate turn right to **San Gimignano**, 10km (6 miles) away, and park outside the walls. The silhouette of the town is not as dramatic as it must have been once, but it is nonetheless striking. Built on a small hilltop, San Gimignano's skyline is punctuated by several tall, rectangular stone towers. They date from the twelfth and thirteenth centuries, and were built by powerful families, both as symbols of their wealth and power, and as defensive strongholds. In its heyday, San Gimignano had as many as seventy towers, now only twelve stand to their original heights.

The Collegiata, on Piazza del Duomo, in the centre of the town stands at the top of a flight of steps and dates from the twelfth century. The interior is richly decorated with frescoes. Scenes from the Old Testament, by Bartolo di Fredi (1367), cover the left wall, and the New Testament, by Barna di Siena (1381), the right. A fresco of the *Martyrdom of St Sebastian* by Benozzo Gozzoli is above the main door, and is flanked by the impressive *Last Judgement* of Taddeo di Bartolo (1397). This already rich collection of frescoes was further enhanced in 1482 when Domenico Ghirlandaio (1449-1495) added three more. His *Annunciation* can be seen in the small loggia to the left of the nave, the other two frescoes are in the Capella San Fino.

Piazza del Duomo is surrounded by fine buildings. On the south side is the Palazzo del Popolo (1288-1323), on the east the Palazzo del Podesta (1239-1337). On Thursday mornings the *piazza* is filled by a lively market, and during the summer arts festival is the venue for recitations and concerts.

The Museo Etrusco e d'Arte Sacre is on the small *piazza* to the left of the Collegiata. Arranged around a courtyard containing Etruscan remains, the museum has a collection of medieval stone carvings, vestments and silver, dating from the thirteenth to fifteenth centuries, as well as illuminated manuscripts of the fourteenth century. The Museo Civico is housed in part of the Palazzo del Popolo and is reached via an external staircase. It has a collection of thirteenth to fifteenth-century Sienese and Florentine paintings, but perhaps

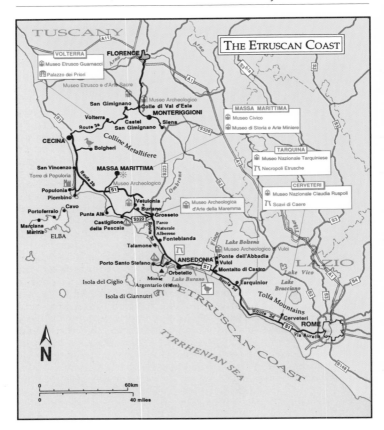

most interesting is the Sala del Consiglio, the Council Chamber. It was frescoed in 1317 by Lippo Memmi and in 1467 by Benozzo Gozzoli, and is believed to be where Dante gave his famous speech, in 1229, defending Florence, and advising San Gimignano to join the Guelph league. The 56m (184ft) high tower above the Palazzo Popolo is also reached from the museum.

Head north out of Piazza del Duomo along Via San Matteo, passing the Torri dei Salvucci, the Palazzo della Cancelleria and the thirteenth-century church of San Bartolo. Near the bottom of the hill, turn right shortly after the Palazzo Tinacci, to the church of Sant'Agostino which is located on a quiet *piazza*, close to the town walls. It dates from the thirteenth century and is built in the Gothic-Romanesque style. The well-lit interior has a single nave and an excellent fresco cycle in the apse. The seventeen frescoed panels illustrate the life of St Augustine, and were painted by Benozzo Gozzoli in 1465. The Cappella di San Bartolo on the right side of the church has a richly-carved altar by B. da Maiano and a fine painting of *Madonna and Saints*, by P. Fiorentino. A door on the left side of the church leads through to an attractive fifteenth-century cloister.

Return to Piazza del Duomo by following the town walls up to the Rocca, a fortress built in 1353, but destroyed by Cosimo I in 1558. The ruined towers are set in a park, overlooking the olive-covered slopes below. To the south of Piazza del Duomo, is another square, the Piazza della Cisterna. It is surrounded by medieval houses and towers, and has a thirteenth-century well at its centre. Via San Giovanni, leads downhill from the *piazza*, through the Arco de Beci. It is the main shopping street in the town and has a good selection of local produce, such as Vernaccia and Chianti wines, Mandorlato fruit cake, and wild boar. The Palazzo Pratellesi on the left, now the public library, dates from the fourteenth century. Further down on the right is the twelfth-century church of San Francesco, which now houses an *enoteca*. There are splendid views from here across the Elsa valley.

The road to **Volterra**, (29km / 18 miles), passes through San Donato and Castel San Gimignano, the latter village having a ruined castle, before joining the SS68. The road gradually climbs up to Volterra which has a commanding position at the top of a hill, 555m (1,820ft) high. Visitors can either park below the walls of the Fortezza, built by Lorenzo Medici in 1472, and still used as a prison, or continue on to Piazza Martiri della Liberta, inside the south walls. Volterra is built

The twin towers of Torri dei Salvucci, San Gimignano

on the site of Etruscan *Velathri* and Roman *Volaterrae*. Many ancient stones have been incorporated into the numerous fine buildings in the town, and excavations have provided the Etruscan museum with an excellent collection.

Museo Etrusco Guarnacci, is on Via Don Minzoni, near the Fortezza at the east end of town. The museum was founded by Mario Guarnacci in 1761 and has an outstanding collection of Etruscan funerary urns, dating from the third century BC onwards. There are over 600 urns altogether, arranged chronologically in 36 rooms on 3 floors. Mostly carved from stone, they are decorated with a variety of subjects, ranging from simple symbols and masks, to complex mythological scenes and funerary processions. While at this end of town it is also worth walking up to the Parco Archeologico Enrico Fiumi, beside the Fortezza, from where there are good views over the town and surrounding countryside.

From the museum Via Don Minzoni leads into the town centre via Piazza XX Settembre, where the little church of Sant'Antonio contains a beautiful altar painting by Priamo della Querce (1442), as well as a sixteenth-century Della Robbia terracotta. To the left of the church, Via Gramsci, the main shopping street, leads up to Piazza dei Priori which is surrounded by thirteenth-century buildings. The Palazzo dei Priori (1208-54) was one of the earliest seats of government in Tuscany, and still houses the offices of the local *comune*. Two rooms on the first floor are open to the public. The council chamber, the Sala del Consiglio, has coats of arms painted on the walls, as well as a fourteenth-century fresco of the *Annunciation and Saints*. The Duomo is behind the Palazzo dei Priori, but can be entered from the *piazza* through a door in the left transept. It was constructed during the twelfth and thirteenth centuries, and has a large, symmetrical interior. The attractive wooden ceiling and the marble ciboria date from the sixteenth century, while the choir stalls are early fifteenth century. The second chapel on the right has a fine painting of the *Annunciation* by Mariotto Albertinelli (1497). Pass out through the main door onto a small *piazza*, containing the octagonal baptistery.

The Pinacoteca Civica is on Via dei Sarti, to the north of the Duomo. Housed in the fifteenth-century Palazzo Minucci-Solaini, the first floor has a well-arranged collection of religious paintings, while the second contains medieval sculptures, ceramics and other artefacts. Continue along Via dei Sarti past the grand fourteenth-century Palazzo Viti on the left, to the black and white striped façade of San Michele. The church is built in the Pisan style, and contains a Della Robbia terracotta *Madonna and Child* to the left of the altar. While walking around the town it is worth looking out for the fine alabaster articles carved by the local craftsmen.

Two kilometres (1 mile) north-east of the town is an area of erosion, known as Balse. It was the site of the Etruscan necropolis, but a few fragments of the Etruscan city wall are all that remain.

Route 3B — Volterra to Massa Marittima

Cecina, 39km (24 miles) west of Volterra, is a popular family seaside resort. The marina and beach resort are 3km (2 miles) from the town centre, and have facilities for water-sports, boating, tennis and target-shooting. The coast, which was reclaimed from malarial marshes, is flat and has long, sandy beaches backed by pine forests. The beach, which stretches south from Cecina as far as San Vincenzo, is dotted with small resorts and camping sites, all easily accessible from the SS1 Via Aurelia. Ten kilometres (6 miles) south of Cecina the SS1 passes an avenue of cypress trees 5km (3 mile) long. It was planted in 1806 and leads to the village of **Bolgheri**, home of the Realist poet, Castagneto Carducci. The Rifugio Faunistico Padule di Bolgheri, also reached from the avenue, is an area of preserved marshland and a bird observatory. The marsh is dry in the summer, but between September and May the seasonal migration brings large numbers of herons, wild ducks and marsh harriers.

San Vincenzo, 24km (15 miles) south of Cecina, marks the start of the Etruscan Riviera. It boasts 5km (3 miles) of sandy beaches, a marina with a capacity of 400 boats, and a range of sports facilities, including horse-riding, tennis, and roller-skating. In February it stages the Carnevale della Riviera degli Etruschi, a masked carnival.

From San Vincenzo follow the small road along the coast towards Piombino. It passes through the Parco Naturale di Rimigliano, a protected area of coastland, covering some 350 hectares (865 acres). Footpaths lead through the pinewoods to unspoilt, sandy beaches. After 12^1/$_2$km (8 miles) take the right turn to **Populonia**, set in a picturesque bay in the most beautiful part of the park. At the southern end of the bay there are remains of an Etruscan necropolis. The tombs, which date from the eighth century up until the second century BC, are built in a variety of styles, although most are of the tumuli type. It takes about forty minutes to make a complete tour of the site.

The Etruscan settlement on the headland, *Pupluna*, based its economy upon copper and had developed into an important town by the sixth century BC. The Romans smelted iron here from ore mined on Elba, between the third century BC and 79BC when it was destroyed by Sulla. Some remains of these ancient settlements can be seen around the present day village of Populonia, at the top of the headland. The road winds up to a carpark at the foot of the Torre di Populonia, a medieval fortress with two crenellated towers, from where there are excellent panoramas of the coast and Elba. The small village, inside fourteenth-century walls, covers the site of the ancient acropolis. There are a handful of souvenir shops, including the Cantina Buia which sells home produced olive oil, grappa, preserves and stone-ground bread. Down a side street on the right, the Museo Etrusco, houses a private collection of local archaeological finds.

Piombino, 15km (9 miles) south of Populonia, is a rather drab, industrial town. The only reason for visiting is to catch a ferry to **Elba**, 11km (7 miles) off-shore. Two ferry companies operate regular services to the main town on the island, **Portoferraio**, but some also call at **Cavo**. The crossing takes about one hour. Elba is 27km (17 miles) long and about 18km (11 miles) wide, and has a mountainous interior. The highest point, Monte Capanne, at the western end of the island, is 1,018m (3,339ft) high and can be reached by cable-car from **Marciana**. The coast is dotted with numerous resorts, which although well visited, are less crowded than those on the mainland during summer. Elba is perhaps best known for being Napoleon's place of exile between 1814 and 1815. Although only in Elba for a short period he had two residences, a modest house in the upper part of Portoferraio, and another below the slopes of Monte San Martino. The latter is a 6km (4 miles) excursion from the town and is signposted off the road to Marciana Marina. Villa Napoleone di San Martino, which was built in front of his country house in 1851, contains a collection of Tuscan paintings in the Pinacoteca Foresiana.

Returning to the mainland at Piombino continue south along the SS1 Via Aurelia for 7km (4 miles) before turning left to Massa Marittima on the SS348. The road continues for 23km (14 miles) passing through an undulating landscape of olive groves and vineyards before arriving at the town. **Massa Marittima**, built on a rocky crag, is divided into two parts, an upper and a lower town. Most of the carparks are in the lower town and it is best to park here as it is only a short climb to the upper town. Inhabited since prehistoric times, the town owes its historical importance to the rich supply of metallic ores in the surrounding hills. These were extensively mined both by the Etruscans and Romans, particularly after the destruction of Populonia. By the eighth century Massa Marittima was a city of considerable influence and wealth, remaining independent up until 1335 when it was taken by Siena.

The gallery of a disused mine, entered from Via Corridoni, on the southern edge of the town, houses the Museo della Miniera. The 700m (765yd) long gallery, which contains the original mining equipment and a collection of local minerals and rocks, can be visited by applying to the Museo Civico on Piazza Garibaldi. Piazza Garibaldi, the centre of the lower town, is surrounded by gracious medieval buildings. The Duomo stands on a stepped terrace at one end. Built on the site of an earlier church, the original Duomo (1229-69) was enlarged into its present form by a Pisan architect between 1287 and 1304. The slender blind arches surrounding the outer walls are typical of the Pisan-Romanesque style as is the large *campanile*. Stone columns divide the simple interior into three aisles. Fragments of thirteenth-and fourteenth-century frescoes decorate the walls, with a cycle depicting the life of St Cerbone, the patron saint of the church, on the wall above the main door. The baptismal font, the Fonte di San Benardino is to the right of the main door. It is decorated with reliefs by Giroldo da Como (1267), and surmounted by a white marble tabernacle of the fifteenth century. Other reliefs, from the eleventh century, are set into the wall to the left of the main door. They are carved from dark stone, and depict the apostles, in a naive but forceful style. Stone-carved reliefs (1324), by Goro di Gregorio, decorate the sarcophagus of St Cerbone in the choir. The fourteenth-century wooden crucifix to the left of the sarcophagus is by Bonaventura, while in the left chapel there is a painting by the Sienese master, Duccio (1316), the *Madonna delle Grazie*. The Palazzo del Podesta, built around 1230, is on the west side of the *piazza*. It houses the Museo Civico which has Etruscan finds from the necropolis at Lago dell'Accesa, (12km/7 miles south of Massa Maritimma), on the ground floor, and a collection of paintings, including work by the fourteenth-century artist, Ambrogio Lorenzetti, on the first floor. The Palazzo Comunale, built in the thirteenth and fourteenth centuries, and the thirteenth-century house and tower of Conti di Biserno are to the left of the museum.

Via Moncine heads uphill from the opposite side of the *piazza* to the Porta alle Silici, the entrance to the upper town. It is set in the fine defensive walls of the Fortezza dei Senesi, which was built by the Sienese following their victory over the town in 1335. A fourteenth-century bridge spans the gap between the wall and the great tower, the Torre del Candeliere o dell'Orlogio. Piazza Matteoti, is the centre of the upper town, and the Palazzo delle Armi with its Renaissance arcaded façade, houses a small museum, the Museo di Storia e Arte Miniere, which records the history of mining and minerals in the region.

*Balestro del Girifalco
in Massa Marittima*

Corso Diaz leaves the piazza from the east side, passing the Antico Frantoio, an old olive press open as a museum, before reaching the church of Sant'Agostino with its Gothic façade and fine cloisters. The Museo dei Consol to the left of the church is dedicated to the Balestro del Girifalco, and has a collection of crossbows, traditional costumes and victory banners from past tournaments. The Balestro is held twice a year on the first Sunday after the 20 May, and on the second Sunday of August. In it the three districts of the town compete in an archery contest, using crossbows and dressed in medieval costume, on Piazza Garibaldi.

Route 3C — Massa Marittima to Ansedonia

From Massa Marittima, return to the main coastal road, the SS1 Via Aurelia, and either continue along it in the direction of Grosseto, as far as the turning to Vetulonia, or take the more picturesque coastal route, the SS322. This leads from **Follonica** through thick pine forests. The road passes by **Punta Ala**, a resort known for its golf course, polo field, and other sports facilities, before reaching **Castiglione della Pescaia**, some 22km (14 miles) from Follonica. The resort is gathered around the marina and has long, sandy beaches and facilities for skin-diving, wind-surfing, water-skiing and boating. The old town is clustered on a hill above the resort, surrounded by thick walls built by the Pisans after their conquest in AD962. There is a pleasant walkway inside the walls which passes under a series of stone arches and vaults, making a complete circuit of the town. There are good views from the ruined fortress at the very top of the hill.

The SP3 heads north-east of Castiglione della Pescaia towards Grosseto, across one of the largest remaining areas of natural marsh on the Tuscan coast. After 12km (7 miles) take the left turn to **Vetulonia**, continuing for a further 11km (7 miles) before reaching the site. Founded in the seventh century BC, Vetulonia was one of twelve cities that made up the Etruscan league. The necropolis is on the lower part of the hill, on either side of a steep track that leads from the right side of the road. The foundations of the three chambers and the passageway are all that remain of the first tomb, the Tomba del Belvedere, at the top of the track. The Tumulo della Pietrera, is on the right, 400m (437yd) down the track, which is just about passable by car. Dating from the seventh century BC, it is much more impressive and consists of a large circular chamber entered through a long stone passageway. The Tumulo del Diavolino, also with impressive vaulting, is a further 400m (437yd) downhill.

The remains of Etruscan *Vetulonia* are 3km (2 miles) uphill from the necropolis, just before the present day village. Excavations started here in 1887 and have uncovered a paved road, water cisterns and the foundations of housing. The village is surrounded by fragments of Etruscan walls, dating the fifth century BC, and offers an outstanding panorama of the coast. From Vetulonia, head downhill towards Grosseto, past the attractive hill-town of **Buriano**.

Grosseto is surrounded by market gardens and modern outskirts, but has an attractive centre, enclosed within a well-preserved, sixteenth-century wall. There is ample parking outside the south wall. The city was founded in the tenth century and remained independent until Siena took control in 1336. Its development, however, was hampered by the surrounding malarial marshes. Periodically throughout its history, the city's population dwindled and it is only since the 1960s and the final draining of the marshes that Grosseto has thrived.

The Duomo stands on a large, cobbled square, Piazza Dante, at the centre of the city. Originally built between 1294 and 1302, it has an attractive striped façade of pink and white stone, a brick *campanile* which was added in 1402 and a sun-dial on the side wall. Just north of the *piazza* is the Museo Archeologica d'Arte della Maremma, which has been recently modernised. It has a collection of artefacts from **Roselle**, 7km (4 miles) north of Grosseto, which up until AD 935 when it was destroyed by Saracens, was the most important settlement in the region. There is also a good collection of Sienese paintings dating from the thirteenth to seventeenth centuries, and works from local churches, on the upper floor. Beyond the museum, the church of San Francesco, on Piazza di Indipendenza, is also worth visiting. Built of brick in the Gothic style, it dates from the thirteenth century and contains a fine fourteenth-century crucifix painted by Duccio and the remains of Sienese frescoes.

An excursion can be made, 16km (10 miles) south of Grosetto, to the Monti dell'Uccellina mountains, in the Parco Naturale di Maremma. No cars are permitted beyond **Alberese** where visitors must apply to the *centro visito* for permission to enter the park. Guided walks of around 5km (3 miles) length are arranged from here, visiting on the way the ruined abbey of San Rabano, and hilltop towers which date from the fourteenth century.

The SS1 Via Aurelia continues south from Grosseto, through Fonteblanda, past the turning to the fashionable resort of **Talamone**, at the southern tip of the park. Eight kilometres (5 miles) south of Fonteblanda, a right turn leads across a causeway to the **Monte Argentario** promontory. Follow the picturesque northern shore for 4km (2 miles) to the busy resort of **Porto Santo Stefano**. Centred around a marina, the resort is a good point from which to visit two small islands, **Isola del Giglio** and **Isola di Giannutri**, which lie roughly 30km (19 miles) offshore. Isola del Giglio, the largest of the two, is hilly and has three small beach resorts, while Isola di Giannutri is more remote, having one village and a ruined first-century, Roman villa. However, the latter island is privately owned, and can only be visited in summer on one of the regular boat tours from Porto Santo Stefano. **Orbetello**, on a causeway midway between Monte Argentario and the mainland, is less popular than Porto Santo Stefano. It is mainly of importance as an eel-fishing

The Castello dell' Osteria at Ponte dell' Abbadia

One of the beach resorts on Giglio island

centre and has an eel festival, the Sagra dell'Anguilla, every August.

Continue through Orbetello to the SS1 Via Aurelia and the Roman site of **Ansedonia**. A right turn off the SS1 climbs up a headland through a secluded residential area to a small carpark, from where a footpath leads to the ruins. The city, named *Cosa* when it was founded by the Romans in 273BC, is situated on a panoramic promontory 113m (370ft) above the sea. The Porta Romana, set in the city wall, is the best-preserved of the gates. Ruins are strewn across the top of the hill and include the forum where the remains of two temples and a basilica can be seen, and the acropolis and Capitol at the very summit from where there are excellent views. Near the ancient harbour at the foot of the promontory is a remarkable channel carved through the natural rock, known today as the Tagliata Etrusca. The harbour is overlooked by a romantic ruined tower, the Torre della Tagliato, where Puccini stayed while composing *Tosca*. The recently-excavated Roman villa, complete with mosaics and wall paintings is also worth visiting.

Route 3D — Ansedonia to Rome

Continuing south of Ansedonia on the SS1 Via Aurelia, Lake **Burano**, a bird sanctuary, is passed on the right. As the domed church of **Montalto di Castro** comes into view ahead, take the left turn to **Ponte dell'Abbadia**. The road passes the Oasi di Protezione di Vulci, another nature reserve, before arriving at the turning right to the Casale dell'Osteria and the sparse ruins of the Etruscan city of *Vulci*. The site can only be visited by applying to the museum in the castle at Ponte dell'Abbadia, a little further along the main road on the right. The castle, surrounded by a pretty moat, was originally built as an abbey in AD809, and contains an interesting collection of archaeological finds from *Vulci*. It has a picturesque location on the high banks of the Fiora river gorge which is spanned by an excellent Roman bridge, built with Etruscan stones. It has a single arch, over 30m (98ft) high. Six kilometres (4 miles) further along the road are the remains of an Etruscan necropolis. Strewn along the east bank of the river, one of the principal tombs is La Tomba Francois, built in the form of a tumulus.

Return to the SS1 Via Aurelia and continue south, passing the sixteenth-century Castello Guglielmi, at the top of the fortified town of Montalto di Castro. **Tarquinia**, is a further 13km (8 miles) south. Three kilometres (2 miles) of well-preserved walls, complete with eighteen towers, encircle the town, and as traffic is restricted in the centre visitors should park outside the main gate.

Although Tarquinia's main attraction is the nearby Etruscan necropolis, the town is very pleasant and has an excellent museum, as well as a charming medieval quarter. The museum is on the left side of Piazza Cavour, just inside the main gate. Housed in the Palazzo Vitelleschi (1436-9), it is one of the most important collections of

Etruscan art in Italy, spanning the period from the seventh century up until the first century BC. The *palazzo*, which is built in the Gothic-Renaissance style, surrounds an inner courtyard. The ground floor rooms leading off the courtyard hold seventh and sixth century BC sarcophagi with finely carved reclining figures on their lids. Upstairs, a beautiful pair of winged horses in the first room date from the fourth to third centuries BC, and were originally part of a monumental frieze on a temple. The other rooms on the first floor contain Etruscan ceramics and bronzes. The best and largest pieces are displayed in the Great Hall. Some of the beautifully decorated, red and black ceramic vases even have the signatures of their Etruscan makers.

Corso Vittorio Emanuele leads uphill from Piazza Cavour to an even larger square, Piazza Matteoti. Two Baroque churches with identical façades face one another on either side of the *piazza*, while in the centre stands a large eighteenth-century fountain. An archway leads beneath the Palazzo Comunale from the left side of the *piazza* to the medieval quarter. Small churches and numerous stone towers lie between the houses on narrow, cobble-stone streets. The church of Santissimi Annunziata was built between the twelfth and thirteenth centuries, and has an attractive rose window and a simple portal, decorated with black and white stone.

Tarquinia's famous necropolis is $1^1/_2$km (1 mile) from the town along the road to Viterbo, where there are parking spaces at the side of the road. The carefully preserved site is set in a large field with footpaths leading from tomb to tomb, each of which is protected under a concrete entrance. There are usually no more than five tombs open at any time and as space is limited there may be some waiting before being able to enter them. Stairs lead underground to the decorated funerary chambers which are protected behind glass. The frescoed scenes depict figures, animals and household objects, which provide both a valuable document of Etruscan life, and of pre-Roman painting. The Etruscan acropolis is visible on the hill to the north-east of the site.

Cerveteri, the other major Etruscan site in the region, is 55km (34 miles) further down the coast. From Tarquinia follow the SS1 Via Aurelia south for 8km (5 miles) before joining the A12 *autostrada* which avoids the slow traffic along the coastal road. After 38km (24 miles) take the exit to Cerveteri and follow the road through modern outskirts to the old town centre.

Cerveteri is built on the site of Etruscan *Kysry*, later named *Caere* by the Romans. With a good harbour at *Pyrgi*, 14km (9 miles) to the west, and a rich source of minerals in the nearby Tolfa mountains, it soon developed into an important trading town, and was at its peak between the eighth and fifth centuries BC. It fell into a decline in 384BC when Syracuse destroyed the harbour, and never regained its former importance, either as a Roman or medieval settlement. Today, Cerveteri is a sleepy town surrounded by medieval walls, which are partly constructed with Etruscan masonry, as is the ruined, twelfth-century fortress in the town centre. The sixteenth-century Palazzo Ruspoli, next to the fortress, houses a collection of archaeological finds from the nearby necropolis. The exhibits are arranged chronologically with finds dating from the ninth to the sixth centuries BC on the ground floor, and those from the sixth to first century BC on the first floor.

The necropolis of Cerveteri, known as the Scavi di Caere, is well-signposted from the town. A narrow road passes through an avenue of pine trees to the carpark at the site entrance. Covering the top of the Banditaccia Hill, the necropolis is both extensive and excellently-preserved, and has a charming natural setting beneath shady pines. At least 2 hours should be allowed for the marked itinerary, *itinerario consigliato*, which leads around the best of the site, but a whole afternoon could easily be spent wandering at random around the 'city of the dead'. The tombs date from the seventh to the first century BC and are built in a variety of different styles. Amongst the oldest are the large mound tombs close to the entrance of the site. They are known as the *fosso* type as they consist of a large tumuli surrounded by a ditch cut into the rock. Some of the very large mounds contain several tombs, such as the mound which has the Tomba della Capanne on one side and the Tomba Vasi Greci on the other. The chambers are not decorated with frescoes, but have attractively carved beds lining the walls, beams across the ceilings and lintels above the doors. The Tomba Rilievi, which dates from the fourth century BC, is named after the rock-carved frieze which surrounds the inner walls. It also has carvings of household objects on the columns in the main chamber. The Tomba dei Capitelli has columns topped with scrolled capitals and a particularly fine carved ceiling. The later tombs at the east end of the necropolis resemble houses and are arranged in rows like streets. La Vie dei Monti Ceriti della Tolfa is one of the largest streets and contains the Tomba della Cornice, named after the cornice which is carved around the funerary chambers.

Visitors have the choice here of either taking the A12 *autostrada* to Rome (35km/22 miles), or continuing up past Cerveteri to Bracciano (18km/11 miles) where chapter 2 can be joined.

Additional Information

Places of Interest

ROUTE 3A
Colle di Val d' Elsa

Museo Archeologico
Palazzo Pretorio
Via di Campana
53034 Colle di Val d' Elsa (SI)
Open: September to May, Saturday
3-5 or 6pm. June to August,
Tuesday to Friday 4-6pm, Saturday
and Sunday 10am-12noon, 4-7pm.
Group visits by appointment: C/o
Colle Turismo
☎ (0577) 923534

Museo Civico
Palazzo dei Priori
Via del Castello
53034 Colle di Val d' Elsa (SI)
Open: September to May, Saturday
3-5 or 6pm. June to August,
Tuesday to Friday 4-6pm.
Saturday and Sunday 10am-12noon,
4-7pm.
Group visits by appointment:
C/o Colle Turismo
☎ (0577) 923534

San Gimignano
*Museo Etrusco e d'Arte Sacre, Museo
Civico e Torre*
Piazza del Duomo
53033 San Gimignano (SI)
Open: winter Tuesday to Sunday
9.30am-12.30pm and 2.30-5.30pm.

Volterra
Museo Etrusco Guarnacci
15 Via Don Minzoni
56048 Volterra (PI)
☎ (0588) 86347
Open: winter Monday to Saturday
9am-2pm, Sunday and holidays
10am-12noon, summer Monday to
Saturday 9.30am-1pm and 3-
6.30pm, Sunday and holidays 9am-
12noon and 3-6pm.

Palazzo dei Priori
Piazza dei Priori
56048 Volterra (PI)
Open: Monday to Saturday 9am-1pm.

Parco Archeologico Enrico Fiumi
56048 Volterra (PI)
Open: winter daily 8.30am-5pm,
summer daily 8am-8pm.

Pinacoteca Civica
Palazzo Minucci Solaini
1 Via dei Sarti
56048 Volterra (PI)
☎ (0588) 87580
Open: winter Tuesday to Sunday
9am-1pm, summer Tuesday to
Sunday 9am-6.30pm.

ROUTE 3B
Populonia
Torre di Populonia
Populonia
57020 Comune di Piombino (LI)
Open: Tuesday to Sunday 9.30am-
12.30pm and 2.30-5.30pm (closed
during bad weather).

Massa Marittima
Museo Civici
Palazzo del Podesta
Piazza Garibaldi
58024 Massa Marittima (GR)
☎ (0566) 902289
Open: summer Tuesday to Sunday
10am-12.30pm and 3.30-7pm,
winter Tuesday to Sunday 9am-
1pm and 3-5pm.

Museo di Storia e Arte Miniere
Piazza Matteoti
58024 Massa Marittima (GR)
Open: Tuesday to Saturday 10am-
12.30pm, Sunday 10am-12.30pm
and 3.30-5pm.

Antico Frantoio
Via Populonia
58024 Massa Marittima (GR)
Open: Tuesday to Sunday 10am-
12.30pm and 3.30-7pm.

ROUTE 3C
Vetulonia
Museo Archeologico
Vetulonia
58040 Comune di Castiglione della
Pescaia (GR)
☎ (0564) 949877

Grosseto
Museo Archeologica d'Arte della
Meremma
Piazza Baccarini
58100 Grosseto (GR)
Open: daily (except Wednesday)
9am-1pm and 4-7.30pm, holidays
9am-1pm.

Alberese
Consorzio del Parco Naturale della
Maremma
Aurelia Antica Localita Pianacce
Alberese (GR)
☎ (0564) 407098
Open: June to September
Wednesday and holidays 9am-5pm.

ROUTE 3D
Ponte dell' Abbadia
Museo Archeologico di Vulci
Castello dell ' Abbadia
01014 Montalto di Castro.

Museo Archeologico di Vulci
Castello dell'Abbadia
01014 Montalto di Castro (VT)
Open: winter Tuesday to Sunday
9am-1.30pm and 2.30-4pm,
summer Tuesday to Sunday 9am-
2pm, 3-6 or 7.30pm.

Tarquinia
Museo Nazionale Tarquiniese
Palazzo Vitelleschi
Piazza Cavour
01016 Tarquinia (VT)
☎ (0766) 856037
Open: Tuesday to Sunday 9am-7pm.

Necropoli Etrusche
01016 Tarquinia (VT)
Open: Tuesday to Sunday 9am-7pm.

Cerveteri
Museo Nazionale Claudia Ruspoli
Palazzo Ruspoli
Piazza Santa Maria
00052 Cerveteri (ROMA)
Open: winter Tuesday to Sunday
9am-2pm. Summer Tuesday to
Sunday 9am-2pm and 4-7pm.

Scavi di Caere
00052 Cerveteri (ROMA)
Open: winter 9am-4pm. Summer
9am-7pm.

Tourist Information Centres

ROUTE 3A
Colle di Val d' Elsa
Pro Loco
Piazza Arnolfo di Cambio 5
53034 Colle di Val d' Elsa
☎ (0577) 921692

San Gimignano
Pro Loco
Piazza del Duomo
53033 San Gimignano (SI)
☎ (0577) 940008

Volterra
Ufficio Informazioni Pro Loco
2 Via G. Turazza
56048 Volterra (PI)
☎ (0588) 86150

ROUTE 3B
Cecina
Pro Cecina
17 Largo Cairoli
57023 Marina di Cecina (LI)
☎ (0586) 620678

San Vincenzo
Azienda Autonoma di Soggiorno e
Turismo
7 Piazza Umberto I
57027 San Vincenzo (LI)
☎ (0565) 57027

ROUTE 3C
Grosseto
Ente Provinciale per il Turismo
Via Monterosa
58100 Grosseto (GR)
☎ (0564) 22534

Porto Santo Stefano
Azienda Autonoma Costa
d'Argento
55A Corso Umberto
58019 Porto Santo Stefano (GR)
☎ (0564) 814208

ROUTE 3D
Tarquinia
Azienda Autonoma dell'Etruria
Meridionale
1 Piazza Cavour
01016 Tarquinia (VT)
☎ (0766) 856384

4

UPPER TUSCANY
AND FLORENCE

This chapter passes through upper Tuscany, from east to west, visiting Florence midway. It takes in some of the smaller hilltop towns so typical of Tuscany, as well as the larger cities with their excellent collections of art and architecture. Despite its popularity, it remains one of the most picturesque regions in Northern Italy, and rewards the visitor with good wine and food, and a wealth of culture.

At Florence visitors who do not wish to continue to Lucca, can either head north to Bologna and join chapter 9, or south to Siena to join chapters 2 or 3. Those who continue to Lucca are able to join chapter 5 at Pisa.

Route 4A — Perugia to Florence

The A1 crosses the plain from Perugia over the hills to Lake Trasimeno. The lake, which covers an area of 128sq km (49sq miles) and is about 6m (20ft) deep, is a popular destination for holidaymakers from the surrounding cities. **Passignano sul Trasimeno** is one of the busiest of the lake resorts and has a marina and good water-sport facilities. The promenade along the lake-edge is lined with cafés, hotels and shops, with the old town, and its fortified gate and attractive clock tower, clustered on the slope behind. The resort has regular ferries (*traghetti*) to the small offshore islands, Isole Minore and Isole Maggiore, as well as other destinations around the lake. The main island, **Isole Maggiore**, has a picturesque fishing village and a thirteenth-century Romanesque church, Chiesa del Salvatore on its western shore, and the church of San Michele Archangelo on its summit.

Follow the A1 along the northern shore of the lake, past the hill town of Tuoro, and turn right onto the SS71 to Cortona. As the road climbs up towards Cortona it passes the grand Renaissance church of Madonna del Calcinaio (1484-1513) with its large, sixteenth-century rose window and beautiful stained-glass. **Cortona**, a further 3km (2 miles), is surrounded by excellent medieval walls built on Etruscan foundations. Follow signs to one of the many carparks outside the walls, either on Piazzale del Mercato or Piazzale

Garibaldi, as the centre is closed to traffic.

Cortona, ancient *Corythus*, was an important Etruscan town up until 390BC when it was taken by the Romans. It was destroyed by the Goths in the fifth century, and only rose to prominence again after the medieval period. During the Renaissance, under Florentine rule, the town gave rise to a number of influential painters including, Fra Angelico (1408), Luca Signorelli (1441) and Pietro da Cortona (1596). Many fine buildings stand testimony to Cortona's importance as a flourishing Renaissance town, including the sixteenth-century Medici fortress, built high above its eastern end. Accessible by road, the fortress can also be reached by a pleasant walkway, Via Crucis, also known as Via Santa Margherita, which is lined with mosaics depicting the stations of the cross by the Italian futurist, Gino Severini (1883-1966), who was born in Cortona. Via Crucis ends at the large nineteenth-century church of Santa Margherita, but the road continues up to the fortress. Built in 1549 on the foundations of an earlier fourteenth-century fortress, the Fortezza Medicea offers superb views and encloses attractive gardens, however, the interior is closed except during summer exhibitions. There are remains of Etruscan walls, dating from the sixth and fifth centuries BC, close by.

The fifteenth-century, Gothic church of San Domenico, at the bottom of Via Crucis, has a number of fine paintings. The apse has a fine altar-piece and there is an excellent triptych by Lorenzo di Niccolo Gerini (1402) in the side chapel. Of the numerous paintings hung along the walls, the *Assumption* by Bartolomeo della Gatta in the third niche on the left is particularly notable. Behind the church are the public gardens and a pleasant promenade with fine views, known as Il Parterre.

In the town centre there are two excellent museums. The first, the Museo dell'Accademia Etrusco, is in Palazzo Casali, on the main square, Piazza della Signorelli. The *palazzo* was originally built in the thirteenth century as the home of the ruling Casali family, but was reconstructed in the sixteenth century. The spacious rooms with their attractive carved fireplaces and doorways, provide a charming setting for the museum collection. It is diverse, ranging from Egyptian mummies and Etruscan pottery, to medieval costumes and fourteenth- to sixteenth-century paintings, including works by L. Signorelli and Pietro da Cortona. There is also a fine collection of Etruscan bronze figurines in the main hall, including a bronze candleholder which dates from the fifth century BC.

The Museo Diocesano, is downhill from Piazza Signorelli on a small square, opposite the seventeenth-century Duomo. Housed in the deconsecrated church of Gesu (1498-1505), the museum has an outstanding collection of paintings, including works by Fra Angelico and L. Signorelli, and artists of the fifteenth-century Florentine school. Of the numerous large paintings by L. Signorelli, the *Deposizione* and the *Comune degli Apostoli* are amongst the finest, but the *Annunciation* by Fra Angelico is the museum's masterpiece.

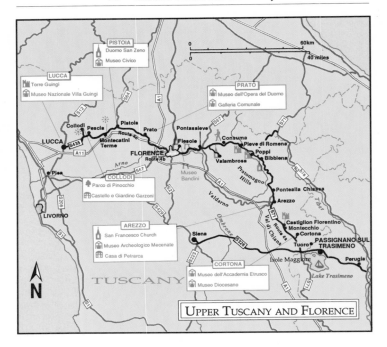

UPPER TUSCANY AND FLORENCE

From Cortona the SS71 passes through **Montecchio**, with its thirteenth-century castle, on the way to **Castiglion Fiorentino**, 11km (7 miles) north of Cortona. It stands on a hillside, overlooked by the ruined, fifteenth-century Cassero fortress. Just before the town centre the road passes the thirteenth-century church of San Francesco, which has attractive cloisters with the remnants of frescoes depicting the life of St Francis. On Piazza Municipio, the town centre, there is a sixteenth-century loggia, designed by Vasari with fine views over the lower part of the town. The Palazzo Comunale on the opposite side of the *piazza* houses a collection of religious paintings which can be viewed during office hours. Below the loggia, the Collegiata di San Giuliano, reconstructed in 1853, houses some fine art works, while the parish church next door has a fresco by L. Signorelli of the *Deposition* (1483).

Arezzo, 17km (11 miles) north of Castiglion Fiorentino, is located at the meeting point of four valleys: the Valdarno, the Casentino, the Val Tiberina and the Val di Chiana. Originally named *Arretium*, it was one of the most important of the twelve cities that made up the Etruscan league. Nothing remains of the Etruscan settlement and much of the medieval and Renaissance city was badly damaged in

World War II. Despite this, and the modern outskirts that have mushroomed around the city, the carefully restored historic centre is attractive.

The church of San Francesco, at the centre of the city, was built during the thirteenth and fourteenth centuries in the Gothic style. The interior has a fine stained-glass window by G. de Marcillat (1524) and magnificent frescoes on its walls. The main apse contains one of the most important fresco cycles in Italy, the *Legend of the Cross* (1453-64) by Piero della Francesco, who was born in Arezzo. The sixteen panels are extraordinarily beautiful, even though they are rather damaged. The fine triptych by Niccolo di Pietro Gerini in the chapel on the right dates from the fourteenth century, while the powerful wooden crucifix which hangs in the main apse is even older, dating from the thirteenth century.

Follow Via Cavour for 100m (110yd) and then turn left up Corso Italia. The street ends at the tall, five-storey *campanile* of Pieve Santa Maria. The church, started in 1140 was not finished until the fourteenth century, and the façade is typical of the Pisan-Romanesque style. The fine carvings decorating the main portal date from 1216. Piazza Grande, behind the church, is surrounded by fine buildings, including the seventeenth-century Palazzo del Tribunale and the elegant arcade, which was designed by Vasari in 1573. There are also a number of picturesque medieval houses, complete with wooden balconies and crenellated towers. On the first Sunday in September,

*The church at
Castiglion Fiorentino*

a medieval jousting tournament, the Giostra del Saracino, is held in the *piazza*, and during the summer, on the first Sunday of every month there is an antiques fair.

Via del Orto heads uphill from Piazza Grande past Casa di Petrarca at number twenty-eight which is believed to be the four-teenth-century poet's home, to the Duomo at the top of the hill. Built of yellow sandstone in the Gothic style, it was begun in the thirteenth century, but not finished until 1510. The stained-glass windows are the work of G. de Marcillat (1519-23). The *campanile* which was built in 1859, overlooks a pleasant park, the Passeggio del Prato. At the far end of the park is the Fortezza Medicea, a vast brick fortress, built for the Medici family to a design by G. and A. da Sangallo in the sixteenth century.

From the Duomo follow signs to Casa di Vasari, number fifty-five, Via XX Settembre. The house, now open as a museum, was designed and frescoed by Vasari between 1540 and 1548, and contains a collection of Tuscan paintings. There are two other museums of interest in the city. The first, the Galleria e Museo Medioevale e Moderno is 200m (220yd) south-west of Casa di Vasari. Housed in a fine fifteenth-century Renaissance *palazzo* the museum has a good collection of paintings, including work by L. Signorelli. The other, the Museo Archeologico Mecenate, to the south of the city, close to the ruins of a Roman amphitheatre, has a collection of local archaeo-logical finds housed in the former sixteenth-century monastery of San Bernardo.

From Arezzo the SS71 heads north, joining the River Arno at **Ponte alla Chiassa**, and following it for 25km ($15^1/_2$ miles) all the way to **Bibbiena**. This small hilltop town was founded by the Etruscans who knew it under the name, *Vipena*. Today it is the main town of the Casentino, the upper Arno valley, and although little remains of its ancient past, it is pleasantly unspoilt. The small church of San Lorenzo in the centre of the town dates from the fifteenth century, and has two terracotta reliefs attributed to the Della Robbia school. The Palazzo Dovizi, on the opposite side of the street, has an attractive Renaissance façade. There are fine views out over the surrounding countryside and to Poppi from the small *piazza* at the top of the town, near the twelfth-century church of Santissimi Ippolito e Donato.

Overshadowed by the Castello dei Conti, **Poppi** lies on a wooded hilltop, 5km (3 miles) north of Bibbiena. The road climbs up past a circular monument, built to commemorate the Austro-Hungarian war of 1918, and passes through the town walls onto Piazza Amerighi. The small hexagonal chapel of Madonna del Morbo, at the centre of the *piazza*, was erected in thanks for the town's deliverance from the plagues of 1530 and 1631. The Castello dei Conti, with its severe 44m (144ft) high tower, lies above the *piazza* on a panoramic terrace. The castle was the seat of the Ghibelline Conti Guidi, who ruled from the eleventh century up until 1440, after which they were allied to Guelph Florence. Built around a courtyard with a fine external staircase, the interior, including an attractive chapel, is decorated with thirteenth- and fourteenth-century frescoes. There is also an impressive library with a collection of 20,000 manuscripts. After visiting the castle it is worth walking along the finely arcaded street, Via Cavour, which leads down to the small church of San Marco from the main *piazza*.

Follow the SS70 from Poppi through picturesque countryside for 9km (6 miles), to the turning right to **Pieve di Romena**. This hilltop *castello*, built by the Guidi family, is mentioned in Dante's *Inferno* and was probably his first place of refuge after being exiled from Florence. Today, only three of the original fourteen towers are still standing, surrounded by crumbling walls and cypress trees.

The SS70 continues in a westerly direction, climbing up to the village of **Scarpaccia**, which is a good base from which to go hiking in the surrounding hills. There are scenic views across the Pratomagno hills as the road continues to wind up to **Consuma**, a small resort built in the Passo di Consuma at a height of 1,060m (3,477ft). Popular in the summer due to its cooler climate, footpaths lead off into the hills, through a pleasant wooded landscape. It is also possible to make a 7km (4 miles) excursion south to visit the tenth-century monastery of **Valambrosa**.

The descent from Consuma into the Arno valley is very scenic with vineyards covering the lower hills, but after **Pontassieve** the valley is marred by industrial development which has spread out from Florence, 18km (11 miles) to the west.

Route 4B — Florence and Fiesole

Florence, the capital of Tuscany and the cradle of the Renaissance, is richly endowed with art treasures, both inside its grand *palazzi*, with their roughly-hewn, rusticated façades, and in its numerous inlaid marble churches. The city, on the banks of the River Arno, is attractively encircled by rolling Tuscan hills. However, despite its picturesque setting, Florence is too large and crowded to have the charm of Tuscany's smaller hilltop towns. The streets roar with traffic and industrial suburbs choke the flatter land to the west, stretching in an unbroken belt as far as Prato. Between spring and autumn the hordes of tourists which visit Florence put additional strain on the city's resources, filling most of the available accommodation. However, for all its drawbacks Florence is too important a city to miss, particularly for art-lovers, and it should be remembered that the option of escaping into the surrounding hills is always available for those who begin to feel frazzled. Fiesole is a short bus-ride to the north and the Chianti region lies just to the south.

Not surprisingly, parking in Florence is fairly difficult, and it is best to approach the city by bus or rail if possible. The main parking

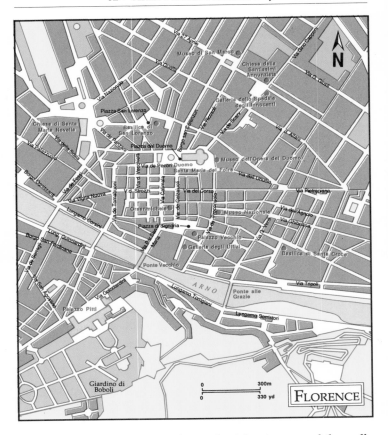

area available to visitors is to the north of the city around the walls of Fortezza da Basso, but it is also worth trying the carpark on Piazza Beccaria on the east side of the city. Getting around the historic centre is relatively easy as the major sights are all within reasonable walking distance of one another. The best place to start a tour is in the city centre on Piazza del Duomo where **Duomo Santa Maria del Fiore**, with its decorative red, green, and white marble façade, stands on the east side of the square. The Duomo was begun in 1296 by Arnolfo di Cambio, but was not consecrated until the completion of Brunelleschi's famous dome in 1436. At the time, it was the largest and highest dome in Italy and was remarkable for being constructed on an octagonal vault, without the aid of scaffolding. The interior is focused around the vast octagonal space beneath the dome, from where a staircase in the left aisle, with 463 steps, leads up to a gallery

A roofscape view of Florence

The awe-inspiring dome of Santa Maria del Fiore cathedral, Florence

with good views of the fresco inside the dome, the *Last Judgement* by G. Vasari and F. Zuccari (1579), before continuing up between the inner and outer shell of the dome to the lantern. The panoramic terrace at the top is some 90m (298ft) above the *piazza* and offers views across the entire city.

The Duomo has fine stained-glass windows, which were designed by Ghiberti, and in the left transept there are two Della Robbia terracottas. The remains of the former twelfth-century Duomo of Santa Reparato can be seen in the crypt where excavations have brought to light fragments of the original frescoes and sections of the masonry. Most of the art works from the Duomo have, however, been transferred to the Museo dell'Opera del Duomo which is at number nine on the *piazza* behind the Duomo. Included in the rich collection of Florentine sculpture housed in the museum is Michelangelo's *Pieta*, which was pieced together by his pupil T. Calcagni after his master, dissatisfied with his achievement, had smashed it. Also worthy of note are the fifteenth-century choir lofts, which were carved by L. della Robbia and Donatello, as well as the original sculptures from the *campanile* by A. Pisano.

The *campanile*, 82m (269ft) high, was started by Giotto in 1334, continued by A. Pisano in 1343, and finished by F. Talentini in 1348. It is possible to climb up the 414 steps to the top of the *campanile*, from where there are good views of the Duomo itself as well as the city. The octagonal baptistery, ornately patterned with green and white marbles, is divided from the Duomo and the *campanile* by a busy road. It was built in the twelfth century and was enormously influential on the subsequent development of Florentine-Renaissance architecture. It has three sets of bronze doors, the oldest of which are those designed by A. Pisano (1330) on the south side, now the main entrance. The north and east doors are by L. Ghiberti, the latter, known as the Doors of Paradise (1425-52), are the better pair, and are considered to be his greatest work. The interior is covered by a large dome with a magnificent thirteenth-century, Venetian mosaic, while the floor is also paved with mosaics, which date from the twelfth to fourteenth centuries.

Head south of the baptistery along Via di Calzaiuoli past the small but highly decorative church of Orsanmichele, where a fine painting of the *Virgin* by B. Daddi (1359) can be seen set in an ornate, Gothic tabernacle by Orcagna. Just south of the church, the street opens out into one of the oldest and most beautiful squares in the city, **Piazza della Signoria**. Along the east side of the *piazza* is the Palazzo della Signoria, also known as **Palazzo Vecchio**, which has a severe Gothic façade topped by crenellations, and a splendid tower, 94m (308ft) high. The *palazzo* was built between 1298 and 1314 by A. di Cambio, but the interior was completely renovated by the great Renaissance polymath G. Vasari in the mid-sixteenth century for the Medici ruler, Cosimo I (1537-74). The main door, flanked by a copy of Michelangelo's *David* to the left and a statue of *Hercules and Cacus* by

B. Bandinelli to the right, leads into a lovely courtyard filled with carved pillars and frescoes, which was designed by Michelozzo in 1470. Stairs lead up from the right side of the courtyard to the grand hall, the Salone dei Cinquecento, which was built in 1496 to accommodate a Venetian-style council of 500 that was established under Savonorala during a brief spell in which the Medici family were expelled from Florence. On the return of the Medici in 1512, Vasari decorated the walls and ceilings with frescoes depicting Medici triumphs and their good deeds and the hall was used as the ducal chamber. A niche at the southern end of the hall holds Michelangelo's statue of *Victory* (1526), originally intended for Julius II's tomb. Next to it a door leads into the Studiolo of Francesco I, a small windowless room, richly encrusted with small paintings and statuettes. It was built for Francesco I Medici who preferred to withdraw from the public eye and pursue his interests in alchemy, metallurgy and technology, rather than govern the city. On the opposite side of the great hall another door leads into the Quartiere di Leone X where Vasari was commissioned to fresco the history of the Medici family on the walls. Continuing up to the second floor the Quartiere degli Elementi is also frescoed by Vasari and contains an excellent collection of Florentine art works, including altar paintings by Masolino and Masaccio, as well as paintings by Venetian artists such as Veronese and Tintoretto. The Quartiere di Eleonora di Toledo, the apartments of Cosimo I's wife, contain a delightful chapel frescoed by Bronzino (1540-45). Last of all is the Sala dei Gigli, the Hall of Lilies, which has a finely coffered ceiling by G. da Maiano and is frescoed by Ghirlandaio (1485).

Loggia dei Lanzi, on the south side of Piazza della Signoria, is an open-air museum of sculptures, of which the *Rape of the Sabine* by Giambologna (1583), the sculptor's last work, is perhaps the most notable. The **Galleria degli Uffizi** lies behind the loggia and extends as far as the banks of the River Arno. The building, which is a long U-shape, was designed by G. Vasari, under Cosimo I in 1560, as the government offices *(uffici)*. In 1581 Francesco I Medici converted the second floor into a gallery to house his impressive family art collection. Today, the collection ranks amongst the greatest in the world and is the most important in Italy. Contained within forty-five rooms it is arranged chronologically, starting in the east wing with thirteenth-century altar-pieces and finishing in the west wing with eighteenth-century paintings. The three wide hallways connecting the rooms hold antique statues and tapestries. Amongst the great many important paintings hung in the gallery are: paintings by Duccio, Cimabue and Giotto in Room 2; *Annunciation* by Simone Martini in Room 3; *Adoration of the Magi* by Gentile da Fabriano; *Battle of San Romano* by Uccello, and *Portraits of Federico di Montefeltro and Battista Sforza* by Piero della Francesca in Room 7; paintings by Filippo Lippi in Room 8; *Primavera* and *The Birth of Venus* by Botticelli in Room 10; *Annunciation* by Leonardo da Vinci; *Adoration of the Magi* by Dürer in Room 20; *Sacred Allegory* by G. Bellini in Room 21; *Madonna with the Goldfinch* and *Leo X with Cardinals* by Raphael in Room 26; *Venus of Urbino* by Titian in Room 28; *Head of Medusa and Bacchus* by Caravaggio in Room 43. The sculpture of a wild boar passed on the way down to the exit is a copy of the Hellenistic original.

Florence's oldest bridge, **Ponte Vecchio**, is a short distance to the west of the Uffizi. Lined with small jewellers' shops along either side, the bridge leads across the Arno to the district of Oltrarno on the south bank. The most important monument in Oltrarno is the **Palazzo Pitti** which lies 300m (328yd) south of the bridge along Via Guicciardini. The palace was built between 1457 and 1466 by the wealthy Florentine, Luca Pitti, to a design by Brunelleschi. It was purchased in 1550 by Cosimo I Medici and was the family seat for almost 200 years to follow. Behind its vast, rusticated façade with projecting wings at either end, is a spacious inner courtyard, designed by B. Ammanati. An entrance on the right side of the courtyard leads into the **Galleria Palatina** which houses further paintings collected by the Medici, dating mainly from the sixteenth and seventeenth centuries, with masters such as Raphael, Andrea del Sarto, Titian and Rubens among them. Many of the rooms in the gallery have frescoes by Pietro da Cortona, the most important of which is the *Four Ages of Man* decorating Room 29. The palace also contains the Museo degli Argenti which has a collection of gold, silver, amber, ivory and jewels belonging to the Medici family, and on the second floor, the Galleria d'Arte Moderna has paintings dating from the nineteenth and twentieth centuries. It is also possible to visit the Appartamenti Monumentali, the State apartments, which are decorated in the style of the eighteenth-century Savoy period.

The Giardino di Boboli laid out in 1560 for Cosimo I Medici, cover the hillside behind the Pitti Palace. A ramp leads up from Ammanati's courtyard to an amphitheatre, above which is Neptune's Fountain. To the right of the fountain, the Vittolone, a wide boulevard lined with statues, leads to the Fontana dell'Oceana which was designed by Giambologna.

Return to the Arno and head east along the river, crossing over Ponte alle Grazie to the beautiful Franciscan **Basilica di Santa Croce**. It was designed by A. da Cambio in 1294, although the marble façade, which looks over a spacious *piazza*, dates from 1863. The interior, lit by a myriad of stained-glass windows, has three spacious aisles with numerous famous funerary monuments to names such as Michelangelo, Machiavelli, and Galileo. The church also contains many fine frescoes in the chapels either side of the main apse. Cappella Peruzzi, the second chapel on the right has frescoes depicting the *Life of John the Baptist* and the *Life of John the Evangelist* by Giotto (1320). Cappella Bardi, the first chapel on the right, also contains frescoes by Giotto, of the *Life of St Francis*, while the painting of St Francis on the altar is by an unknown artist and dates from the thirteenth century. The apse itself holds a fine fourteenth-century crucifix and has the *Legend of the Cross* (1380) frescoed on the walls by A. Gaddi. The fourth chapel on the left is frescoed by B. Daddi (1330) and holds a terracotta altar by G. della Robbia, while in the fifth chapel on the left the *History of St Silvester* covers the walls. Further frescoes can be seen in the chapels in the right transept: the Cappella Castellani is frescoed by A. Gaddi and the Cappella Baroncelli is by his father, T. Gaddi, while the sacristy is now a postcard shop and the sacristy corridor, designed by Michelozzo, leads to a leather school.

The cloisters along the right side of Santa Croce contain the Cappella de Pazzi which was designed by Brunelleschi for the De Pazzi family in 1430 and has a number of terracottas by Della Robbia embedded in its walls. Along the left side of the cloister is the Chiostro Antico, where there is a collection of inscriptions and tombs, while along the right side is the **Museo dell'Opera di Santa Croce**. The museum holds a collection of fresco fragments, stained-glass, and Della Robbia terracottas, as well as a fresco of the *Last Supper* by T. Gaddi and a crucifix by Cimabue, both of which are in the former refectory.

Neptune's Fountain, Florence

Leave Piazza Santa Croce from the east corner and follow Borgo dei Greci to Piazza San Firenze where the **Museo Nazionale**, also known as the Bargello, can be visited. Built between 1254 and 1346 as the magistrates courts, today the Bargello houses an important collection of Florentine sculpture. The ground floor contains sculptures by Michelangelo and Cellini; the first floor has some of Donatello's most important works, as well as bas-reliefs by Brunelleschi and Ghiberti designed for the doors of the baptistery; while the second floor holds Della Robbia terracottas and an excellent collection of Renaissance bronzes.

To visit the monuments in the northern part of the city, return to the Duomo and follow Borgo San Lorenzo north of the baptistery, to Piazza San Lorenzo. The **Basilica di San Lorenzo**, on the west side of the *piazza*, was built between 1425 and 1446 by Brunelleschi for the Medici family. The simple interior is typical of the Renaissance style and has two attractive pulpits supported on columns, designed by Donatello, on either side of the central aisle. The monumental chapel behind the church, **Cappelle Medicee**, was designed by Vasari as a grand burial place for the Medici dukes. To the left of the church is the Laurenziana library which was founded by Cosimo I Medici and designed by Michelangelo. Cross the *piazza*, which is filled with market stalls selling leather and souvenirs, to **Palazzo Medici-Riccardi** and turn left along Via Cavour from where the *palazzo* can be entered. Built between 1440 and 1460 this fine *palazzo* with its great rusticated walls was designed by Michelozzo for the founder of the Medici dynasty, Cosimo Il Vecchio. It is now the seat of the *prefettura*, although it is possible to visit the chapel which holds Gozzoli's *Journey of the Magi* (1459), and also the gallery of Medicean portraits.

Follow Via Cavour north for 400m (437yd) to Piazza San Marco, crossing over to the **Museo di San Marco** which is on the north side. Housed in the former Domenican monastery designed by Michelozzo in 1437, the museum is devoted to Fra Angelico who lived here from 1435 to 1445 and contains the greatest collection of his work in Italy. Entering the Cloister of Sant'Antonino take the first door on the right into the Ospitzio dei Pellegrini, the Pilgrim's Hospice. It contains a superb collection of Fra Angelico's paintings including the *Tabernacolo dei Linaioli*, a beautiful altar piece made for the linen-maker's guild and set in a marble frame designed by Ghiberti, the *Armadio degli Argenti* which is made up of thirty-five small panels depicting the story of Christ, and an excellent *Deposition*. The Great Refectory, on the west side of the cloister, holds numerous paintings by other artists of the sixteenth and seventeenth centuries, while the Chapter House along the south side has a large fresco of the *Crucifixion* by Fra Angelico. Next door to the Chapter House stairs lead up from the cloister to the Dormitory which contains forty-four cells each with a fresco by Fra Angelico. At the top of the stairs is Fra Angelico's beautiful *Annunciation* while the cells are arranged along three corridors surrounding a courtyard. Along the north corridor is the library, commissioned by Cosimo Il Vecchio, which contains an important collection of manuscripts illuminated by Fra Angelico amongst others. At the end of the north corridor, on the right, is Cosimo Il Vecchio's cell, made up of two small rooms, the first with a fresco of the *Crucifixion*, and the other with the *Adoration of the Magi*.

Leave Piazza San Marco from the east side, following Via C. Battisti to Piazza della Santissimi Annunziata. This fine square, designed by Brunelleschi, has an equestrian statue of Duke Ferdinand I at the southern end and is surrounded by porticoed buildings. The Confraternita dei Servi di Maria extends along the west side, the **Galleria dello Spedale degli Innocenti** with its terracotta medallions by A. della Robbia along the east side, while the **Chiesa della Santissimi Annunziata** fills the north side. The church was first built in 1250, but was re-designed in 1444 by Michelozzo. Its porticoed façade, which was added in 1604 by A. da Sangallo, leads into an atrium, known as the Chiostrino dei Voti. The walls of the atrium are covered by numerous impressive frescoes including works by the early Mannerist painter, A. del Sarto. The interior with its fine Baroque ceiling also contains frescoes, amongst the most important of which is the fourteenth-century *Annunciation* in the first chapel on the left.

The **Museo Archeologico** lies just to the east of Chiesa della Santissimi Annunziata, along Via della Colonna. It is one of the most important archaeological collections in Italy and contains finds from Etruscan, Greek and Roman sites as well as an Egyptian museum on the first floor.

For those with time it is well worth visiting the **Chiesa di Santa Maria Novella** on the western side of the city, near the rail station. The pretty, inlaid marble façade overlooks a spacious square, Piazza di Santa Maria Novella, where two obelisks are supported on the backs of bronze tortoises by G. da Bologna (1608). The church was built for the Domenican order in the thirteenth and fourteenth centuries and contains numerous fine frescoes, amongst the most famous of which is Masaccio's *Trinity* (1425), in the third chapel on the left. Also of note is the *Last Judgement* decorating the Strozzi Chapel in the left transept and the excellent frescoes by Ghirlandaio which illustrate the *Lives of St John the Baptist and the Virgin* in the main apse.

Fiesole, on a hill 8km (5 miles) north of Florence, is an easy and pleasant excursion either by the No 7 bus from Piazza San Marco, or by car. Founded by the Etruscans in the seventh century BC, the town prospered as Roman *Faesulum*, up until AD405 when it was destroyed by the Goths. After further invasions by the Lombards (AD539-40), the town gradually grew up again, but was suppressed by Florence in 1125. Today, the small town has a cheerful character, as well as some attractive Roman ruins and fine medieval buildings. The long *piazza* at the centre of the town, Piazza Mino da Fiesole, has the fourteenth-century Palazzo Pretorio at one end and the Duomo with its tall *campanile* at the other. The *campanile* was built in 1213, while the Duomo, first erected in 1028, was rebuilt during the thirteenth and fourteenth centuries. Inside, the nave is lined with columns, some with Roman capitals, and there is a fine fresco cycle, depicting the *Life of St Romulus*, the patron saint of the church, in the main apse. The triptych on the altar is by Bicci di Lorenzo (1440), and there are also fine triptychs in both of the side chapels.

The Museo Bandini, next to the Duomo, has a collection of paintings from the fourteenth and fifteenth centuries, including fine works by T. Gaddi and other Tuscan artists. The entrance to the Zona Archeologico is opposite the Museo Bandini. The Museo Archeologico, just to the right of the entrance, houses an interesting and well-displayed collection of artefacts found during the excavations, which began in 1809. The ruins, which mainly date from the first century BC, are picturesquely located on a gentle slope surrounded by olive trees. The best-preserved structure is the theatre which was reconstructed by Claudius (AD41-54), and later modified by Septimus Severus (AD193-211). With a seating capacity for 3,000 spectators, the theatre is still used during the summer arts festival, the Estate Fiesolana, which is held in July and August. A path leads down from the theatre to the ruins of a Roman baths, complete with pool, arched windows and hypercaust system. Further down, a balcony gives views of the fine Etruscan walls built with cyclopean stonework. The scant remains of the temple nearby, are also Etruscan, although they were built over by the Romans.

For a panorama of Florence follow Via San Francesco from the Duomo up to a terrace below the convent of San Francesco. The convent was founded by the Franciscan order in 1399 on the site of the Etruscan acropolis. Its Gothic church contains a number of fine paintings, as does the sacristy next door.

The monastery of San Domenico is below Fiesole, about halfway along the main road to Florence. Built between 1406 and 1435, it has a rather gloomy Baroque interior. However, in the first chapel on the left there is a magnificent painting of the *Virgin and Angels* (around 1430) by Fra Angelico, who lived at the monastery.

Route 4C — Florence to Pisa

Prato, 14km (9 miles) west of Florence, is best reached along the A11 motorway. It is a large, industrial city, but it has a well-preserved *centro storico* within easy walking distance of the carparks on Piazza Mercatale and Piazza Sant'Antonio. Prato has been an industrial centre since Roman times, when it was known as *Pagus Cornius*. From the thirteenth century up until the end of the fifteenth, it was known throughout Europe for its woollen textiles, but began its present rapid expansion in the late nineteenth century.

The Duomo, considered one of the finest in Tuscany, stands on a vast *piazza* at the northern edge of the old city. It was built during the thirteenth and fourteenth centuries, to designs by G. Pisano (1385-1457) and others, and is strikingly decorated with green and white stone. The façade has an attractive portal with a terracotta by A. della Robbia (1489) in the lunette. The fine exterior pulpit, designed by Donatello and Michelozzo (1428-38), is still used for the traditional display of the Sacro Cingolo (Holy Girdle) at religious festivals. The Cappella del Sacro Cingolo, inside the cathedral on the left, is decorated with frescoes by Agnolo Gaddi (1392). The nave, divided by attractive, green stone columns, has a cycle of frescoes depicting the *Life of St Stephen and John the Baptist*, by Filippo Lippi (1452-66), while the frescoes in the Cappella dell'Angelo Custode are attributed to Paolo Uccello.

The Palazzo Vescovile, next door, which is built around a charming Romanesque cloister, houses the Museo dell'Opera del Duomo. The collection is made up of paintings, including work by P. Uccello and F. Lippi, and the original carvings by Donatello from the external pulpit of the Duomo.

Via Mazzoni leads south from the Duomo to Piazza del Comune, which is dominated by the crenellated façade of Palazzo Pretorio. Although the *palazzo* dates back to the thirteenth century, it has had many additions, including the grand external staircase which was built in the sixteenth century. Today, the grand apartments, with their high, panelled ceilings and frescoed walls, house the Galleria Comunale with its collection of fourteenth- and fifteenth-century paintings. Via Guasti leads to Piazza San Domenico and its church which was founded in 1283. The church contains the Museo di Pittura Murale, a museum of frescoes removed from other local churches.

The sturdy fortress in the centre of the old city, the Castello dell'Imparatore, was built in 1248 for Frederick II and offers good views of the city from its walls. The nearby Renaissance church of Santa Maria delle Carceri, with its polychrome marble stonework, was designed by G. da Sangallo (1484-92), in the style of Brunelleschi and is built on a Greek cross plan.

From Prato take the A11 20km (12 miles) west to **Pistoia**, another large industrial city. The modern outskirts that have grown up around the old historic centre are themselves surrounded by a wide belt of rich horticultural land. The old city, within its fortified walls, has some fine architecture, including many churches with green and white striped stonework in the Pisan-Romanesque style.

It is possible to park inside the city walls, although the very centre, around Piazza del Duomo is pedestrianised. Duomo San Zeno on one side of the vast *piazza* has a tall, thirteenth-century *campanile*, and a façade with rows of small arcades which dates from the twelfth century. The elegant portal, added in the fourteenth century, is decorated with blue, yellow and white glazed terracottas by A. della Robbia (1505). The main point of interest in the seventeenth-century interior is the famous silver altar in the Cappella di Sant'Iacopo. It was started in 1287, but not finished until 1487, by which time it was decorated with over 600 figures.

To the right of the Duomo is the thirteenth-century Palazzo del Podesta, decorated with heraldic shields, while opposite stands the baptistery. This remarkable octagonal building was designed by A. Pisano (1338-59) and is constructed of alternating bands of green and white stone. There is a lively fruit and vegetable market behind the baptistery. On the far side of the *piazza*, is the fourteenth-century Palazzo Comunale, part of which houses the Museo Civico. Joined by a bridge, built in 1637, to the Duomo, the *palazzo* has a façade of green stone and has a large collection of paintings on three floors. The first floor contains thirteenth to sixteenth-century paintings by the Pistoian and Florentine schools. The second floor has a collection of local modern art, and the third floor has paintings and antiques of the seventeenth to nineteenth centuries. A centre devoted to the Italian sculptor, Marino Marini (1901-80), which was formerly housed here, has now moved to Palazzo del Tau on Corso Silvano Fedi.

The Ospedale del Ceppo, north of the *piazza*, on Via F. Pacini, has an interesting façade, decorated with a large and colourful bas-relief in terracotta by G. della Robbia (1525). Among the many churches throughout the city, the three most notable are: Sant'Andrea, with its fine pulpit carved by G. Pisano (1298-1301); San Giovanni Forcivitas with its attractive, striped exterior; and Madonna del'Umilita which has a high dome, resembling Brunelleschi's in Florence, designed in 1561 by Velsari.

The A11 continues west to Montecatini Terme, 15km (9 miles) from Pistoia, although it is also possible to take a more picturesque route along the SS435, through the fortified town of Serravalle. **Montecatini Terme** is one of the most elegant and famous spas in Europe and has over 200 hotels. There are eight principal curative establishments: the Tamerici, Torretta, Regina, Tettucio, Rinfresco, Leopoldine, Giulia and Grocco. The treatment involves drinking the mineral spring water, taking mud baths, hot baths and inhalations according to the prescription of the specialists each establishment employs. The period of treatment varies, but is usually in excess of 2 weeks. The centre of the resort, only open to traffic at certain hours (clearly posted at the road entrance), is along Viale Verde, a wide promenade lined with luxuriant gardens, music halls, cinemas and restaurants. The street ends at one of the most impressive establishments, the Terme Tettucio. Built in 1927, it is neo-classical in style with vast white columns forming shady arcades above polished marble floors. A large wooded park, La Panteraie, stretches over an area of 12 hectares (30 acres) around the Terme, providing clients with a beautiful environment in which to walk and exercise. At the top of the park is another prestigious establishment, the Terme la Toretta, which apart from its treatment facilities, has seven red clay tennis courts and a swimming pool. For a panoramic view of the spa, take the *funicolare* from Viale A. Diaz to **Val di Nievole** (290m/951ft).

As well as all this Montecatini Terme also has the fastest 800m (875yd) horse-racing track in Europe and an 18-hole golf course at **La Pievaccia**.

The A11 *autostrada* is the quickest route to Lucca, but those who prefer a more scenic drive should take the SS435 to Pescia, passing **Uzzano** with its medieval fortress. The road enters **Pescia** through an eighteenth-century gate and crosses the river to the main square, Piazza Mazzini, on the west bank of the river. The Palazzo dei Vicari, originally built between the thirteenth and fourteenth centuries is one of the many attractive buildings that line the *piazza*. Pescia, well-known for its floriculture, particularly the cultivation of carnations, has a large flower market and is the venue of the Bienale de Fiore, an important flower fair held on even years.

Collodi 6km (4 miles) west of Pescia, is best known for its Parco di Pinocchio. The park, created in 1951 to commemorate Carlo Lorenzini (1826-90), who under the pen-name of Collodi, invented Pinocchio, contains scenes from the tales of Pinocchio and a labyrinth. On the steep hillside overlooking Collodi is the Castello e Giardino Garzoni. Built for the Garzoni family in 1633, the house is set at the top of a fine garden, which is arranged symmetrically around a monumental staircase, on a series of steep terraces. Guided tours of the interior (summer only) include the room where Napoleon is believed to have slept, and the kitchens where Collodi grew up as a boy.

After returning to the SS435, continue west to **Lucca** (20km/12 miles), parking inside the city walls on any of the numerous small *piazza*, or in the main carpark on Piazza Napoleone. The 4km (2 miles) of well-preserved wall and eleven bastions that encircle the city were built between 1504 and 1645, although Lucca's history has been traced back as far as the Iron Age. It was made a Roman colony in 180BC, it remained relatively unimportant until the Lombard Dukes, who conquered Tuscany in AD568, made it their capital. After a period of peace and prosperity in the medieval period, it passed through a half-century of turmoil when it was fought over by the Pisans, between 1314 and 1369. After it was freed by Emperor Charles IV in 1369, peace was restored and Lucca flourished, continuing as an aristocratic republic up until 1799. Today it is a large provincial capital. The well-preserved historic centre of the city has numerous attractive streets and squares, and many interesting monuments.

Duomo San Martino is in the southern part of the old city, close to Piazza Napoleone. The original construction of 1060 was rebuilt in its present Romanesque form during the twelfth century. The attractive white marble façade, decorated with green marble inlay, has a fine portico containing beautiful carved reliefs by N. Pisano. The *campanile* in the right corner of the façade was added in 1262. The vast Gothic interior contains many important works of art. Just inside the main door stands the thirteenth-century, equestrian statue of *St*

Martin Dividing his Cloak, which originally adorned the façade. In the middle of the left aisle, the Tempietto del Volto Santo, an octagonal chapel designed by M. Civitali in 1484, contains an extraordinary wooden crucifix. Legend has it that the carving was started by Nicodemus, miraculously completed by an angel, then lost at sea before turning up on the Italian coast at *Luni*. In fact its origins are unknown, although it is thought to date from the eleventh century. On the 13 September, during the candlelit procession of the Festa di Santa Croce, the crucifix is paraded around the town, draped in sumptuous gold and black velvet. In the left transept stands the beautifully carved tomb, the Tomba di Ilaria del Caretto (1408) which is considered Jacopo della Quercia's best work. Also of note are the fine sections of polychrome paving which date from the fifteenth century, and Tintoretto's *Last Supper* in the third chapel on the right. Other works of art from the Duomo can be seen in the thirteenth-century Casa del Duomo, on the small *piazza* behind the *campanile*.

Piazza San Michele in the centre of the town, 400m (437yd) north-west of the Duomo, is dominated by the beautiful green and white façade of San Michele in Foro. Dating from 1145, the façade is ornately decorated with inlaid marble animals and row upon row of uniquely patterned columns. The newly-restored, gilt statue of the *Madonna and Child* in the top right corner of the façade is by M. Civitali (1480). The plain stone interior contains fine paintings, including the *Four Saints* by F. Lippi on the right of the main apse, and an attractive twelfth-century wooden curcifix in the apse itself, attributed to the Luccan school.

Leave Piazza San Michele along Via Roma and turn left up Via Filungo, the most elegant shopping street in the city. Near the end of Via Filungo, turn right into Piazza di Mercato which is built on the foundations of a second-century Roman amphitheatre, and retains its original shape. A hundred metres south-east of the *piazza* is a tall tower, the Torre Guingi, from where there are excellent views of the city. Visitors with the time and energy needed to climb all the steps should make this short detour, others should proceed directly to the large church of San Frediano, to the north-west of the *piazza*. Built between 1112 and 1147, the upper façade has a beautiful, Byzantine-style mosaic of the *Ascension* which was restored in the nineteenth century. The interior of the church is plain, but it has a very large, central aisle, divided by fine marble columns, some of which are antique. To the right of the main door, there is a beautifully carved font which dates from the twelfth century. The blue and white glazed terracotta on the wall behind it is by A. della Robbia. The finely carved altar in the fourth chapel on the left is by Jacopo della Quercia.

The city's national museum, Museo Nazionale Villa Guingi, is a 20 minute walk from the centre. Located near the east gate in the city walls, the museum is housed in a fine *villa*, built for the Guingi family in 1418. It stands on a *piazza* opposite the large fourteenth-century church of San Francesco. The museum is on two floors. The ground

Market day at the Piazza San Michele, Lucca

This Byzantine-style mosaic can be seen on the façade of San Frediano Church, Lucca

floor has a collection of Roman to medieval stone carvings, including reliefs by M. Civitali. The first floor contains the *pinacoteca* where there are many fine works of art from the local churches, among the best of which are a set of inlaid panels depicting scenes from Lucca.

Additional Information

Places of Interest

ROUTE 4A
Cortona
Museo dell'Accademia Etrusco
Palazzo Casali
52044 Cortona (AR)
☎ (0575) 62767
Open: winter Tuesday to Sunday 9am-1pm and 3-5pm. Summer Tuesday to Sunday 10am-1pm and 4-7pm.

Museo Diocesano
Piazza del Duomo
52044 Cortona (AR)
☎ (0575) 62830
Open: winter Tuesday to Sunday 9am-1pm and 3-5pm. Summer Tuesday to Sunday 9am-1pm and 3-6.30pm.

Fortezza di Girifalco
52044 Cortona (AR)
Open: summer daily 10am-7pm.

Arezzo
San Francesco Church
Piazza San Francesco
52100 Arezzo (AR)
Open: winter daily 8.30am-12noon and 2-6.30pm. Summer daily 8.30am-12noon and 1.30-7pm.

Casa di Petrarca
28 Via del Orto
52100 Arezzo (AR)
Open: Monday to Friday 10am-12noon and 3-5pm, Saturday mornings 10am-12noon.

Casa di Vasari
55 XX Settembre
52100 Arezzo (AR)
Open: Monday to Saturday 9am-7pm, holidays 9am-1pm.

Galleria e Museo Medioevale e Moderno
8 Via San Lorentino
52100 Arezzo (AR)
Open: Tuesday to Saturday 9am-2pm, holidays 9am-1pm.

Museo Archeologico Mecenate
10 Via Magaritone
52100 Arezzo (AR)
Open: Tuesday to Saturday 9am-2pm, holidays 9am-1pm.

ROUTE 4B
Places of Interest in Florence

Duomo Santa Maria del Fiore
Piazza Duomo
50100 Firenze (FI)
☎ (055) 294514
Open: daily 10am-5pm.

Cupola del Brunelleschi
Cattedrale Santa Maria del Fiore
Piazza Duomo
50100 Firenze (FI)
☎ (055) 2302885
Open: Monday to Saturday 10am-5.40pm.

Museo dell'Opera del Duomo
9 Piazza Duomo
50100 Firenze (FI)
☎ (055) 2302885
Open: winter Monday to Saturday 9am-6pm. Summer Monday to Saturday 9am-7.30pm.

Campanile di Giotto
Piazza Duomo
50100 Firenze (FI)
☎ (055) 2302885
Open: winter daily 9am-5.20pm. Summer daily 8.30am-7.30pm.

Palazzo Vecchio
Piazza Signoria
50100 Firenze (FI)
☎ (055) 2768465
Open: Monday to Friday 9am-7pm.
Holidays 8am-1pm.

Galleria degli Uffizi
6 Loggiato degli Uffizi
50100 Firenze (FI)
☎ (055) 218341
Open: Tuesday to Saturday 9am-7pm. Holidays 9am-1pm.

Galleria Palatina e Appartimenti
Monumentali
Palazzo Pitti
Piazza Pitti
50100 Firenze (FI)
☎ (055) 210323
Open: Tuesday to Saturday 9am-2pm, holidays 9am-1pm.

Basilica di Santa Croce
Piazza Santa Croce
50100 Firenze (FI)
☎ (055) 244619
Open: Monday to Saturday
7.30am-12.30pm and 3-6.30pm,
Sunday 3-5pm.

Museo dell'Opera di Santa Croce
16 Piazza Santa Croce
50100 Firenze (FI)
☎ (055) 244619
Open: winter daily except
Wednesday 10am-12.30pm and 3-5pm. Summer daily except
Wednesday 10am-12.30pm and
2.30-6.30pm.

Museo Nazionale del Bargello
4 Via del Proconsolo
50100 Firenze (FI)
☎ (055) 210801
Open: Tuesday to Saturday 9am-2pm. Holidays 9am-1pm.

Basilica di San Lorenzo
Piazza San Lorenzo
50100 Firenze (FI)
☎ (055) 216634
Open: daily 7am-12noon and 3.30-6.30pm.

Museo di San Marco
Piazza San Marco 1

50100 Firenze (FI)
☎ (055) 210741
Open: Tuesday to Saturday 9am-2pm, Sunday and holidays 9am-1pm.

Cappelle Medicee
Piazza Madonna degli
Aldobrandini
50100 Firenze (FI)
☎ (055) 213206
Open: Tuesday to Saturday 9am-2pm. Holidays 9am-1pm.

Biblioteca Medicea Laurenziana
9 Piazza San Lorenzo
50100 Firenze (FI)
☎ (055) 210760
Open: Monday to Saturday 10am-1pm.

Palazzo Medici Riccardi
1 Via Cavour
50100 Firenze (FI)
☎ (055) 27601
Open: daily except Wednesday
9am-1pm and 3-5pm. Holidays
9am-12noon.

Chiesa della Santissimi Annunziata
Piazza Santissimi Annunziata
50100 Firenze (FI)
☎ (055) 298034
Open: daily 7am-12.30pm and 4-6.45pm.

Galleria dello Spedale degli Innocenti
12 Piazza Santissimi Annunziata
50100 Firenze (FI)
☎ (055) 243670
Open: daily, except Wednesday,
9am-2pm. Holidays 8am-1pm.

Museo Archeologico
36 Via della Colonna
50100 Firenze (FI)
☎ (055) 2478641
Open: Tuesday to Saturday 9am-2pm. Holidays 9am-1pm.

Chiesa di Santa Maria Novella
Piazza Santa Maria Novella
50100 Firenze (FI)
☎ (055) 210113
Open: daily (except Sunday am) 7-11.30am and 3.30-6pm.

Florence: Useful Information

Tourist Information Centre
Azienda di Promozione Turistica
16 Via Manzoni
50100 Firenze (FI)
☎ (055) 294514
Open: daily 10am-5pm.

Emergency Telephone Numbers
Emergencies (Soccorso Pubblico di
Emergenza) 113
Police (Carabinieri Pronto
Intervento) 112
Fire (Vigili del Fuoco) 115
Ambulance (Ambulanza) 118
Car Breakdown (Soccorso Stradale)
116

Medical
Ambulance
☎ (055) 212222/215555

Arcispedale di Santa Maria Nuova
Piazza Santa Maria Nuova 1
50100 Firenze (FI)
☎ (055) 27661

Dial 192 to find out pharmacies
open outside regular hours.

Postal Services
Central Post Office
Palazzo delle Poste
Via Pellicceria
50100 Firenze (FI)
Open: (General postal services)
Monday to Friday 8.15am-7pm.
Saturday 8.15am-12noon.
(Telegraph and telephone service)
24 hours a day.
Telegraph Office
Central Railway Station
50100 Firenze (FI)
Open: 24 hours a day.

Travel
A.T.A.F. (City Bus)
Information Office
Piazza del Duomo 57r
50100 Firenze (FI)
☎ (055) 580528

C.A.P. (Provincial Bus)
Piazza Stazione
Via Nazionale 13r
50100 Firenze (FI)
☎ (055) 214637

F.LLI LAZZI (Provincial Bus)
Piazza Stazione
50100 Firenze (FI)
☎ (055) 215155

CO.PI. T (Provincial Bus)
Piazza Santa Maria Novella
50100 Firenze (FI)
☎ (055) 215451

SITA (Provincial Bus)
Viale dei Cadorna 105
50100 Firenze
☎ (055) 47821

Ufficio Informazioni Ferrovie Dello
Stato
(Railway Information Office)
Central Railway Station
50100 Firenze (FI)
☎ (055) 278785
Open: daily 7am-9.30pm.

Peretola Airport
50100 Firenze (FI)
☎ (055) 373498

Car Hire
Avis (Car Hire)
Borgognissanti 128r
50100 Firenze (FI)
☎ (055) 213629/298826

Europcar (Car Hire)
Borgognissanti 53r
50100 Firenze (FI)
☎ (055) 293444/294130

Hertz (Car Hire)
Via M. Finiguerra 33r
50100 Firenze (FI)
☎ (055) 298205/282260

Maggiore (Car Hire)
Via M. Finiguerra 11r
50100 Firenze (FI)
☎ (055) 210238

Automobile Club d'Italia
☎ (055) 666500

Radio Taxi SO.CO.TA
☎ 4798

Radio Taxi CO.TA.FI
☎ 4390

Other Places of Interest

Fiesole
Zona Archeologico
50014 Fiesole (FI)
☎ (055) 59477
Open: winter daily except Tuesday
10am-4pm. Summer daily 9am-
5pm.
Book and postcard shop.

Museo Bandini
Piazza Mino da Fiesole
50014 Fiesole (FI)
☎ (055) 59061
Open: winter daily except Tuesday
10am-1pm and 3-6pm. Summer
daily except Tuesday 9.30am-1pm
and 3-7pm.

ROUTE 4C
Prato
Museo dell'Opera del Duomo
49 Piazza del Duomo
50047 Prato (FI)
☎ (0574) 29339
Open: daily except Tuesday
9.30am-12.30pm and 3-6.30pm.
Holidays 9.30am-12.30pm.

Galleria Comunale
Palazzo Pretorio
Piazza del Comune
50047 Prato (FI)
☎ (0574) 452302
Open: daily 9.30am-12.30pm and 3-
6.30pm. Holidays 9.30am-12.30pm.

Museo di Pittura Murale
San Domenico
50047 Prato (FI)
Open: Sunday and holidays
9.30am-12.30pm. To visit the
museum on weekdays contact the
Azienda Autonoma di Soggiorno e
Turismo (see address under Tourist
Information Offices).

Pistoia
Duomo San Zeno
Piazza del Duomo
51100 Pistoia (PT)
Open: daily 7am-12noon and 4-
7pm. Holidays 7am-1pm and 4-
7pm.

Museo Civico
Palazzo Comunale
Piazza del Duomo
51100 Pistoia (PT)
☎ (0573) 371214
Open: Tuesday to Friday 9am-1pm
and 3-7pm. Holidays 9am-1pm.

Collodi
Parco di Pinocchio
51017 Collodi (PT)
☎ (0572) 429342
Open: daily 8am-sunset.

Castello e Giardino Garzoni
51017 Collodi (PT)
Open: winter gardens daily 8am-
1pm and 2.30-4.30pm. House
Saturday 2.30-4.30pm. Summer
gardens and house daily 8am-sunset.

Lucca
Museo Nazionale Villa Guingi
Via della Quarquonia
55100 Lucca (LU)
☎ (0583) 46033
Open: Tuesday to Sunday 9am-2pm.

Tourist Information Centres

ROUTE 4A
Passignano sul Trasimeno
Pro Loco
Piazza Garibaldi
06065 Passignano sul Trasimeno
(PG)
☎ (075) 847495

Cortona
Azienda Autonoma di Soggiorno e
    Turismo
72 Via Nazionale
52044 Cortona (AR)
☎ (0575) 603056 or 630353

Arezzo
Ente Provinciale per il Turismo
116 Piazza Risorgimento
52100 Arezzo (AR)
☎ (0575) 23952 or 23953

Bibbiena
Azienda Autonoma di Soggiorno e
    Turismo
Via Cappucci
52011 Bibbiena (AR)
☎ (0575) 593098

ROUTE 4B
Fiesole
Azienda Autonoma di Soggiorno e
    Turismo
45 Piazza Mino da Fiesole
50014 Fiesole (FI)
☎ (055) 598720

ROUTE 4C
Prato
Azienda Autonoma di Soggiorno e
    Turismo
48-52 Via Cairoli
50047 Prato (FI)
☎ (0574) 24112

Pistoia
Ufficio Informazioni
Piazza del Duomo
51100 Pistoia (PT)
☎ (0573) 21622

Azienda Autonoma di Soggiorno e
    Turismo
66 Viale Verdi
Montecatini Terme
51016 Pistoia (PT)
☎ (0572) 70109

Lucca
Ente Provinciale per il Turismo
2 Piazza Guidiccioni
55100 Lucca (LU)
☎ (0583) 41205

5

LIGURIA AND PIEDMONT

C hapter 5 heads north from Pisa along the coast, following the
    Apuan Alps, which supplied Rome and the Renaissance with
their marble, through elegant resorts with palm-lined bays, to
Genoa, the largest port in Italy. After Genoa the route heads inland
through the little visited region of the Langhe, where there are excellent
wines, cheeses and medieval castles, to Turin, capital of Piedmont.

At Turin visitors can choose, either to continue along the routes in
chapter 6, or make excursions to the Gran Paradiso natural park and
the Valle d'Aosta.

Route 5A — Pisa to Carrara

Pisa is a large city, known throughout the world for its leaning tower,
but little else. Despite this, the city is well-endowed with monuments, most of which date from the time when it was one of the
world's leading naval powers. Known to the Romans as *Julia Pisana*,
the city first rose to prominence in the ninth century after its naval
victory over the Saracens. By the eleventh century Pisa controlled the
entire coast from Portovenere to Civitavecchia, and in 1114 it took
Sardinia, Corsica and the Balearic Islands, and dominated sea trade
in the western Mediterranean, as well as having links with Istanbul
and Tunis. From the eleventh to the thirteenth centuries Pisan art and
architecture flourished. Nicola Pisano (around 1220-84) and his son
Andrea (Giovanni) Pisano (around 1290-1348) did much to enhance
the Pisan-Romanesque, and later Pisan-Gothic styles, with their
sculptural and architectural work. Unfortunately, in 1284, Pisa's
entire navy was destroyed by the Genoans at Meloria, near Livorno,
signalling the decline of the city, which eventually fell into Florentine
hands in 1406. Under the Florentines, and after widespread malaria,
the city was reduced to fewer than 8,500 inhabitants, and it was only
with the rise of Cosimo I Medici in the sixteenth century, that Pisa
once again prospered. Pisa's university dates from this period, as
does the fine Renaissance architecture seen in the city centre today.

Unlike most other Italian cities, the Duomo is not in the centre of
the city, but to the north, on Piazza dei Miracoli. There is ample

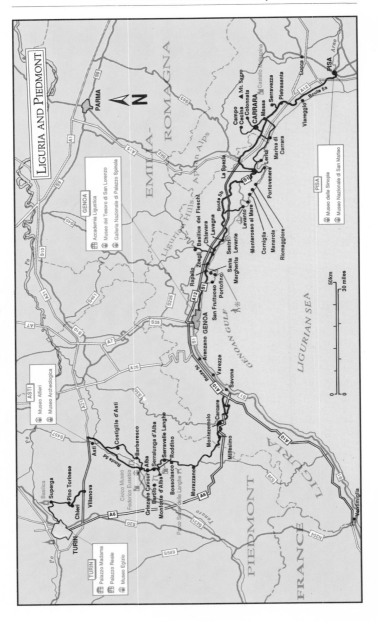

parking nearby, along the city walls. The grassy *piazza* contains four major monuments: the Duomo; the baptistery; the cemetery and the Campanile (leaning tower). Unfortunately, the tower has been closed as it is considered dangerous, and becomes more so by 1mm each year. When last measured it stood to a height of 54.80m (180ft) on the north side, and 55.65m (182.5ft) on the south. Construction work on the tower was started in 1152, but stopped when the building was little more than 10m (33ft) off the ground, as there was already significant subsidence. In 1275, when the tower showed no signs of falling down, the building work continued, at an angle.

The Duomo, at the centre of Piazza dei Miracoli, has also suffered from subsidence, but leans far less obviously than the tower. It was built in 1064 by Buscheto and is the earliest example of Pisan-Romanesque architecture, typified by the rows of columns adorning the façade. The lower façade is decorated with panels of inlaid stone, while the three grand but simple portals are flanked by columns and have beautiful bronze doors, recast in 1595 by Giambologna. The vast interior has five aisles, divided by columns with Corinthian capitals, with black and white striped arches above. The central aisle has a beautifully coffered ceiling, but the masterpiece is G. Pisano's

The leaning tower of Pisa in the 'Field of Miracles'

pulpit (1302-11) which stands on eleven columns, and is exquisitely decorated with finely sculpted reliefs. The bronze lamp, which hangs from the ceiling nearby, is said to have inspired Galileo (1564-1642) who was born in Pisa.

The baptistery, opposite the Duomo, was started in 1152 and completed under the direction of N. and G. Pisano, between 1260 and 1284, although the dome was not added until the fourteenth century. Of its four portals, the one facing the Duomo is the most ornate, having carvings of the Apostles, but the greatest works of art are inside. The beautifully carved pulpit by N. Pisano (1260), which stands on seven columns on the left of the interior, is decorated with five reliefs that mark the beginning of the Gothic style in Italy. The octagonal, white marble font, inlaid with mosaic, which stands in the centre of the baptistery is by Guido da Como (1246).

The Camposanto, a walled cemetery, lies along the north side of the *piazza*. The cemetery was founded in 1203 when Archbishop Ubaldo de Lanfranchi brought soil from the hill of Golgotha, near Jerusalem, to enable Pisans to be buried in holy ground. The cemetery was enclosed within a cloister in 1278 by Giovanni di Simone and was the preferred resting ground for the Pisan nobility throughout the medieval and Renaissance periods. The Camposanto was hit by Allied bombs in 1944, irreparably damaging the cycle of twenty-three frescoes painted between 1340 and 1470, by B. Gozzoli amongst others, on the walls of the cloister. The sketches for the frescoes are kept in the Museo delle Sinopie, on the opposite side of the *piazza*.

The Museo dell'Opera del Duomo, with its fine collection, including sculptures by N. and G. Pisano, is housed in the former Chapterhouse, opposite the Campanile. The building, which dates from the thirteenth century, has an attractive cloister and was opened as a museum in 1986.

To visit the rest of Pisa, leave the Piazza dei Miracoli from the corner near the Museo dell' Opera del Duomo, and head in a southeasterly direction to Piazza del Cavalieri. The *piazza* is named after the Order of the Knights of St Stephen which was founded in 1561 by Cosimo I, mainly to combat piracy in the Mediterranean. Palazzo Cavalieri, on the north side of the *piazza*, was designed by Vasari in 1562 as the headquarters of the Order, and is intricately decorated with sgraffitto. The church of Santo Stefano dei Cavalieri, next to the *palazzo*, was also designed by Vasari.

Piazza Garibaldi, the hub of the city, is 350m (383yd) south of Piazza dei Cavalieri, on the north bank of the Arno river. Follow the left embankment, the Lungarno Mediceo past the Palazzo Toscanelli, where Byron stayed between 1821 and 1822, to the Museo Nazionale. The museum is housed in the former monastery of San Matteo, founded by the Benedictines in 1027. It contains an important and wide-ranging collection, including ancient sarcophagi, Pisan sculpture, Tuscan painting and ceramics, as well as work from Northern European schools.

Returning to Piazza Garibaldi, cross the river on the Ponte di Mezzo, the oldest bridge in the city, and follow the right embankment, Lungarno Gambacorti, to the small Gothic church of Santa Maria della Spina. Dating from 1323, the richly decorated exterior of the church is adorned with carvings from the Pisano workshop.

To avoid the built–up area around Pisa, and the string of modern coastal resorts, such as **Viareggio**, take the A12 motorway as far as the Versilia exit, 30km (19 miles) north of the city. **Pietrasanta**, just east of the motorway, is an important marble-working centre. Duomo San Martino (1330), which stands on the main *piazza*, along with the Gothic church of Sant'Agostino, has an attractive façade constructed of the local marble. **Serravezza**, a further 5$\frac{1}{2}$km (3 miles) inland, is another important marble-working centre.

Return to the SS1 Via Aurelia and continue northwards to **Massa**, the provincial capital. Situated in the Frigido river valley, the town was the seat of the Malaspina Duchy from 1442 to 1790. The Renaissance Castello Malespina, which was built on the foundations of a medieval castle, stands high on a rocky promontory at the southern end of the town. It has a collection of archaeological finds from Paleolithic to Roman times, and there are fine views from its loggia.

The road to **Carrara** crosses the Frigido river and then winds up into the Apuan foothills on SS546, the Dir di Fossidinuovo. After 7km (4 miles) a series of hairpins lead down into the town which is built on the banks of the River Carriona. Encircled by a dramatic wall of mountains Carrara is close to some of the largest marble quarries in the world. The Romans named the town *Kar*, meaning stone, but there are no ancient remains, and the town has an atmosphere more like that of Genoa rather than anywhere in Tuscany.

· Duomo Sant'Andrea, located on a quiet *piazza*, north of the town centre, was built between the eleventh and fourteenth centuries. It was constructed from the local marble and has two attractively carved Romanesque portals, and a fourteenth-century Gothic rose window. The simple interior is divided into three aisles by columns with fine capitals, and the pulpit, which dates from the sixteenth century is inlaid with coloured marble. On the *piazza*, near the Duomo, is a sixteenth-century statue of Neptune, which is a memorial to the Genoan ruler, Andrea Doria, and the house where Michelangelo stayed when choosing his marble.

Carrara is a good base from which to visit some of the three-hundred working quarries, known as *cave*, in the surrounding mountains. There are footpaths up from the town into the mountains, but they are long and steep and it is better to make the initial ascent by car. **Collonata**, the most easily accessible of the quarries is 8km (5 miles) east of the town. Named after the Roman slaves who worked in the quarry, this is where Michelangelo chose the marble for his statue *David*. A longer, but very scenic excursion can be made up to **Campo Cecina**, 20km (12 miles) north of the town. The road winds up the wooded slopes of the Apuan Alps to a height of 1,469m

(4,818ft) with outstanding panoramas of the coast. The summit of Mount Sagro is 280m (918ft) above the car park and can only be reached on foot.

The road to La Spezia from Carrara passes the Museo di Marmo after 3km (2 miles). It contains a collection of different types of marble and illustrates the methods of quarrying and cutting the stone.

Route 5B — Carrara to Genoa

The beautiful coastline around the Gulf of Spezia has attracted numerous poets over the years, and is often referred to as 'The Gulf of Poets'. The tranquillity of the gulf may have been disturbed somewhat in recent years by the industrial growth around the port at La Spezia, but this has done little to dent the popularity of this part of the Italian coast. From Carrara the most direct route to Lerici is along the SS1 to **Sarzana**, turning left shortly after the town onto the SS331. However, a more picturesque route can be followed by taking the coastal road from **Marina di Carrara** to **Ameglia**, 10km (6 miles) to the west. From Ameglia follow signs to **Montemarcello**, which lies at the mouth of the gulf. A footpath leads from the village out to the limestone cliffs of Punta Bianca, the most south-easterly tip, from where there is a fine panorama. The coast as far as Lerici has been designated a natural park, and the road winds through an unspoilt landscape, above the small resorts of **La Serra**, **Fiascherino**, and **Tellaro** where D.H. Lawrence lived from 1913 to 1914.

Lerici, forever associated with Shelley, is $9^1/_2$km (6 miles) north-west of Montemarcello. Set around a beautiful bay, it still retains something of the character of a fishing village although it is now a busy and affluent resort. The harbour fortress was built by the Pisans in the thirteenth century, and along with the one at Portovenere, used to guard the entrance to the gulf. Enlarged by the Genoans in 1555, it now stands guard over Lerici's modern marina. The coast beyond Lerici becomes increasingly built up as it approaches La Spezia, and those who do not wish to visit it, or the west coast of the gulf, are advised to by-pass the city, by heading uphill from Lerici to join the A12 motorway, rejoining the coast at Levanto in order to visit the Cinque Terre.

La Spezia, has little to attract the visitor apart from the usual services available in a large city. The coast to the west of the city, however, has great charm. **Portovenere**, on the tip of the headland, is surrounded by unspoilt coast, and looks out to the **Isola Palmaria**, one of a cluster of islets, a mere 114m (125yd) offshore. Boat trips can be taken to visit the blue grotto from where Byron started out on his famous swim to visit Shelly at Lerici. The two smaller islands, **Isola del Tino** and **Isola del Tinetto**, both have romantic ruins and are also accessible by boat. In the summer, boat excursions can be made to the

(Opposite) Riomaggiore's charming harbour is surrounded by steep, narrow streets

Cinque Terre, which are less than 10km (6 miles) up the coast. A well-marked footpath, which takes about 3 ¹/₂ hours also follows the coast up to the Cinque Terre from Portovenere.

Levanto, known as the 'gates to Cinque Terre' is a pleasant town with good water-sport facilities, a large sandy beach and a regular train service to La Spezia which stops at each of the five **Cinque Terre** villages. The character of these tiny fishing villages has been preserved by their remarkably inaccessible locations. The train line which connects them, only emerges from the tunnel briefly at each of the villages, and at the moment only three can be reached by road, but plenty of boats leave from Levanto during the summer. It is also possible to walk along the coast from Levanto on footpath number one, joining footpath number ten at the Punta Mesco, which leads to Monterosso al Mare, the first of the Cinque Terre villages. Visitor's keen on hiking round the region should buy Club Alpino Italiano's '*Carta dei Sentieri delle Cinque Terre*' (1:40,000), which clearly shows all the footpaths between Levanto and La Spezia. It is well worth walking at least some part of the coast, as the scenery is outstanding with terraced vineyards rising steeply from the rocky shore.

Monterosso al Mare, the largest of the Cinque Terre villages is built around two sandy bays divided by a fortress. Restaurants serving seafood are clustered in the narrow streets surrounding the small black and white striped façade of the parish church. It is accessible by car and there are good water-sport facilities. The next village, **Vernazza**, one of the most picturesque of the Cinque Terre, is built on such a steep slope that when the train stops, both its ends remain in the tunnel. The houses in **Corniglia** are stacked up steeply on the slope behind the wide sandy beach, while in **Manarola**, they are clustered around a sheltered harbour, full of brightly coloured fishing boats. **Riomaggiore**, the last of the Cinque Terre villages, also has a charming harbour surrounded by steep, narrow streets. The vineyards between all the villages provide grapes for the local white wines, such as Sciacchetra, and a grape festival is held in Riomaggiore in the middle of September.

From Levanto, the SS332 winds up for 15km (9 miles) to join the SS1 Via Aurelia. Follow the road west for 18km (11 miles) along the Ligurian foothills to **Sestri Levante**. The elegant resort surrounds two palm-lined bays: the western one is known as the Baia delle Favole (Bay of Fables); and the eastern one, overlooked by the Romanesque church of San Nicolo (1151), as the Baia di Silenzio (Bay of Silence). The hilly promontory, is covered by a wooded park, the Parco dell'Albergo dei Castelli. Grand hotels are set amongst the trees and on the hill at the top there is a tower, which is said to be where Marconi experimented with the first short wave transmitter.

The SS1 Via Aurelia continues westwards along the coast, to the right turn to **Basilica dei Fieschi**. Four kilometres (2 miles) north of Lavagna, this attractive Gothic church was founded in the thirteenth century by Sinibaldi Fieschi, who was born in Lavagna and later became Pope Innocent IV. It stands on a small, neglected *piazza*, opposite the Fieschi *palazzo* (1252). The church is decorated with black and white stone work and has a fine rose window and a vast *campanile*.

Lavagna and **Chiavari** are both busy industrial towns and have little of interest for the visitor. The SS1 Via Aurelia climbs uphill above Chiavari, where there are fine views across the Gigullio Gulf to Portofino, before winding down to **Zoagli**, a lively holiday resort. Continue along to the elegant resort of **Rapallo**, where Ezra Pound once lived, and take the small coastal road to **Santa Margherita**. Tall, painted houses surround the palm-lined bay of this sophisticated resort. There are many smart hotels and boutiques, and the harbour is usually full of luxury yachts, but there is little in the way of any beach. **Portofino**, 5km (3 miles) south of Santa Margherita, is even more chic. During peak season, cars queue for at least 2km (1 mile) along the coast road and it is better to take a bus from Santa Margherita, or walk. The gulf is exceptionally beautiful, and Portofino has a charming setting at the end of the headland. The headland, has been designated a natural park, and offers plenty of opportunities for those interested in walking. A footpath leads from Portofino, past the church of San Giorgio and the sixteenth-century Fortezza di San Giorgio, which now houses a small gallery, to the Punta del Capo, at the tip of the promontory, from where there are excellent views. The tiny hamlet of **San Fruttuoso**, also connected by footpath to Portofino, is overshadowed by a ruined tenth-century, Benedictine monastery, San Fruttuoso di Capodimonte.

Route 5C — Genoa

Genoa, 43km (27 miles) east of Santa Margherita, is Italy's largest commercial port. The SS1 Via Aurelia passes through extensive suburbs before arriving at the Fiera Internazionale where there is a large parking area and a bus service into the city centre.

Commerce must be in the Genoan's blood, as Ligurians began trading with the Phoenicians and Greeks from here in the sixth century BC. After it was taken by the Lombards in AD641, Genoa gradually increased its hold over Mediterranean trade, and became one of the largest and most powerful cities in Europe, with a colonial empire that included the Crimea, Syria and North Africa. In the twelfth century it captured Sardinia and Corsica, and went on in the thirteenth century to defeat its rivals, the Pisans (1284) and the Venetians (1298). The city continued to flourish up until the sixteenth century when rather ironically, following the discovery of the Americas (1492) by Genoan-born Christopher Columbus (1447-1506), sea-trading routes changed. Prosperity was restored only much later with the opening of the Suez Canal. Today the city has all the character of a busy port.

A tour of the city can be divided into three parts: the area around

Piazza Ferrari and the east of the city; the port area; and around Via Garibaldi and the west of the city. Piazza Ferrari is like the hub of a vast wheel with streets radiating out in all directions. Designed in the nineteenth century by Carlo Barabino, it has a monumental fountain at its centre. Of the surrounding buildings, the **Accademia Ligustica** on the north-east corner is one of the finest. It houses a large gallery of fifteenth- to nineteenth-century Ligurian paintings.

Follow Via Dante, south-east to Piazza Dante and the small, ivy-covered Casa di Columbo. The house was actually built in the eighteenth century on the site where Columbus was believed to have lived, but behind it are the pretty cloisters of Sant'Andrea, which date from the twelfth century. Behind the cloisters stands Porta Soprana (1155-60), one of the finest gates in the medieval city wall. Follow Via Porta Soprana from the gate, past the ornately decorated, sixteenth-century church of Sant'Ambrogio, to Palazzo Ducale. Built from white stone around a U-shaped courtyard, this grand edifice was the city Doges' residence. **Piazza San Matteo**, one of the oldest and most charming parts of the city, lies directly behind the *palazzo*. A sense of harmony is created through the use of black and white stone in all the buildings on the *piazza*, including the church, which was built in 1278. Andrea Doria who ruled Genoa in the sixteenth century, lived at number seventeen.

Head downhill from Piazza San Matteo and turn left along Via Scurreria to **Cattedrale San Lorenzo**. Consecrated in 1118, it has a grand façade of black and white alternating bands of marble, flanked by towers. The interior is divided into three aisles by large columns. The cathedral was damaged during World War II and an unexploded shell, fired by the British navy in 1941, can be seen in the right aisle. The Cappella di San Giovanni Battista (1450-65) in the left aisle contains fine statues by M. Civitali and A. Sansovino. The cathedral treasury, housed in the **Museo del Tesoro di San Lorenzo**, at the back of the church, has numerous precious reliquaries, including a first-century Roman glass bowl, a golden Byzantine cross and a silver casket (1436-45) said to contain the ashes of St John the Baptist.

The port area is reached by following Via San Lorenzo downhill from the cathedral to Palazzo San Giorgio. Traffic speeds by the upper windows of the *palazzo* on the *sopraelevata*, a busy flyover, getting good views of its *trompe l'oeil* frescoes. The Banco di San Giorgio, one of the first banks in the world, stood here in 1407, but the present building, which is now used by the port authorities, was erected in 1571. **Piazza Caricamento**, next to the *palazzo* is backed by the Portici di Sottoripa. This tenth-century arcade is crowded with market stalls, shops, cafés and street traders, as it must have been throughout its history. Via San Luca, which runs parallel behind it, is one of the narrow streets in this district where there is something of the atmosphere of the bazaar. It is lined with small shops selling cut-price shoes and clothes, and is always thronging with people. Midway along the street, is the little church of San Luca, from where

signposts indicate the whereabouts of **Palazzo Spinola.** The eight- ⊞
eenth-century *palazzo* is now a museum and visitors can wander
around the richly decorated interior hung with numerous paintings
of the period. Return to Via San Luca, and continue along it, branching left down Via Fossatello. From Piazza Fossatello, Via del Campo,
a colourful street of small food shops, leads up to the medieval Porta
dei Vacca and the western part of the city.

Follow Via dei Fontane up to the immense, neo-Classical façade of
Santissima Annunziata. The interior is one of the most ornate in
Genoa. Dating from 1522, it is a lavish concoction of inlaid marble, ⊞
gilt and stucco. **Palazzo Reale,** 200m (218yd) west of the church, on
Via Balbi, was built in the seventeenth century. The apartments are
sumptuously decorated with frescoes and contain a collection of
paintings and period furniture, and there is even a Hall of Mirrors,
the Galleria degli Specchi.

Return along Via Balbi to Santissima Annunziata, and head south-
east along Via Bensa for 150m (164yd) before turning right down Via
Cairoli. After 300m (328yd), the street joins Via Garibaldi, which is
lined with sixteenth-century *palazzi*. It was designed by Galeazzo
Alessi as a residential area for the wealthy nobility of Genoa and each
palazzo is perfectly preserved, complete with inner courtyards and
monumental staircases. At the start of the street, Palazzo Bianco
(number 11) and Palazzo Rosso, opposite it (number 18), are open as
museums. **Palazzo Bianco,** built in 1565 for Nicolo Grimaldi, houses ⊞
a collection of paintings by the Genoese school, that date from the
twelfth to the eighteenth centuries. There is also some work by the
Dutch and Flemish schools, including paintings by Van Dyck who
began his career in portraiture in Genoa. **Palazzo Rosso** (1671-7),
built for the Brignole family, and beautifully decorated with frescoes, also has a collection of paintings. Although mostly from the
northern Italian schools there are also a number of portraits by Van
Dyck of Genoan aristocrats. Continue along Via Garibaldi, past the
eleven other *palazzi*, and turn left into Piazza del Portello. Cross
under the *piazza* and head up the flight of steps next to the funicular
station on the opposite side. The **Museo Chiossone,** in the gardens ⌂
on this hill has an outstanding collection of oriental art. The collection, left to the museum by the painter Edoardo Chiossone (1832-98),
consists mainly of Japanese art, The peace of the surrounding park
is a pleasant relief from the bustle of the city, and there are good
views across to the port.

Route 5D — Genoa to Turin

Route 5d takes the visitor to Turin through the Langhe region. While
the region is rich in wine and scenic countryside, there is little of
major importance and those short of time might prefer to go directly
from Genoa to Turin on the motorway.

The quickest way to get out of Genoa and its surrounding suburbs
is to take the A10 *autostrada*, by following signs to Ventimiglia. The

motorway passes two attractive resorts, **Arenzano** and **Varazze**, before reaching the large industrial town of **Savona**, 45km (28 miles) west of Genoa. Shortly after Savona, turn off the A10 and take the A6 *autostrada* in the direction of Turin. The first part of this road is very impressive as it crosses high over wooded valleys on graceful arching viaducts. After passing through an almost 3km (2 miles) tunnel at Alt Stazione, leave the motorway by the Altare Carcare exit and follow the SS28 to the old medieval town of **Millesimo**. An attractive fourteenth-century bridge with a tower, the Ponte de Gaietta, crosses the River Bormida nearby. The SS28 then winds up a series of steep bends, passing a ruined fortress, into Piedmont. At **Montezemolo** a small road leads right, along the top of a ridge of hills, above the valleys of the Langhe, for 20km (12 miles) to **Murazzano**. This quiet market town is a centre of Pecorino cheese-making and has a well-attended Friday market in the *piazza* below the fortified tower. Continue on to Bossolasco, 9km (6 miles) north of Murazzano, passing a safari park, the Parco Safari delle Langhe, on the left. **Bossolasco** wins local prizes for being the best kept village in the region, and each house has a rose tree in front of it. It is a good base from which to go hiking in the Langhe, and itineraries are available from the local *comune*. Continue through scenic country-side to **Serravalle Langhe**, with its tall church tower, and turn left to Roddino shortly afterwards. Just before reaching Roddino, a sharp right turn leads to Serralunga d'Alba, although visitors can choose to carry on through Roddino, for 5km (3 miles) to **Monforte d'Alba**, a well-preserved medieval village.

   Serralunga d'Alba, on a hilltop, 6km (4 miles) north of Roddino is in the heart of a famous wine-making region, and Barolo, Barbaresco, and Barbera d'Alba wines can all be tasted in the village's *bottega del vino*. The fine castle on the top of the hill was built in 1340, and is surrounded by a ring of medieval buildings, including a small parish church which dates from 1100. The castle's entrance is well defended with a portcullis and beams that can be drawn out of the wall to barricade the door. The great hall inside has the original fourteenth-century wooden ceiling and a small chapel. Upstairs are the kitchens and the soldiers' quarters, where a series of slits and thickly shut-tered windows are set into the walls. The castle is believed to be connected by an underground tunnel to the castle in Barolo, 8km (5 miles) west of Serralunga d'Alba.

   The road to Alba continues on past another medieval castle at **Grinzane Cavour**. It dates from the thirteenth century and there are tours of the distillery, bottlery and kitchens. On the first floor is a small restaurant and wine bar.

   Alba is a further 7km (4 miles) along the *strada vini d'Alba*, where there are plenty of places to buy the local wines. Alba, has the best white truffles in Italy, a fact that has done much to establish the reputation of its cuisine. There is a popular festival of gastronomy on the last weekend in November, where truffles are served with nearly everything. Known as the Sagra del Tartufo di San Martino, it takes place on Piazza Risorgimento in the town centre. The *piazza* is also the venue for an annual donkey race, the Palio degli Asini, which is held on the first Sunday of October. It is a tradition that dates back to the thirteenth century and originated as a satire of Asti's annual horse race. The buildings round the square also date back to the medieval period, although the Duomo was not built until the late fifteenth century. While the red brick exterior is not very impressive, inside there are attractive stained-glass windows, and beautifully inlaid choir stalls (1512). The main shopping street, Via Vittorio Emanuele II, which leaves the *piazza* from the west side, contains several fine medieval *palazzi*. The small local museum, Civico Museo Federico Eusebio, is a short distance up Via Paruzza on the left.

The most direct way from Alba to Asti (30km/19 miles) is along the SS231. Those interested in the wines of the region may prefer to take the smaller roads along the east bank of the River Tanaro. At **Barbaresco**, which produces one of Italy's best red wines, there is an *enoteca* in a disused church and a ruined castle. **Costigliole d'Asti**, 10km (6 miles) further north-east, is another wine-making village.

Asti is a large, sprawling town, best known for its sparkling wines. There is ample parking space both on the Campo del Palio, and on Piazza Alfieri at the centre of town. The arcades on the west side of the *piazza* lead through to Collegiata San Secondo, a Romanesque-Gothic church, which was built between the thirteenth and fifteenth centuries. The lower façade is Romanesque and has three stone-carved portals, while the upper façade is Gothic and is built of brick. It stands on the site of a much earlier ninth-century church, the only remains of which are in the crypt. The interior of the church has a paved floor which dates from the thirteenth and fourteenth centuries, and frescoes of the same period in the chapel on the right.

As the two other monuments of interest lie at opposite ends of Corso Vittorio Alfieri, which stretches for 1¹/₂km (1 mile) through the middle of the town, it may be better to visit them by car. The Cattedrale is just north of Piazza Cairoli, at the westernmost end of the street. It was built between 1309 and 1354 in the Romanesque-Gothic style, and has a fine *campanile*. The interior is Baroque and is decorated with eighteenth-century frescoes. The Battistero di San Pietro is at the eastern end of Corso Vittorio Alfieri. Built on an octagonal ground plan, the baptistery dates from the twelfth century and stands alongside the fifteenth-century church and cloisters of San Pietro in Consavia. The church is deconsecrated and now houses an archaeological museum.

With little of particular interest between Asti and Turin, it is best to take the A21 motorway and avoid the worst of the traffic. Those who wish to visit the basilica of **Superga** should leave the motorway at Villanova, and take the SS10 through **Chieri** to **Pino Torinese**, from where it is clearly signposted. The domed basilica is impossible to miss as it towers above the countryside, on the summit of a hill

670m (2,198ft) high. It was commissioned by Vittorio Amedeo II to celebrate the end of the Turin Siege, and designed by F. Juvarra (1717-36). The dome is an impressive 65m (213ft) high and there is a fine panorama of Turin from the terrace in front of the basilica's grand façade. The interior of the basilica is beautifully decorated, while the crypt contains the tombs of several of the Kings of Sardinia. One of the most impressive tombs is that of Carlo Emanuele II, son of Vittorio Amedeo, and second king of Sardinia. It is decorated with bas-reliefs depicting the Battle of Guastalla (1734), and three fine statues.

The castle at Serralunga d'Alba

Turin is surrounded by extensive suburbs and getting in and out of the city is not easy. Nor is parking. Head for Piazza Vittorio Veneto, on the west bank of the River Po, where there is a large carpark which is within walking distance of the centre. Otherwise the choice is either to park further out and use the public transport system, or search for a short term metered space in the city centre.

Even though the city is spread over a wide area, getting around is quite easy as there is a good tram and bus system. The streets are flat and well laid, making it a spacious and orderly city. Most of it dates from the nineteenth century, when King Vittorio Emanuele II made it his capital, although the settlement goes back to Roman times.

Piazza Castello, named after the fifteenth-century castle at its centre, is at the heart of the city. Most of the buildings surrounding the *piazza* date from the eighteenth and nineteenth centuries, including Palazzo Madama, which was built onto the rear of the castle to a design by F. Juvarra, between 1718 and 1721. The *palazzo* houses the Museo Civico di Arte Antica, which has a collection of medieval sculptures and carvings, paintings by the Piedmont school, and eighteenth-century furniture, glass and ceramics. There is another museum on the north side of the *piazza*, the Armeria Reale. It contains the Royal armoury collection of the House of Savoy, one of the most important collections of sixteenth to nineteenth century arms in Europe. **Palazzo Reale**, which was built for the Savoy rulers in 1660, is to the north of Piazza Castello, set back on Piazza Reale. The massive building, which was not completed until 1865, encloses a central courtyard and stands in front of a large park. Part of it is open as a museum, and a monumental staircase designed by F. Juvarra leads up to the apartments. They contain a collection of porcelains and paintings, and numerous statues of the Savoy princes, as well as their original eighteenth-century furnishings.

To visit the **Duomo** return to Piazza Reale in front of the *palazzo* and go through the arch on the right. The Duomo, which is set into the west side of Palazzo Reale, was built between 1491 and 1498. It has a Renaissance façade, and an attractive *campanile* with a stone top that was added by F. Juvarra in 1720. The interior is lined with ornate altar chapels, and at the back of the church, the Cappella della Sacra Sindone, houses the famous Turin shroud. To the left of the Duomo are the scant remains of a Roman theatre, while on the opposite side of the road is a restored section of the first-century Roman wall, known as the Palatina. It has a gate with four arches, flanked by towers and statues of Caesar and Augustus in front.

The **Museo Egizio** lies 400m (437yd) south of Piazza Castello, along Via Roma, a wide street lined with fashionable shops. Housed in the Baroque Palazzo dell'Accademia delle Scienze (1678), the museum has one of the most important collections of Egyptian art in Europe. The main exhibit on the ground floor is the reconstructed rock temple of Ellesija, which dates from 1450BC and is decorated with bas-reliefs. On the first floor there is a large collection of mummies, tombs, wooden statuettes and papyri, from the site of Heliopolis. On the second floor there is another museum, the Galleria Sabauda, which houses the Savoy collection of art. It contains fifteenth- and sixteenth-century paintings by the Piedmont school, other paintings by the Tuscan and Venetian schools, and works by Dutch and Flemish artists, as well as medieval furniture.

Piazza San Carlo, to the south of the museum, is lined with seventeenth-century arcaded buildings with smart cafés. At the far end of the long, rectangular *piazza* is a pair of identical churches, San Carlo and San Cristina. At the centre of the *piazza* there is an equestrian statue, dedicated to Emanuele Filiberto.

✳ The monumental spire, Mole Antonelliana, is west of Piazza Castello, close to Via Giuseppe Verdi. It was built in 1863 as a monument to Italian unity and stands to a height of 165m (541ft). A lift can be taken to the cupola (85m/279ft) from where there are fine views of the city. For local colour make the short excursion north of Piazza Castello to Piazza della Repubblica, where there is a daily market. An antiques market, known as the Balon, is held here on Saturdays. The Parco del Valentino, on the left bank of the Po to the south of the city centre, has a number of attractions. There is a large exhibition centre which hosts shows of an international calibre, as well as the biennial motorshow. There is also the Borgo Medioevale, a reproduction of an Aostan medieval village, and the Castello del Valentino. The *castello* was constructed between 1630 and 1660, in the style of a sixteenth-century French château.

Additional Information

Places of Interest

ROUTE 5A
Pisa
Museo delle Sinopie
Piazza del Duomo
56100 Pisa (PI)
☎ (050) 560547
Open: winter daily 9am-1pm, 3-5pm
Summer daily 9am-1pm, 3-7pm.

Museo dell 'Opera de! Duomo
Piazza Arcivescovado 6
56100 Pisa (PI)
☎ (050) 560547
Open: winter daily 9am-5pm
summer daily 9am-7.30pm.

Museo Nazionale di San Matteo
Lungarno Medieceo
56100 Pisa (PI)

☎ (050) 541865
Open: Tuesday to Saturday 9am-7pm. Holidays 9am-1pm.

Massa
Castello Malaspina
54100 Massa (MA)
Open: winter Tuesday to Sunday 2-5pm. Summer Tuesday to sunday 9am–12 noon, 4–7pm.

Carrara
Museo di Marmo
Via XX Settembre
54033 Carrara (MA)
Open: Monday-Saturday 10am-1pm, 4-7.30pm.

ROUTE 5C
Genoa
Pinacoteca dell'Accademia Ligustica di Belle Arti

5 Piazza de Ferrari
16100 Genova (GE)
☎ (010) 581957
Open: Monday to Saturday 9am-1pm.

Museo del Tesoro di San Lorenzo
Piazza San Lorenzo
16100 Genova (GE)
☎ (010) 296695
Open: Tuesday to Saturday 9.30-
11.45am and 3-5.45pm.

Galleria Nazionale di Palazzo Spinola
1 Via di Pellicceria
16100 Genova (GE)
☎ (010) 294661
Open: Tuesday to Saturday 9am-
5pm. Sunday and Monday 9am-1pm.

Galleria di Palazzo Reale
10 Via Balbi
16100 Genova (GE)
☎ (010) 206851
Open: daily 9am-1.30pm.

Galleria di Palazzo Bianco
11 Via Garibaldi
16100 Genova (GE)
☎ (010) 291803
Open: Tuesday to Saturday 9am-
7pm. Sunday 9am-12noon.

Galleria di Palazzo Rosso
18 Via Garibaldi
16100 Genova (GE)
☎ (010) 282641
Open: Tuesday to Saturday 9am-
7pm. Sunday 9am-12noon.

*Museo d'Arte Orientale Edoardo
 Chiossone*
Villetta Dinegro
16100 Genova (GE)
☎ (010) 542285
Open: Tuesday to Saturday 9am-
6pm. Sunday 9am-12.30pm.

ROUTE 5D
Bossolasco
Parco Safari delle Langhe
12060 Bossolasco (CN)
☎ (0173) 791142
Open: Monday to Saturday 10am-
12noon and 2-6.30pm. Holidays
10am-7pm.

Serralunga d' Alba
Castello
12051 Serralunga d'Alba (CN)
☎ (0173) 53358
Open: winter Tuesday to Sunday 9am-
12noon and 2-6pm. Summer Tuesday
to Sunday 10am-12noon and 2-5pm.

Grinzane Cavour
Castello Cavour
12051 Grinzane Cavour (CN)
Open: castle daily 9am-12noon and 2-
7pm. *Enoteca* daily except Tuesday
9am-12noon and 2.30-6.30pm.

Alba
Civico Museo Federico Eusebio
Via Paruzza
12051 Alba (CN)
☎ (0173) 30092
Open: daily except Friday, Sunday
and Monday afternoons, 9am-
12noon and 3-6pm.

Asti
Museo Alfieri
Palazzo Alfieri
Corso Vittorio Alfieri
14100 Asti (AT)
Open: Tuesday to Saturday 10am-
12noon and 3.30-5.30pm. Holidays
10am-12noon.

Museo Archeologico
Complesso del Vecchio San Pietro
14100 Asti (AT)
Open: Tuesday to Saturday 9am-
12noon and 3-6pm. Sunday 10am-
12noon.

Superga
Superga Basilica
10100 Superga (TO)
☎ (011) 890083
Open: winter daily except Friday
10-12.30pm and 3-5pm. Summer
daily except Friday 8am-12.30pm
and 2.30-7.30pm.

Palazzo Madama
Museo Civico di Arte Antica
Piazza Castello
10100 Torino (TO)
Open: Tuesday to Saturday 9am-
7pm. Sunday 10am-1pm and 2-7pm.

Turin
Palazzo Reale
Piazza Castello
10100 Torino (TO)
☎ (011) 4361557 or 4361455
Open: winter palace daily 9am-
1pm, gardens daily 9am-5.30pm.
Summer palace daily 9am-1pm.
Gardens daily 9am-7pm.

Cappella della Sacra Sindone
Duomo
10100 Torino (TO)
Open: Tuesday to Saturday
8.30am-12noon and 3-5pm.
Holidays 9.45am-12noon.

Museo Egizio
Palazzo dell'Accademia delle
    Scienze
10100 Torino (TO)
☎ (011) 537581 or 544091
Open: Tuesday to Sunday 9am-2pm.

Galleria Sabauda
Palazzo dell'Accademia delle
    Scienze
10100 Torino (TO)
☎ (011) 547440
Open: Tuesday, Thursday and
Saturday 9am-2pm. Wednesday
and Friday 2.30-7.30pm. Sunday
guided tours only.

Tourist Information Centres

ROUTE 5A
Pisa
Ufficio Informazione Turistiche
Piazza del Duomo
56100 Pisa (PI)
☎ (050) 560464

Carrara
Ente Provinciale per il Turismo
14 Piazza II Giugno
54033 Carrara (MS)
☎ (0585) 70668

ROUTE 5B
La Spezia
Ente Provinciale per il Turismo
47 Viale Mazzini
19100 La Spezia (SP)
☎ (0187) 36000

Levanto
Azienda Autonoma di Soggiorno e
    Turismo
Piazza Colombo
19015 Levanto (SP)
☎ (0187) 808125

Monterosso al Mare
Pro Loco
Via Fegina
19016 Monterosso al Mare (SP)
☎ (0187) 817506

Rapallo
Azienda Autonoma di Soggiorno e
    Turismo
9 Via Diaz
16035 Rapallo (GE)
☎ (0185) 51282

Portofino
Azienda Autonoma di Soggiorno e
    Turismo
35-7 Via Roma
16034 Portofino (GE)

ROUTE 5C
Genoa
Ente Provinciale per il Turismo
11 Via Roma
16100 Genova (GE)
☎ (010) 581407

ROUTE 5D
Alba
Pro Loco
19 Via Vittorio Emanuele
12051 Alba (CN)
☎ (0173) 497118 or 362807

Asti
Ente Provinciale per il Turismo
34 Piazza Alfieri
14100 Asti (AT)
☎ (0141) 50357

Turin
Ente Provinciale per il Turismo
226 Via Roma
Piazzetta CLN
10100 Torino (TO)
☎ (011) 535181

6

THE NORTHERN LAKES

C hapter 6 takes in five of Italy's large northern lakes, as well as several smaller ones. Each one has its own character and individual landscape, whether it is steep and rocky, or gently undulating, but they all enjoy a mild climate with refreshing mountain breezes in the summer. The major resorts offer good facilities for the watersport enthusiast, while smaller villages have picturesque harbours and narrow winding streets. All of the lakes have good ferry services and should be used wherever possible, or take one of the boat tours arranged in the larger resorts. As a contrast to the natural beauty of the lakes, the route also visits several fine cities with impressive local architecture and good collections of art.

The route ends at Riva, at the northern tip of Lake Garda. From here visitors can either make a circular tour of the lake, returning southwards along its western shore, to join chapter 8 at Verona, or continue north to the Dolomites in chapter 7.

Route 6A — Turin to Lake Orta

The most interesting route from Turin to Lake Orta is along the foothills of the Alps, from where a number of excursions can be made into the mountains. Leave Turin on the A5 motorway and continue along it for 25km ($15^1/_2$ miles) to the San Giusto Canavese exit. From here follow signs to **Aglie**, the first place of interest on the route. The road climbs up through the grounds of Castello d'Aglie, a vast eighteenth-century mansion, to a circular *piazza*. Fourteen of the 365 rooms in the mansion, which are decorated with frescoes and furniture of the period, are open to the public, as are its beautiful gardens. Other fine buildings surround the *piazza* including an attractive eighteenth-century church.

Head straight along Aglie's porticoed high street, and either continue along the route to Ivrea, 20km (12 miles) to the north-east, or make an excursion west to the **Gran Paradiso** national park. Visitors to the park should follow signs to **Cuorgne** (11km/7 miles), from where the road climbs up the Orco river valley for 18km (11 miles) to the southern boundary of the park. The Gran Paradiso

Massif, at the centre of the park, rises to a height of 4,061m (13,320ft) and offers excellent opportunities for high altitude hiking. Since the park was formed in 1922, great care has been taken to preserve its natural flora and fauna, and endangered species such as the ibex have greatly increased in number.

Ivrea is at the entrance to the Aosta valley, and visitors who wish to travel on to Switzerland or France, or make an excursion to visit Aosta and the northern side of the Gran Paradiso park, can take the A5 motorway from here. The river Dora Baltea flows through the centre of **Ivrea** and is crossed by the road to the right of the eighteenth-century bridge, Ponte Vecchia. The ruined *castello* on the hill above was built for Amedeo VI in 1358. It stands next to the Duomo which has two attractive towers that date from the eleventh century. Ivrea is the home of the Olivetti company and in their premises, just outside the town on the road to Castellamonte, stands the church of San Bernardino, which contains excellent frescoes of the *Life of Christ* by G.M. Spanzzotti (1485).

The Serra d'Ivrea, which stretches for 25km (15^1/$_2$ miles) east of the town, is one of the largest moraines in Europe. Deposited by glaciers during the last Ice Age it forms a series of steep ridges that separates Ivrea from Biella, 30km (19 miles) to the north-east. The most scenic route leaves Ivrea along the SS26, passing **Montalto Dora** with its impressive fortress, before turning right to Andrate at Borgofranco. It climbs up through chestnut woods to **Croce Sera** (853m/2,798ft), just past the lovely village of **Andrate**. The road winds on through a string of small alpine villages to **Netro** where there is a Romanesque church, dating from the eleventh century. After **Graglia** it crosses the Torrente Elvo and heads down through **Occhiepo** into Biella.

Biella, is a busy modern town on the bank of the River Cervo. There is little of interest, apart from the tenth-century baptistery next to the Duomo, and visitors should head up to **Biella Piazzo**, the historic centre. It lies along the top of the hill above the town, and is linked by a funicular, that climbs up from Piazza Curiel (west of the Duomo). It is a tranquil spot and has several fine fifteenth- and sixteenth-century buildings.

There are two routes visitors can choose to follow from Biella to Varallo. The first is the easiest and most direct, but there is little of interest on the way. It follows the SS142 to **Gattinara** and the SS299 north up the Sesia river valley. The second is longer and considerably more difficult, but offers spectacular panoramas of the Alps. It heads up the Cervo river valley, through **Andorno** and continues up to the resort of **Bielmonte**. From here follow the SS232 through **Trivero** to **Borgosesia**, after which it too follows the Sesia river to Varallo.

Varallo is a small, unspoilt town nestled in a green valley beneath steep wooded hills. It is well worth spending some time wandering around the attractive narrow streets, keeping an eye out for the various Valsesia specialities sold in the local shops, such as mortadella, black sausage, and Toma cheese. The town has two churches containing important works by locally-born Gaudenzio Ferrari (1471-1546).

Varallo's other attraction is the sanctuary of **Sacro Monte**, which stands high above the town. It can either be reached by walking up the steep path from Madonna delle Grazie, or by driving up from the east end of town. The sanctuary was started in 1486 by a Friar Minor as a 'new Jerusalem', but was not completed until the seventeenth century. There are forty-four chapels altogether, each containing a life-size tableau illustrating the life of Christ. G. Ferrari was just one of the many artists involved and his statue stands at the entrance to the complex. A footpath leads from chapel to chapel, ending up in the *piazza* in front of the basilica. Built between 1641 and 1728, the basilica has a grand marble façade and a highly ornate interior, where every facet is encrusted with stucco and gilt. The focal point is the richly decorated domed apse, which is adorned with 800 statuettes and an estimated 4,000 frescoed figures. The chapel below the apse contains a wooden effigy of the sleeping Virgin, originally brought from the Orient in the fifteenth century.

An excursion can be made to **Alagna**, 36km (22 miles) west of Varallo, on the SS299. It is located at the foot of Monte Rosa (4,634m/ 15,199ft), which is the second highest peak in the Alps. A *funivia* climbs up as far as Punta Indren (3,260m/10,693ft) from where there is an outstanding panorama that takes in the Gran Paradiso national park, Mont Blanc, and even the peaks of the Appenines on exceptionally clear days.

The first of the northern lakes, **Lake Orta**, lies 24km (15 miles) east of Varallo. It is reached by a picturesque road, past the chapel of Madonna di Loreto, which is frescoed by G. Ferrari, and through the elegant town of **Civiaso**. After climbing over the Passo della Colma, at a height of 942m (3,090ft), the road descends to **Alzo**, where the lake comes into sight for the first time. The church of Madonna del Sasso, built on the peak above Alzo, offers even finer views.

Pella has a lovely position on the lake edge, looking across to the island of San Giulio (see below) which can be reached by hiring a boat from the promenade. The village is little visited, and does not have the facilities of other resorts on the lake, but has a charming unspoilt character. By contrast, **Orta San Giulio**, on the opposite shore, reached by the SS229 from **Gozzano**, is the best-equipped and most popular of the lake resorts. Beautifully positioned on the tip of a small peninsula, the centre is closed to traffic, and narrow, cobbled streets lead down from the carpark to the main *piazza* at the water's edge. At the centre, the fine Palazzo della Comunita (1582) stands raised above a loggia. *Motoscafi*, motorboats leave from the jetty to the island of **San Giulio**, while larger ferries take visitors on cruises round the lake. The island is named after the saint who cleared it of serpents and has a basilica in his honour. It was built between the eleventh and thirteenth centuries, and has a beautifully carved, black marble pulpit that dates from the eleventh century, as well as the

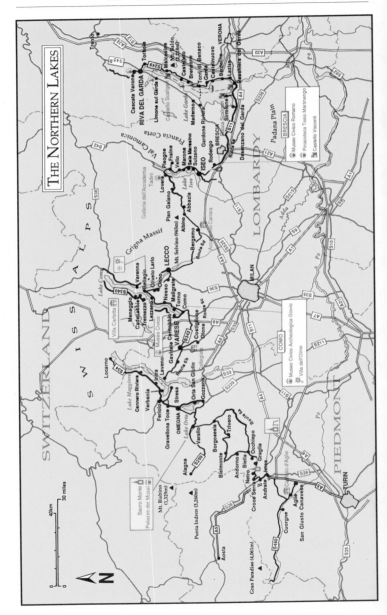

Pella

remnants of fifteenth- and sixteenth-century frescoes. **Sacro Monte**, is a popular excursion, being only $1^1/_2$km (1 mile) from Orta San Giulio. Similar to the sanctuary at Varallo, it is less impressive, as it has only twenty chapels. It was started in 1591, but not completed until the late eighteenth century, and is dedicated to St Francis.

The SS229 continues along the lake edge, passing through **Pettenesco**, from where there is a good view of Pella, before reaching **Omegna**. Pleasantly situated at the northern end of the lake, the town has a well-preserved historical centre, as well as facilities for sailing and waterskiing. A panoramic excursion can be made from the town to the Mottarone mountain top, 21km (13 miles) to the east. The mountain lies between Lakes Orta and Maggiore, and from the summit, which is 1,419m (4,654ft) high, there are outstanding views of both lakes, as well as of the Alps.

Route 6B — Lake Maggiore to Varese

Lake Maggiore is 10km (6 miles) north-east of Lake Orta. It is the second largest lake in Italy, covering an area of 212sq km (82sq miles), although the northern tip crosses the border into Switzerland. The lake is long and narrow, being no wider than $4^1/_2$km (3 miles) at any point. A complete circuit of the lake by road involves a journey of 165km (102 miles), and it is better to visit only the central area by car, taking ferries to the more far-flung parts.

To visit the western shore, south of the Toce river, follow the SS33 from **Gravellona Toce**, through Feriolo, to the elegant resort of **Baveno**. Its reputation goes back to the early nineteenth century, and Queen Victoria who spent the spring of 1879 in Villa Bianca, was just one of the many illustrious figures who stayed here. Grand hotels and villas, surrounded by ornamental gardens line the shore, looking out across the lake to Verbania. Continue down the lake on the SS33, towards Stresa ($4^1/_2$km/3 miles), passing Isola Bella and Isola Pescatori, two of the famous **Borromean Islands**, which lie a short distance from the lake edge, midway between the two resorts. Ferries leave regularly to both islands, but **Isola Bella**, which lies just 400m (437yd) offshore, is the most popular. Only 320m (1,050ft) long, it is covered by the ornate, terraced gardens that surround Palazzo Borromeo. The *palazzo* which can be visited on a guided tour, was built for Count Carlo Borromeo in 1632, and has a richly decorated, Baroque interior. **Isola Pescatori**, the island of fishermen, has none of the grandeur of Isola Bella, but its picturesque streets and small church have a certain charm.

A *funivia* leads up to **Mottarone** (1,491m/4,890ft) from the lido on the outskirts of Stresa. The mountain can also be reached by a road which leaves from **Gignese**, where there is an umbrella museum, passing through the Giardino Alpino, that contains over 2,000 species of Alpine plants. The last stretch of the road up Mottarone is privately owned and a toll is charged.

Stresa is the most famous resort on Lake Maggiore, and is associated with a long list of well-known names which include, Stendahl, Flaubert, Goethe, Wagner and Shaw. Palatial hotels, such as the Iles Borromees and the Regina Palace, grace the water front, and an elegant promenade leads through pretty flower gardens along the lake edge. The grounds of Villa Pallavicino, one of the many fine villas in the resort, are open to the public and contain a zoo. Excursions on ferries can be made from Stresa to the southern arm of the lake. **Arona**, 13km (8 miles) south of Stresa, is the largest of the resorts. It has a well-preserved historic centre and a picturesque harbour. A colossal bronze statue of Carlo Borromeo, Archbishop of Milan (1565-84), stands on a hill, just north of the town.

To explore the upper arm of Lake Maggiore, return to Feriolo, where a road crosses the Toce river, to the SS34 and **Verbania**. **Pallanza**, the first part of Verbania, looks out across the lake to Baveno and the Borromean islands from its attractive quayside. A pedestrianised street leads up a steep hill through the old town centre to the Museo del Paesaggio. The collection is wide ranging and includes fifteenth- and sixteenth-century frescoes and archaeological finds from the region. Villa Taranto is just round the headland from Palanza, set amidst an enormous botanical garden. Laid out on the northern slopes of the Castagnola promontory by the Scotsman, Captain Neil McEacharn in 1931, the gardens are rated amongst the best in the world. They cover 16 hectares ($39^1/_2$ acres) and have 7km (4 miles) of paths, and over 20,000 different species of exotic plants. A recommended route leads around the best of the garden from the carpark at the main gate. **Intra**, the second part of Verbania has little of interest, but ferries leave from here to the Borromean Islands, and a pleasant excursion can be made to **Isola Madre**, with its eighteenth-century *palazzo* and large botanical garden. Ferries also make excursions further up the northern arm of Lake Maggiore, where **Cannero Riviera** is the most attractive resort. Visitors who wish could drive completely around the top of Lake Maggiore, through Switzerland, visiting Locarno on the way. Otherwise they should take the car-ferry from Intra across the lake to Laveno.

At Laveno follow signs to Varese on the SS394, through Gavirate. Just outside the town, on the road which skirts along Lake Varese, stand the cloisters of Voltorre. Continue along the shore before turning left into the town. **Varese** has several historical monuments but they have been largely swamped by the rapid growth of the modern town. Palazzo Estense, on Via Sacco, is now the *municipio*. This eighteenth-century building has frescoes by G.B. Ronchelli in the Salone Estense. Behind it are extensive public gardens, in the middle of which is the Museo Civico, which contains a collection of archaeological finds ranging from prehistoric to Roman times, and a *pinacoteca* with paintings by the Lombard school, dating from the seventeenth and eighteenth centuries. While walking through town one gets glimpses of a large and ornate *campanile*. It belongs to San Vittore, a late sixteenth-century basilica to the north of the town centre, on Piazza Monte Grappa. Those who have the time to visit the basilica will be rewarded with the sight of the baptistery, the oldest building in town. It dates from the twelfth century, and contains the remains of frescoes from the fourteenth and fifteenth centuries.

An excursion can be made 16km (10 miles) south of Varese on the SS233 to Castiglione Olona. **Castiglione Olona** was the home of Cardinal Branda Costiglioni (1350-1443), who commissioned the construction of the numerous Renaissance style monuments seen in the town today. His home, Palazzo Branda, is on Piazza Garibaldi at the centre of the town. It is decorated with frescoes and contains a small collection of paintings. The cardinal is buried in the church, the Chiesa di Villa, on the opposite side of the *piazza*. It was built between 1430 and 1441, in the style of Brunelleschi, Florence's greatest architect, and colossal statues of St Anthony and St Christopher flank the portal. Cardinal Castiglioni's finely carved tomb stands in the apse. Via Cardinal Branda leads uphill from the church to the Collegiata, which is at the top of the hill on the right. Constructed on the site of a former castle in 1421, the façade has a fine rose window and an attractive Venetian-Lombard relief above the main portal.

Going to school on Lake Maggiore

Route 6C — Varese to Lake Como

Como is 32km (20 miles) east of Varese along the SS342. It is a busy, modern city surrounded by extensive outskirts, but the centre, which is closed to traffic, has a delightful setting at the south-west tip of Lake Como, the third largest of the northern lakes, and one of the most beautiful. The carpark outside the city wall along Viale Lecco is the most convenient, but it is quickly filled, and visitors may have to head for one of the four underground carparks, known as *autosilo*.

Like so many Italian cities, the Duomo is at the heart of the city centre. Work began on its construction during the fourteenth century, but it was not completed until the eighteenth, when F. Juvarra added the impressive green dome. Fine statues by T. and G. Rodari (1453) adorn the richly decorated marble façade. The portals in the side walls are beautifully carved, and are inlaid with pink and grey marble. The vast interior is divided into three aisles by immense sixteenth-century tapestries that are hung between the columns. Numerous fine paintings line the walls, including works by B. Luino and G. Ferrari, and each small chapel has a finely carved altar. In the *piazza*, to the left of the Duomo's façade, stands the Broletto, the town hall, which dates from 1435. Supported on a vaulted loggia, it has a fine façade of alternating bands of pink, grey and white marble, with mullioned windows and an attractive balcony. The vast tower of grey stone that also stands on the *piazza* is the Torre Comunale, which was built in 1215.

The mountainous landscape around Lake Como is best appreciated by boat trip

Como, nestled amongst the mountains surrounding the lake

Follow Via Plinio towards Piazza Cavour on the lake edge. The sweeping bay, criss-crossed by ferries and hydrofoils, is surrounded by wooded hills. At the west end of the bay stands the Tempio Voltiano, which was built in 1927, and contains a small museum dedicated to locally-born Alessandro Volto, after whom the volt was named. The museum is set in a pleasant park and can be reached along the promenade that stretches around the bay.

To visit the Museo Civico, return to the Duomo, and walk up Via Vittorio Emanuele II, a busy shopping street, past the small church of San Fedele. Built between AD914 and 1335, this church is a good example of the Lombard-Romanesque style, and has a fine portal, which is decorated with bas-reliefs. Continue along Via Vittorio Emanuele II to Piazza Medaglie where the Museo Civico is housed in Palazzo Giovio (1536). It has an archaeological collection which ranges from prehistoric to Roman times, as well as paintings dating from the sixteenth to eighteenth centuries.

Lake Como, shaped like an inverted 'y', has a mountainous shoreline over 170km (105 miles) long. The best way of exploring the lake is by making excursions by boat from Bellagio, at the confluence of the lake's three arms. However, before leaving Como it is worth making the short excursion by road to the resort of **Cernobbio**, on the western lake edge 5km (3 miles) north of the city. The road passes Villa dell'Olmo, a fine, neo-classical mansion, built for the Odescalchi family in 1782. The gardens are open to the public, but the interior can only be visited when it is hosting an exhibition. Cernobbio itself lies at the foot of Monte Bisbino and has a colourful harbour with fine views over the lake. The summit of Monte Bisbino (1,329m/4,359ft), which is partly in Switzerland, can be reached by road from Cernobbio. There is a rewarding panorama of the lake at the top, as well as views over the Swiss Alps. Visitors who wish to explore further up the coast from Cernobbio should not miss Villa d'Este, the home between 1815 and 1817, of Caroline Brunswick the Princess of Wales, and the elegant resort of **Moltrasio**.

After returning to Como, follow signs to Bellagio on the SS583 Lariana. The road winds up the inside of the lake's western arm along the base of the Brianza hills. The scenery is spectacular, sheer mountains covered with lush vegetation plunge almost vertically into the lake. There are many picturesque villages to stop at on the way, but **Torno**, clustered around a sheltered harbour, is one of the prettiest. At **Nesso**, 17km (11 miles) north of Como, an excursion can be made up into the Brianza hills by following the small road to **Pian del Tivano** a good picnic spot with views of the lake. Continuing along the shore to **Lezzeno**, the road passes the only island on the lake, **Isola Comacini**, and hugging the cliffs, winds the remaining 7km (4 miles) to the elegant resort of **Bellagio**.

Follow the road through the outskirts of Bellagio, past Villa Melzi d'Eril and its fine landscaped gardens, and park along the waterfront near the lido. The promenade leads past the ferry port to Piazza

Mazzini which is surrounded by elegant arcaded buildings and smart cafés. Cobbled lanes lead up the hill behind the *piazza* to the town centre, while Via E. Vitali heads along to the tip of the promontory, La Punta Spartivento, where there is a small harbour. The hill above Bellagio is covered by the lush gardens which surround eighteenth-century Villa Serbelloni. The villa is privately owned, but the gardens are open to the public.

Several excursions can be made from Bellagio to other resorts on the lake by taking one of the regular ferries that leave from the port near the lido. **Tremezzo**, on the lake's western shore, is one of the most popular destinations. It has a wealth of eighteenth-century villas set amongst beautiful gardens, and fine views across to Bellagio and the Grigne Massif. At the north-east end of the town is the famous Villa Carlotta (1747). It contains a good collection of paintings and sculptures, including works by the Venetian artist, A. Canova (1757-1822). The beautiful gardens, arranged along the lake edge, are a riot of colour, particularly in April and May when the rhododendron and azaleas are in flower. **Cadenabbia**, another attractive resort, just north of Tremezzo, can also be reached by boat, as can **Menaggio**, 4km (2 miles) further along the lake shore. With its cool summertime breezes, it is a good base for exploring the dramatic shore of the lake's northern arm. On the eastern shore of the lake, opposite Menaggio, is the small, resort of **Varenna** with its narrow streets, attractive gardens and thirteenth-century parish church.

The route continues along the SS583 Lariana, down the inside of the eastern arm of the lake, from Bellagio to Lecco. This part of the lake, known as Lago di Lecco, is exceptionally scenic. The Grigna mountains rise dramatically from the water on the opposite shore, and the road winds through steep olive groves, passing through the picturesque hamlets of **Oliveto Lario** and **Onno**, both of which make olive oil. At Onno it is possible to follow the small road, signposted to Asso, up into the Brianza hills where there are plenty of good opportunities for hiking. The SS583 Lariana continues through **Maligrate**, from where Lecco and its tall *campanile* can be seen at the end of the lake. The road crosses the River Adda, which is the lake's main source, passing a fourteenth-century bridge on the right.

Lecco is backed by the steep Grigna mountains which are one of its main attractions. They are popular with rock climbers, as well as hikers, and a *funivia* leads up from the north-east side of town to **Piani d'Erna**. Well-marked footpaths of graded difficulty spread out into the hills from here. Lecco is the birthplace of one of Italy's most famous authors, Alessandro Manzoni. His book *I Promessi Sposi (The Betrothed)* is still widely read, and the eighteenth-century villa where he lived, on Via Amendola, contains a small museum (closed for restoration at time of writing) in his memory. On the last Sunday of May a long procession is held in his honour.

Route 6D — Lecco to Lake Iseo

At this point visitors may wish to join chapter 9 at Milan, which is just over 50km (31 miles) south of Lecco, however, chapter 6 continues to Bergamo on the SS342. The road passes through **Pontida**, where there is a fourteenth-century Benedictine abbey, before reaching Bergamo, 33km (20 miles) south-east of Lecco.

The medieval towers of old **Bergamo** look down from their hilltop position over the modern city built in the Lombard plain below. Head straight through modern Bergamo to the upper part of the city, known as Citta Alta. Park around the city gates at either end of the old town as the centre is pedestrianised, continuing on foot up to the main square, Piazza Vecchia. The *piazza* is at the heart of the city, yet pleasantly isolated from the noise of traffic. People stand chatting around the central fountain, probably much as they have always done, at least since the Venetian mayor presented it to the city in 1780.

The *piazza* was the civic centre of the town up until the nineteenth century and contains many fine public buildings. The grand white *palazzo* along the bottom of the *piazza*, now the public library, was built as the town hall in 1604. The most impressive building, however, is the Palazzo della Ragione which stands on three wide vaulted arches and has fine Gothic windows, as well as an attractive balcony overlooking the square. The original twelfth-century build-

Piazza Vecchia, Bergamo

ing was reconstructed between 1538 and 1545 after it was destroyed by fire. A fine external staircase leads up to the main door from the base of the Torre del Comune in the corner of the square. The unusual inscribed lines in the pavement below the arches were used to calculate the times of the solstices.

Continue through the arches to Piazza del Duomo, another charming square surrounded by fine monuments. Oddly enough, the Duomo (1459), on the left, is not as impressive as the basilica of Santa Maria Maggiore at the back of the square and the domed Cappella Colleoni to its right. The basilica dates from the twelfth century and its plain Romanesque exterior is enriched by the two beautifully carved porches, added in the fourteenth century by Giovanni da Campione. Carved stone lions, their backs finely polished by the generations of children who have played on them, support the columns of the main portal which leads into the Baroque interior.

The Cappella Colleoni, to the right of the basilica, has an outstanding façade. The chapel was designed by G. A. Amadeo in 1472 for B. Colleoni, Captain General of the Venetian Republic, and is typical of the Lombard-Renaissance style. Colleoni's grand sarcophagus, also designed by Amadeo, stands inside, surmounted by a gilt equestrian statue. The sarcophagus to the left is that of Colleoni's daughter, Medea, who died in 1470. The interior of the dome is decorated with frescoes, painted in 1732 by G.B. Tiepolo.

The baptistery (1340), on the right side of the *piazza*, originally stood inside the basilica, but it was dismantled in 1660, and left to collect dust until its reconstruction in its present position in 1898. It contains finely-carved reliefs by G. da Campione and is beautifully decorated with red Verona marble.

The Accademia Carrara is below the eastern extremities of the city walls and can be reached by a flight of steps that lead down from the Porta Sant'Agostino. It was built in 1810 and has fifteen large rooms, which contain one of the most important collections of art in Italy. Many of the paintings, of which there are well over a thousand, are by the Venetian school, dating from the fifteenth to seventeenth centuries, but the collection is wide ranging and includes works by other Italian and European masters too.

Leaving Bergamo, follow signs to Clusone on the SP35 Valle Seriana road. This picturesque route visits Lake Iseo, but visitors who are short of time may prefer to head straight for Brescia on the A4 *autostrada* from Bergamo. After 13km (8 miles) the SP35 passes through **Albino** from where a *funivia* can be taken up to the mountain resort of **Selvino**, at a height of 965m (3,165ft). After crossing the river in the centre of Albino, turn right onto the SP39 to Abbazia and Casazza. **Abbazia** is named after the thirteenth-century Cistercian abbey which is passed to the right of the road, after which the road winds up to Col Gallo (764m/2,506ft), where there is a small thermal spa resort, **Casale**. The road then descends through another spa, **Piano Gaverina**, before reaching the SS42. Turn left and follow the road to **Spinone al Lago**, which lies at the southern end of Lake Endine. Spinone al Lago looks out across this small lake surrounded by gentle hills, to a romantic fifteenth-century castle on the opposite shore, Castello dei Suardi. Both boats and wind-surfs are available for hire at the lake edge. Follow the shore to **Pian Gaiano** at the northern tip of the lake and follow signs right to Riva del Sotto on the SP77. The road zigzags over the hills through the village of Zorzino, to **Riva del Sotto**, a small resort at the edge of **Lake Iseo**. The lake, known to the Romans as *Lacus Sebinus*, covers an area of 62sq km (24sq miles). It is long and narrow, measuring no more than 5km (3 miles) at its widest point, and forms the boundary between the provinces of Bergamo and Brescia. The western shore of the lake, known as Sebbina Occidentale, is very steep towards the northern end, and in places the cliffs plunge vertically into the water. The 7km (4 miles) drive from Riva del Sotto to Lovere on the SS649 is dramatic as the road is literally carved into the cliff face at several points.

Lovere, at the northern tip of Lake Iseo, is picturesque despite being fairly industrial. The main square, Piazza XII Martiri lies along the waterfront and is surrounded by elegant houses and cafés. Frequent ferries call at the jetty, from where regular tours of the lake and its three islands can be made during the summer. On Piazza Garibaldi, at the south end of the bay, the Galleria dell'Accademia Tadini, housed in a finely arcaded, neo-Classical *palazzo*, contains a collection of Lombard and Venetian paintings dating from the fifteenth to seventeenth centuries. The rest of the town, spread up the hill behind the bay has several attractive old buildings such as the fifteenth-century church of San Giorgio and the nearby tower, Torre Soca.

The SS510 leaves Lovere through industrial suburbs which stretch almost as far as Pisogne, 7km (4 miles) east. However, after crossing the Oglio river, the lake's main source, into the outskirts of **Pisogne**, it is worth turning off the main road to visit the small church of Santa Maria della Neve, signposted left from the train station. The church, which was built in the fifteenth century, contains a remarkable series of frescoes by G. Romanino (1532-4). Good views of the lake can be had by following the small road beyond the church to the attractive mountain village of Fraine. A slightly longer excursion, 34km (21 miles) from Pisogne, can be made up the Val Camonica on the SS42 to **Capo di Ponte**, which is at the centre of the Parco Nazionale delle Incisioni Rupestri. The park contains an area of rock engravings which cover an extraordinary time span from as far back as the Neolithic age up until Roman times. Over 200,000 engravings have been so far catalogued, and on the Naquane rock, which is reached by a footpath from the site entrance, there are 876 figures alone.

The route continues along the eastern shore of the lake, known as Sebbina Orientale, on the SS510. **Vello** is reached after passing through a series of tunnels. From here a short detour can be made up into the hills to the Parco Regionale Geotopo to see the *Piramide di*

Erosione. Follow a steep and winding road, the SP32, above Vello to the site, which lies in a valley a short distance from the carpark. A footpath leads down over 100 steps to the eroded cones. Like the famous fairy chimneys of Cappadocia, they were formed by a boulder protecting the softer rock beneath it from erosion. Over time the boulder is left high in the sky supported on a slender cone. Above the valley on a high craggy edge perches the small village of **Cislano**.

Return to the lake shore and continue south along the SS510, through **Marone**, from where hikers can climb up into the hills above the lake, on the footpath marked to Croce di Marone (1,166m/ 3,824ft). Shortly after passing the church in **Sale Marasino** a pleasant excursion can be made by following the small road on the left to Villa Martinengo with its fine gardens, and the nearby remains of a first-century Roman villa. The largest island on the lake, Monte Isola, lies just offshore from Sale Marasino but those who wish to visit it should continue on to **Sulzano**, where boats leave from nearby the lido. **Monte Isola** is the largest island on Lake Iseo, and surprisingly the largest on any lake in Europe. Three and a half kilometres (2 miles) long, most of the population live in one of the four villages on the island. The largest is **Pescheria Maraglio**, but even here there are no cars and life continues peacefully with most people being dependent on fishing and net-making. There are plenty of good hiking opportunities for the visitor; a 9km (6 miles) path encircles the island, another climbs up to the small chapel, the Santuario della Ceriola at the summit (600m/1,968ft). From here there are good views of the lake and the two other islands, Isola Loreto to the north and Isola San Paolo to the south.

Continue along the lake shore on the SS510 through the resort of **Pilzone**, where there is an underground cave 200m (218yd) long, the Buca del Quai. **Iseo**, the main resort on the lake lies a few kilometres further south. The road passes by the ruined Castello Oldofredo to its left, before reaching the main *piazza* at the lake edge. The town has a cheery holiday atmosphere, with busy cafés filling the *piazza*. Visitors who are here in spring should make the excursion to **Torbiera**, a preserved area of natural marshland to the west of Iseo, which is covered in a carpet of pink and white lilies at this time.

Route 6E — Lake Iseo to Lake Garda

Leave Lake Iseo by following the SS510, through the attractive wine-growing region of **Franciacorta**, to Brescia, 23km (14 miles) southeast of Iseo. Just before reaching the outskirts of Brescia, it is worth stopping by at **Rodengo**, where there is a fifteenth-century Cluniac monastery with three large cloisters, decorated by local Brescian artists, including G. Romanino.

Trying to find somewhere to park in **Brescia** can be difficult. The *autosilo*, underground carpark, on Piazza Vittoria is central but busy, and it may be easier to park around the city walls. The largest carpark, the Vecchio Orta Mercato, is outside the south city wall, a 10 minute walk from the centre. Once parked and out of the traffic, Brescia is a charming city, well-endowed with fine monuments.

Start a tour at Piazza della Loggia, just to the west of the centre. Surrounded by elegant Venetian buildings, the *piazza* takes its name from the vast loggia which supports the Palazzo Comunale at one end. The *palazzo* was built between 1492 and 1574 in the Lombard-Venetian style, although its unusual, high roof was not added until 1769, following a fire. The lower storey was designed by Bramante, the upper by Palladio and Sansovino, and the façade has several powerful busts set into it, the work of various Brescian stone masons. Palazzo dell'Orologio, at the opposite end of the *piazza*, is distinguished by its attractive clock tower. The large round face, painted by G. Lamberti (1547), is beautifully decorated with astrological symbols, and on top there are two figures, similar to those of St Mark's in Venice, ready to strike the bell.

Visitors should next head for Piazza del Duomo, reached by following Via X Giornale from the south-east corner of Piazza della Loggia, turning left after 150m (154yd). The *piazza* contains two cathedrals, Duomo Nuovo and Duomo Vecchio, which stand next to one another along the east side. Duomo Nuovo, a massive structure of white marble, was started in 1604, but not finished until 1825, when the great dome, the third highest in Italy, was added by L. Cagnola. It dwarfs the Duomo Vecchio, also known as the Rotunda, a comparatively modest, circular building, dating from the twelfth century. The interior, which has remnants of frescoes on the walls

A venture into an Italian market can lead to some surprising finds

and domed ceiling, is encircled by an attractive colonnaded ambulatory. The raised presbytery was added in the fifteenth century, and as can be seen by looking through the glass panels set in the floor, stands on the remains of first-century Roman mosaics. The painting of the *Assumption* at the altar is by the Brescian artist, Moretto, as are other paintings in the chapel on the right. Beneath the presbytery, steps lead down to the crypt of San Filastrio, where there are numerous Roman and Byzantine columns.

On the *piazza* to the left of Duomo Nuovo stands the Broletto, the town hall. It was built between 1187 and 1230 when Brescia was an independent commune, and surrounds a picturesque courtyard with a seventeenth-century fountain at its centre. The building still houses the offices of the local *comune*, but the tower is open to the public.

Walk behind the Broletto and follow Via dei Musei, to the impressive façade of the Tempio Capitolino, the best remaining structure of the Roman settlement, *Brixia*. The temple, which dates from AD73, stands on the north side of the former Roman forum, known today as Piazza del Foro. It contains the Museo Civico Romano, which has a vast number of Roman inscriptions and carved stone fragments in the three large chambers on the ground floor, and a well-displayed collection of other archaeological finds on the first floor. The collection includes ancient pottery, coins, and detached Roman fresco fragments, but the most stunning exhibits are the bronzes. There are six gilded heads of Roman emperors from the second and third centuries, and an excellently-preserved winged Venus which dates from the first century.

Continue along Via dei Musei to visit the Museo Cristiano (closed for restoration at time of writing), a collection of ecclesiastical art objects housed in the former sixteenth-century church and monastery of Santa Giulia. To reach the city's art gallery head downhill from the temple, along Piazza del Foro, passing the scant remains of the first-century forum on the left. Continue downwards along Via Gallo, crossing over Corso Magento, one of the main shopping streets in the city, before reaching Piazza Moretto. The gallery, Pinacoteca Tosio Martinengo, is housed in the twenty-two rooms, many with their original *trompe l'oeil* ceilings, of a sixteenth-century *palazzo*. Amongst the most important paintings in the gallery are those by the Renaissance master, Raphael, hung in Room VII. The collection is also noteworthy for its fifteenth and sixteenth-century paintings by masters of the Lombard school, such as V. Foppa, and earlier works, including frescoes, by the Brescian school, which date from the twelfth century.

Visitors with time can head for the gardens in the north-east corner of the city, surrounding Castello Visconti. The castle, which commands fine views over the city, was originally built in 1343, but was reconstructed in the fifteenth and sixteenth centuries. It contains the Museo Risorgimento, dedicated to the unification of Italy, as well as the Luigi Marzoli arms collection and the Cidnea Observatory. There is also a small zoo within the grounds.

Lake Garda lies a little over 25km (15^1/$_2$ miles) east of Brescia and can be reached either by the A4 motorway or by the SS11. It has been popular since the Romans, who knew it as *Benaco*, first built summer villas on its shores and is the most visited of Italy's lakes. It is also the largest, having an area of 370sq km (142sq miles). Situated between the Dolomites and the Padana Plain, the lake enjoys a mild climate and has a rich Mediterranean-type flora, and abundant olive and citrus groves. The greatest concentration of resorts are clustered around the gentle terrain at the southern end of the lake, the northern end being steeper and less accessible. It is a 142km (88 miles) drive completely round the lake, so the route only goes round the bottom of the lake and up its eastern shore, Riviera degli Olivi. Places of interest on the western shore can be visited by boat.

The first place to be visited on the lake is **Desenzano del Garda**. The narrow lanes in the town slope down to an attractive bay at the southern end of the lake, and a row of smart hotels and cafés look out over the busy marina. The resort has a wide range of sports and leisure facilities, and in the summer there are regular boat tours of the lake from the jetty. At the northern end of the bay, just inland, stands Villa Romana, a small museum built over the polychrome mosaic floor of a third-century Roman villa.

Sirmione, just over 5km (3 miles) from Desenzano del Garda, has one of the most picturesque locations on the lake, at the tip of a long narrow headland. However, during the summer it gets very crowded, and the seventy or more hotels are fully booked, and long queues build up at the carparks. During peak season, it is a much easier solution to visit Sirmione by ferry and so arrive at the central *piazza*. Visitors with vehicles must park outside the resort, but the walk to the village entrance, is rewarded by the sight of the thirteenth-century Venetian castle, built by the Scaligeri family. Swans glide around its fine moat and a drawbridge leads across to the interior, which is open as a museum. Head north through the centre of the resort, where ice cream parlours, pizzeria and souvenir shops compete for space, to the tip of the peninsula which is covered by a park. Luxury hotels are dotted throughout the park, and at its centre there is a modern spa, built over hot springs where the temperature of the water is 70°C (158°F).

From Sirmione, follow the SS11 along the southern shore of the lake for 15km (9 miles), crossing the boundary from Lombardy into Veneto at **Peschiera del Garda**. The town lies in the south-west corner of the lake at the mouth of the River Mincio. As the road crosses the river, it passes by a well-preserved fortress built on an island in the middle. Named the Fortezza del Quadrilatero, after its quadrilateral shape, it was originally built in the fifteenth century, although the present structure dates from the time of the Austrian occupation in the nineteenth century.

Visitors may wish to make the 23km (14 miles) excursion to Verona from here (see chapter 8), the route however heads north on the SS249, signposted to Garda. The road passes the Gardaland amusement land at **Castelnuovo**, before joining the lake at **Caneva**, a resort known for its good water-sports facilities. **Lazise**, 10km (6 miles) north of Peschiera del Garda, has a fine fortified wall and the remains of a Scaligeri castle. The attractive houses in the centre are clustered around a deep sheltered harbour, from where boats can be hired.

Following the SS249 north, the road passes through the well-known wine growing region of Bardolino. **Bardolino** itself, $5^1/_2$km (3 miles) north of Lazise, is a pleasant resort as well as being a centre of the local red wine, which is celebrated at the grape festival held between 15 September and 5 October. **Garda**, a few kilometres further on, is one of the better-established of the lake's resorts. Fine Venetian buildings surround an attractive harbour, and the nearby beaches offer good facilities for those interested in water-sports. The road continues north around a mountainous headland, which can be ascended by *funivia* from **Costabella**. There are fine panoramas across the lake from the delightful beaches around **Punta San Vigilio** at the tip of the headland.

As the road continues north the terrain gradually becomes rockier with the great mass of Monte Baldo looming nearer. The lake also becomes increasingly narrow, and **Torri del Benaco**, with its four-teenth-century Scaligeri castle, is a good point from which to make a boat excursion to the opposite shore. Car ferries cross regularly to Maderno, from where **Gardone Riviera**, the main resort on the western shore, and the nearby whimsical villa of Gabriele d'Annunzio, can be visited.

Continuing along the Rivera degli Olivi, the road passes through **Brenzone** where it is worth stopping to see the fifteenth-century frescoes in the Romanesque church of San Zeno. Further north, **Castelleto**, a centre of olive oil-making, has a picturesque harbour with lovely views across the water to the steep rocky shore on the opposite side. At **Malcesine**, 11km (7 miles) further north, there is a well-preserved, fourteenth-century Castello Scaligeri, built on a crag above the lake edge, which houses a museum about the lake as well as a collection of arms. A *funivia* can be taken from above the town up to the Selva Pezzi Parc, a nature reserve and botanical gardens, just below the summit of Monte Baldo (2,218m/7,275ft). There are good footpaths marked for hiking on Monte Baldo and the views are spectacular.

North of Malcesine, the coast is sheer, and after passing through a series of rock-carved tunnels, the road crosses into the mountainous region of Trentino Alto Adige. The mountains, increasingly steep and craggy, close in on both sides of the lake and there are no villages until **Torbole**, a health resort, built on the River Sarca, the main source feeding the lake. The road crosses the river and passes through another tunnel to **Riva del Garda**. This elegant resort, set at the foot of Monte Brione, has a lovely harbour surrounded by painted houses and public gardens. At one side of the harbour, on a small island joined by a drawbridge, stands a twelfth-century castle, containing a small museum (closed for restoration at time of writing). The streets leading inland from the harbour are also very attractive, with fine medieval houses along Via Fiume and grand Venetian *palazzi* along Via Mattei. A fat, round tower, the Apponale, built in 1220, looks over the town from the steep slopes of La Rocchetta (1,521m/4,989ft). Riva is a good point from which to go hiking on Monte Brione and the tourist office has maps of the local footpaths. A popular excursion 4km (2 miles) north of Riva is to **Cascata Varone**, a spectacular waterfall that cascades down over 90m (295ft) from Lake Tenno.

Before leaving Lake Garda, visitors may wish to make an excursion along the western shore to **Limone sul Garda**, 10km (6 miles) south of Riva, along the SS45Bis. This quiet resort takes its name from the beautiful lemon groves surrounding it. A panoramic drive can be made from Limone sul Garda up to the Tremosine plateau, from where visitors are rewarded with some of the best views of the lake. Visitors have the choice of continuing south along the western shore, or returning to Riva, and heading 40km (25 miles) north to the start of chapter 7 at Trento.

Additional Information

Places of Interest

ROUTE 6A
Aglie
Castello d'Aglie
10081 Aglie (TO)
☎ (0124) 330102
Open: Thursday, Saturday and Sunday 9am-1pm and 2-7pm.

Varallo
Palazzo dei Musei
Via Don Maio
13019 Varallo (VC)
Open: summer only, daily except Friday 10am-12noon and 3-6pm.

San Giulio
Basilica San Giulio
Isola San Giulio
28016 Lago d'Orta (NO)
Open: Tuesday to Sunday 9.30am-12.30pm and 2-7pm. Monday 11.30am-12.30pm and 2-7pm.

ROUTE 6B
Gignese
Museo dell'Ombrello
28042 Gignese (NO)
☎ (0323) 20444 or 20067
Open: summer only Tuesday to Sunday 10am-12noon and 1.30-6pm.

Isola Bella
Palazzo Borromeo
Isola Bella
28049 Lago Maggiore (NO)
☎ (0323) 30557
Open: March to October daily 9am-12noon and 1.30-5pm.

Stresa
Villa Pallavicino
28049 Stresa (NO)
Open: March to November 8.30am-7pm.

Pallanza-Verbania
Ente Giardini Botanici Villa Taranto
28048 Pallanza-Verbania (NO)
☎ (0323) 556667
Open: daily 8.30am until sunset.

Pallanza
Museo del Paesaggio
Palazzo Dugnani
Via Cavour 40
28048 Pallanza (NO)

Open: winter Saturday and Sunday
10am-12noon, 3-5pm. Summer
Tuesday to Sunday 10am-12noon,
3-6pm.

Varese
Museo Civico
Villa Mirabello
Palazzo Estense
21100 Varese
Open: Tuesday to Saturday
9.30am-12.30pm, 2-5.30pm. Sunday
9.30am-12.30pm.

Castiglione Olona
Collegiata
21043 Castiglione Olona (VA)
Open: Tuesday to Saturday 10am-
12noon and 3-6pm. Holidays 10am-
12.30pm, 2.30-6pm.

Museo
Palazzo Branda
21043 Castiglione Olona (VA)
Open: Monday to Saturday 9am-
12noon and 2.30-5.30pm. Holidays
3-6pm.

ROUTE 6C
Como
Tempio Voltiano
22100 Como (CO)
Open: winter Tuesday to Saturday
2-4pm. Summer Tuesday to
Saturday 10am-12noon, 3-6pm.

Museo Civico Archeologico Giovio
1 Piazza Medaglie d'Oro
22100 Como (CO)
Open: winter Tuesday to Saturday
9.30am-12noon and 2-5pm. Sunday
9.15am-12noon. Summer Tuesday
to Saturday 9.30am-12noon and
2.30-5.30pm. Sunday 9.15am-12noon.

Villa dell'Olmo
Via Cantoni
22100 Como (CO)
Open: daily except
Sunday and holidays.

Bellagio
Villa Serbelloni
22021 Bellagio (CO)
Open: March to October, Tuesday
to Sunday.

Tremezzo
Villa Carlotta
22019 Tremezzo (CO)
☎ (0344) 40405
Open: March to October daily.

ROUTE 6D
Bergamo
Accademia Carrara
Piazza dell'Accademia
24100 Bergamo (BG)
☎ (035) 399426
Open: daily except Tuesday
9.30am-12.30pm, 2.30-5.30pm.

Lovere
Galleria dell'Accademia Tadini
Palazzo Tadini
14 Piazza Garibaldi
24065 Lovere (BG)
Open: May to October Monday to
Saturday 3-6pm. Holidays 10am-
12noon and 3-6pm.

ROUTE 6E
Brescia
Museo Civico Romano
57 Via dei Musei
25100 Brescia (BS)
☎ (030) 46081
Open: Tuesday to Sunday 9am-
12.45pm and 2-5pm.

Pinacoteca Tosio Martinengo
Piazza Moretto
25100 Brescia (BS)
Open: Tuesday to Saturday 10am-
12.45pm and 2-6pm.

Castello Visconti
25100 Brescia (BS)
Open: Tuesday to Sunday 9am-
12noon, 2-5pm.

Malcesine
Castello Scaligeri
37018 Malcesine (VR)
Open: winter Saturday, Sunday
and holidays 9am-5pm. Summer
daily 9am-8pm.

Desenzano del Garda
Villa Romana
Via Scavi Romana
25015 Desenzano del Garda (BS)
Open: Tuesday to Sunday 9am-5.30pm.

Sirmione
Rocca Scaligeri
25019 Sirmione (BS)
Open: winter Tuesday to Sunday
9am-1pm. Summer Tuesday to
Sunday 9am-1pm and 2.30-6.30pm.

Tourist Information Centres

ROUTE 6A
Ivrea
Azienda Autonoma di Soggiorno e
  Turismo
1 Corso Vercelli
10015 Ivrea (TO)
☎ (0125) 424005

Varallo
Azienda Autonoma di Soggiorno e
  Turismo
Corso Roma
13019 Varallo (VC)
☎ (0163) 51280

ROUTE 6B
Baveno
Azienda Autonoma di Soggiorno e
  Turismo
5 Piazza Dante
28042 Baveno (NO)
☎ (0323) 24632

Stresa
Azienda di Promozione Turistica
  del Lago Maggiore
72 Via Principe Tomaso
28049 Stresa (NO)
☎ (0323) 30150

ROUTE 6C
Como
Azienda Promozione Turismo
17 Piazza Cavour
22100 Como (CO)
☎ (031) 262091

Bellagio
Azienda Autonoma di Soggiorno e
  Turismo
Lungolago
22021 Bellagio (CO)
☎ (031) 950204

Lecco
Azienda Autonoma di Soggiorno e
  Turismo
6 Via Nazario Sauro
22053 Lecco (CO)
☎ (0341) 362360

ROUTE 6D
Bergamo
Azienda Turismo
Vicolo Aquila Nera
Citta Alta
24100 Bergamo (BG)
☎ (035) 232730

Lovere
Pro Lovere
2 Piazza Vittorio Emanuele
24065 Lovere (BG)
☎ (035) 962488

Iseo
Azienda Autonoma di Soggiorno e
  Turismo
2 Lungolago Marconi
25049 Iseo (BS)
☎ (030) 980209

ROUTE 6E
Brescia
Azienda di Promozione Turistica
  del Bresciano
34 Corso Zanardelli
25100 Brescia (BS)
☎ (030) 43418

Sirmione
Azienda Autonoma di Soggiorno e
  Turismo
8 Viale Marconi
25019 Sirmione (BS)
☎ (030) 916114

Riva del Garda
Azienda Autonoma di Soggiorno e
  Turismo
Giardini Spiagia degli Olivi
38066 Riva del Garda (TN)
☎ (0464) 554444

7

THE DOLOMITES

The Dolomites, named after the French geologist, Deodat de Dolomieu, who first analysed their rock in 1788, are a thrilling sight. With more than a dozen peaks over 3,000m (9,840ft) high, wherever you are in the Dolomites the scenery is spectacular. Good, albeit steep roads, give easy access to the main mountain groups, and numerous well-marked and well-trodden footpaths criss-cross the region, with the six main hiking paths, the Alte Vie, traversing from north to south. Many of the major peaks can be reached by cable car, which as they generally leave from near the roadside, make it very easy for visitors to get high up into the mountains. As well as helping hikers in the summer, they are used in the winter to ferry skiers up to the slopes.

Starting from Lake Garda, the route heads north into South Tyrol, officially known as Alto Adige, to join the Great Dolomites Road, which crosses the massif eastwards from Bolzano to Cortina d'Ampezzo. The route then heads south to the Venetian plain. It should be noted, however, that as the Great Dolomites Road takes in several of the highest passes, it can only be guaranteed to be snow-free from June to late September.

Route 7A — Riva to Bolzano

From Lake Garda, the road to Trento, the SS45Bis, passes through **Arco**, a health resort, charmingly positioned in the Sarche river valley. It is a popular hiking area and a pleasant walk can be made up from the town, through steep olive groves, to the castle. Continue for 5km (3 miles) north of Arco to the junction of the SS86, where visitors who have time can make a pleasant detour along the Val di Cavedine. The road winds steeply up towards the castle of **Drena**, before branching left and crossing a rocky plateau to the small Lake Cavedine. It continues on through **Pergolese** before rejoining the SS45Bis at Sarche. The road passes three small lakes, **Toblino** with its *castello*, **Santa Massenza**, and **Terlago**, before climbing up to **Passo Cadine** (494m/1,620ft) from where it is downhill all the way to Trento. Those who enjoy hairpin bends can take the tortuous road to

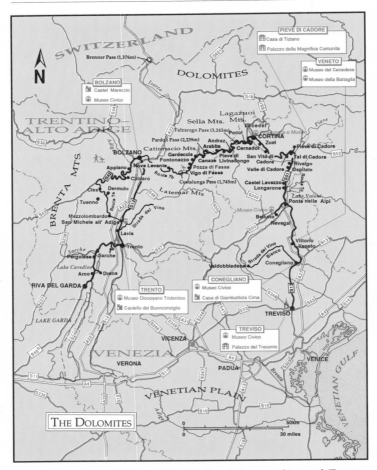

The Dolomites

Monte Bondone (2,091m/6,858ft) from the outskirts of Trento. Others may prefer to take the *funivia* from Ponte San Lorenzo in the city centre.

Trento, capital of the semi-autonomous province, Trentino Alto-Adige, lies on the banks of the Adige river, encircled by mountains. It was ruled by a series of prince-bishops from 1004 to 1801, who hosted the Council of Trent, held in three sessions between 1545 and 1563. The council signalled the start of the Counter Reformation in Italy, a movement that was to drastically change the history of the Catholic church. Much of the architecture of this time has survived and the city's monuments show an interesting mix of styles as the Austrians ruled Trento, from 1813 to 1918. The bright green tiled roofs of some of the buildings strike a cheerful note and are typical of the region.

The easiest place to park is in one of the multi-storey carparks in the city centre. Follow signs to *autosilo*, or Europa, one of the largest carparks. The heart of the city is Piazza del Duomo, a fine square surrounded by colourful Renaissance houses, including the ornately frescoed Palazzo Gazuffi. The Palazzo Pretorio on the north side dates from the thirteenth century and has a fine façade pierced by Gothic windows and topped by crenellations. It houses Museo Diocesano.

Duomo San Vigilio, filling the south side of the *piazza*, was built in the thirteenth century in the Lombard-Romanesque style, although the *campanile* with its bulbous green cupola was added in the sixteenth century. Inside, the main aisle is lined with royal tombs and sixteenth-century funerary monuments. The chapel on the right, Cappella del Crocifisso, contains the crucifix before which the Trent treaties were proclaimed.

Leave Piazza del Duomo from the north side and follow Via Belenzani. The street is lined with Renaissance buildings, a graceful blend of Austrian and Venetian architecture, and is a lively shopping area. After 150m (164yd) turn left to visit Santa Maria Maggiore (1520), one of the principal meeting places of the Council of Trent. It has a striking *campanile*, but the interior although spacious is rather

The Dolomites, one of Italy's natural wonders

plain. Return to Via Belenzani and continue along it to Via G. Manci. Turn right and follow the street for 350m (383yd) to the high walls of Castello del Buonconsiglio. The castle, which was the residence of the prince-bishops from the thirteenth up until the sixteenth centuries, is long and narrow. The walls enclose a series of inner courtyards, constructed at different times, the northern end with its original defensive tower of the thirteenth century being the oldest. Pass through the gardens to the vaulted basement of the castle, the main part of which was built by the prince-bishop Bernardo Cles (1485-1539), an important patron of the arts. Fragments of frescoes by G. Romanino can be seen in the vaulted entrance hall and a finely frescoed staircase leads up to the Museo Provinciale d'Arte in the castle's apartments. The panelled ceilings, pink and white stone floors, and majolica stoves have all been carefully preserved, and the Sala Grande has a magnificent coffered ceiling. In the Torre dell'Aquila, there is a fresco cycle depicting the twelve months of the year which dates from the fifteenth century. A separate entrance in the northern end of the castle leads into the Museo Risorgimento where there is a collection devoted to the unification of Italy and the liberation of Trentino from the Austrians in 1918.

Those with time may wish to visit the monument to Cesare Battisti (1875-1916) who was executed by the Austrians for being a traitor. This circular monument, known as Doss Trento, can be seen from the city on the hillside above the Adige, 3km (2 miles) north-west of the centre.

Bolzano, the next place of major interest on Route 7a, is 51km (32 miles) north of Trento. The most direct way there, is on the A22 motorway, but a more scenic route can be taken through the mountains along the Val di Non. Those who wish to take this route should follow the SS12 to **Lavis**, where a short excursion down a *strada del vino* can be made to sample the Trentino wines. Continue north along the SS12 to **San Michele all'Adige**, another centre of wine-making, at the entrance to the Val di Non. Visit the Museo degli Usi e Costumi della Gente Trentina, of Trentino folklore. housed in an ex-Augustine monastery, next to the ornately decorated church of San Michele. Turn left at San Michele all'Adige onto the SS43. It crosses the River Toce and follows a gentle valley to **Mezzolombardo**, a small wine-making town, under the rocky peak of Monte (885m/2,903ft), which can be ascended by *funivia*. Continue north along the SS43 gradually climbing up to **Dermulo** at a height of 548m (1,797ft). From here a pleasant detour of 21km (13 miles) can be made to Lake Tovel, a picturesque lake surrounded by mountains. The route continues north from Dermulo on the SS43dir, gradually climbing up through an alpine landscape dotted with villages, to the **Mendola Pass** (1,363m/4,471ft). The pass stands on the boundary between Trentino and Tyrol, and once over it German is used as widely as Italian. The road winds down a series of hairpin bends, past the wine-making town of **Caldarola**, to **Appiano**, where there is a fine castle, and continues on through orchards for the last 10km (6 miles) to Bolzano.

Bolzano, the 'door to the Dolomites', is the capital of South Tyrol and a popular base for hiking, climbing and skiing. It lies at the confluence of the Adige and Isarco rivers, and is linked to Austria by the A22 motorway which climbs over the Brenner Pass (1,375m/ 4,510ft) to Innsbruck. The road enters the city from the south, crossing River Isarco to a large carpark within easy walking distance of the centre. The Duomo is in the central square, Piazza Walther. It was consecrated in 1184, but apart from a Romanesque portal, the building dates from the fourteenth to sixteenth centuries. The fine roof is decorated with coloured tiles and the interior contains an attractive raised presbytery with an ambulatory behind it. On the left side of the presbytery is a carved Gothic pulpit, while on the right are the remains of frescoes dating from 1424.

Follow Via Posta from in front of the Duomo, to Piazza Domenicani, named after the great Domenican church that stands on the left. The church was originally founded in the 1270s, but was reconstructed during the fourteenth century. Built of brick, the massive structure has a plain interior, apart from the chapel on the right of the apse which contains a cycle of frescoes (1330-35) in the style of the Giotto school.

Head north of Piazza Domenicani to Piazza dell'Erbe, where there is a colourful fruit and vegetable market. From the east side of the *piazza* it is well worth wandering along Via dei Portici which is lined by arcaded houses dating from the sixteenth to eighteenth centuries. From the west side of the *piazza*, follow Via del Museo for 250m (273yd) to Museo Civico on the left. The museum has a large and varied collection, arranged on three floors, ranging from prehistoric stone tools to nineteenth-century paintings. Not to be missed are the Tyrolean wood carved reliefs from churches, the collection of nine-teenth-century majolica stoves from the Val di Non, and the Tyrolean folk costumes which rate amongst the best in the region.

Those interested in the region's wine-making should visit the thirteenth-century Castel Mareccio, to the north of the centre, where wines can be tasted. Many visitors to Bolzano are keen hikers and there are a number of good walks that can be made in the immediate vicinity as well as in the surrounding mountains. The Talfer Prom-enade runs for about 1km ($^1/_2$ mile) along the left bank of the Talfer river, while the Oswald Promenade follows the Hortenburg hills to the wine-making village of **Santa Magdalena**, $2^1/_2$km ($1^1/_2$ miles) away. The Guntschna Promenade heads up hill for 2km (1 mile) to the panoramic terrace on Monte Guntschna. Alternatively a *funivia*, which leaves from Via Renon, can be taken up to **Soprabozen** (1,255m/4,116ft), from where footpaths lead across the plateau to the Ritner Horn. Another *funivia* leaves from the east end of town, climbing up to Colle (1,100m/3,608ft) where there are pleasant footpaths through the woods.

Route 7B — Bolzano to Belluno

The main road across the Dolomites, the *Strade delle Dolomiti*, was built in 1909 and the route joins it at Val di Fassa after following the Val d'Ega for some distance from Bolzano. The journey from Bolzano to Cortina d'Ampezzo on the east side of the Dolomites is 132km (82 miles) and as the terrain is virtually all mountainous visitors are advised to break the journey and stay overnight in one of the many resorts along the route.

The entrance to **Val d'Ega** lies 3km (2 miles) east of Bolzano. Follow the SS241 across the Isarco river, passing a thirteenth-century castle, before entering the valley gorge. After climbing up for 16km (10 miles) to **Ponte Nova** (872m/2,860ft), the gradient increases as the road ascends the slopes to the popular resort of **Nova Levante**, at an altitude of 1,182m (3,877ft). Continue up the steep winding road past **Carezza al Lago**, between the Latemar and the Catinaccio mountains, to the **Costalunga Pass** (1,745m/5,724ft), the first major pass on the route. The views as the road descends are superb, and on clear days the Marmolada is visible in the distance. **Vigo di Fassa** (1,382m/4,533ft), a popular ski-resort, stands at the foot of Mount Ciampedie (1,997m/6,550ft), the summit of which can be reached by cable car from the resort.

After Vigo di Fassa the route joins the SS48 Great Dolomites Road which follows the Val di Fassa through numerous ski resorts. Just north of **Pera di Fassa** a steep road climbs up to the **Gardeccia** refuge (1,948m/6,389ft) in the Catinaccio mountains on the left. From here

A colourful fruit and vegetable market at Piazza dell' Erbe in Bolzano

Cortina d'Ampezzo is one of Europe's top winter resorts

hikes can be made up to several of the nearby peaks, the highest of which, Catinaccio d'Antermoia, stands at 3,002m (9,846ft). Continue along the SS48 through **Mazzin**, and **Campestrin** where there is an attractive church to **Fontonazzo** (1,380m/4,526ft), one of the largest ski resorts in the valley. Continue up, crossing the River Duron to **Campitello**, from where a cable car climbs up to **Col Rodello** (2,387m/7,829ft) on the slopes of the Sella mountains.

The popular resort of **Canazei** stands at the head of the Val di Fassa, encircled by some of the most famous of the Dolomite peaks, including the Catinaccio, the Sella and the Marmolada. Visitors who wish to make the excursion to the Marmolada (3,342m/10,962ft), the tallest peak in the Dolomites, should follow the signposted road from Canazei for 12km (7 miles) to Lake Fedaia, at the foot of the great mountain. Cable cars take visitors up to the edge of the glacier, but the summit of the mountain can only be reached by those wearing crampons.

The SS48 Great Dolomites Road zig-zags steeply up above

Canazei for 12km (7 miles) to the **Pordoi Pass** (2,239m/7,344ft), the highest pass in the Dolomites. The resort at the pass stands below the rocky mass of Sass Pordoi (2,950m/9,676ft) which, although scaled by cable car is also popular with climbers. The road down from the Pordoi Pass pirouettes through over thirty hairpin bends in less than 9km (6 miles) into the Val Cordevole below.

The road follows the gently sloping valley, passing numerous ski resorts, before climbing up above **Arabba**, through a picturesque landscape, to **Pieve di Livinallongo** (1,470m/4,822ft). This attractive resort with its old-fashioned albergos and Gothic church has fine views of the Civetta (3,218m/10,555ft) and Pelmo (3,168m/10,391ft) peaks to the south-east. **Andraz**, a few kilometres further on, is also pleasant and has a pretty, white church. From here the SS48 climbs steeply up to **Cernadoi** where the ruins of a tenth-century strong-hold can be seen perched on a rocky outcrop. The road continues to climb, crossing the River La Mierla, up to the **Falzarego Pass** (2,105m/6,904ft), from where there are more panoramic views. Cable cars run up the Lagazuoi mountains (2,746m/9,007ft) on the left and Mount Averau (2,648m/8,685ft) on the right. A few kilometres down the other side of the pass another cable car climbs up to the **Cinque Torri** refuge (2,137m/7,009ft), from where there are fine views across the valley to the Tofane mountains. The road winds down criss-crossing over the Lagozuoi river before following the Falzarego river through the **Gioia Pass** to **Pocol**, a busy resort. It continues its descent through **Lacedel**, passing the turning on the left to **Prati Tofane** (1,776m/5,825ft). A pleasant excursion can be made up to the *prati*, which is a high mountain pasture from where cable cars lead up to the dramatic peaks of the **Tofane** mountains, the tallest of which is 3,243m (10,637ft) high. The SS48 winds on down, the green roof of the church in Cortina d'Ampezzo coming into view shortly before the road makes its final descent into the town.

Cortina d'Ampezzo lies in the broad Boite river valley, encircled by the craggy peaks of the Dolomites. It is one of the top winter resorts in Europe and has excellent sports facilities, including an ice-skating stadium that was built for the 1956 Olympics and numerous pistes for skiing and sledging. It is also a popular centre from which to go hiking, and in the summer, Dolomite excursions are organised for all levels of walkers, from children to experienced climbers. As in many of the resorts in the Dolomites the town is linked with the surrounding mountains by *funivia*, making it possible for hikers to start high up in the mountains and gradually work their way back to Cortina. Funivia Faloria leaves from Via Marconi at the south end of town and climbs in two stages to refuge Mandres, then refuge Faloria (2,120m/6,954ft). Funivia Mietres leaves from Verocai at the north end of town, and also climbs in two stages, first to refuge Col Tondo and then refuge Mietres (1,710m/5,609ft). Funivia Tofana leaves from behind the ice-skating stadium at the north end of town, and climbs in three stages to refuge Col Druscie (1,770m/5,806ft), then refuge Ra Valles (2,282m/7,485ft), and last of all to the dizzy heights of refuge Cima Tofana (3,243m/10,637ft). The town itself has the predictable character of a prosperous resort with modern chalets and luxury boutiques lining the main street, Corso d'Italia. The *farmacia* at number 151 and the eighteenth-century Parocchiale church in the town centre, are about all that remains of old Cortina. Also of interest is the small museum and gallery, Casa de Ra Regoles, behind the tall *campanile* of the church.

Leave Cortina d'Ampezzo on the SS51, south in the direction of Belluno. Look out for the Olympic ski jump on the right at **Zuel** just outside the town. The road passes through an area known as the Cadore where some of the people still speak the original Ladin dialect. The history of the Ladini people goes back to Roman times when soldiers were sent by Tiberius to fend off Celtic invaders. The soldiers settled here with their families on a permanent basis, and the Ladin dialect, or Romansch, which is also spoken in parts of Switzerland and other corners of the Tyrol, has been handed down ever since. The first of the Cadore villages, **San Vito di Cadore**, is 11km (7 miles) south of Cortina d'Ampezzo. Located in the shadow of Monte Pelmo (3,168m/10,391ft), it is an attractive mountain resort with stone-tiled houses and a quaint parish church. Continue along the SS51, down the Boite river valley, passing through other pleasant Cadore villages to **Venas di Cadore**, 22km (14 miles) south of Cortina d'Ampezzo. This small, neatly-kept town stands above a picturesque lake, Lake Valle di Cadore. The SS51 winds past the lake to **Valle di Cadore**, beneath the great peak of Antelao (3,624m/11,887ft). It is worth stopping here briefly, if only to see the central square which is surrounded by attractive wooden houses with balconies. Continue down the SS51 to **Tai di Cadore**, from where it is well worth making the short excursion, off left, to **Pieve di Cadore**, Titian's birthplace, which lies along a ridge above an artificial lake. Head for the central *piazza* with its nineteenth-century statue of Titian. The small parish church on the *piazza* holds a *Madonna and Saints* painted by Titian, but the artist's house is a short walk downhill along Via Arsenale. It is an attractive building with overhanging eaves and a wooden balcony, and contains a small museum. Behind Titian's statue in the main *piazza* is the Palazzo della Magnifica Comunita. It was built in 1525 and houses an archaeological museum. Pieve di Cadore is also the home of Father Christmas for Italian children who address their mail to a modest house in the forest on the hill above the town.

Return to the SS51 which heads south along the Pieve river gorge, past **Rivalgo** and **Ospitale**, to **Castellavazzo**, where visitors should turn right to visit the town centre. The town was known to the Romans as *Castrum Laebati* and the *municipio* on the central *piazza* has a fine Roman sarcophagus in its hall. The town also has an attractive church with a fine domed *campanile*. Continue south along the SS51, past **Longarone** which was rebuilt in 1963 after a tidal wave from

Valle di Cadore, beneath the great peak of Antelao

Lake Vaiont swept through the town, killing around 2,000 people. To the south of Longarone, the valley gradually widens and becomes increasingly industrial. The next place of interest on the route is the town of Belluno, reached by turning right at **Ponte nelle Alpi**.

Route 7C — Belluno to Treviso

Situated at the southernmost edge of the Dolomites, the charming town of **Belluno** is built at the confluence of two rivers, the Piave and Ardo. It is an interesting town with genuine character and a number of fine buildings, mainly dating from the fifteenth century, when it was under Venetian rule. The town is centred around Piazza Martiri, a long and narrow *piazza* with parking spaces along one side and an arcade of shops on the other. From the *piazza* head south through the public gardens and Piazza Castello, to Piazza del Duomo. The Duomo, also known as Basilica di San Martino, has a striking *campanile* with a green cupola designed by F. Juvarra in 1743. The building was designed in the sixteenth century by T. Lombardo, but it has undergone considerable alteration since, and the interior, which contains paintings by the Venetian school, is Baroque.

More interesting, is the fine façade of Palazzo dei Rettori, on the north side of the *piazza*. Constructed in 1491 in the Venetian-Gothic style, it stands on a robust arcade with two rows of windows and balconies, and has a wide clock tower at one end. The other tower on the *piazza* is joined to Palazzo Vescovile and was built as part of the twelfth-century town fortress.

Leaving the *piazza* from the east side, look out for Palazzo dei

Guristi with its fine loggia on the right. It houses the Museo Civico, which is made up of two parts: one a collection of local archaeological finds ranging from prehistoric to Roman times; the other a collection of paintings, mainly by the Venetian school. Continue past the museum for a short way to Piazza del Mercato. This small *piazza*, located in the most picturesque quarter of the town, is surrounded by fine porticoed buildings dating from the Renaissance, and has an attractive fountain at its centre (1410) which is dedicated to San Lucano. Follow Via Rialto, north of the *piazza*, to the medieval town gate, Porta Doiona, which is dedicated to San Lucano. Follow Via Rialto, north of the *piazza*, to the medieval town gate, Porta Doiona, which was built in 1289, and enlarged in the fifteenth century.

Visitors who wish to visit the Gothic church of San Stefano should continue through the gate, across Piazza Vittorio Emanuele, and follow Via Roma for 200m (218yd) north. The church was built in 1486 and is mainly visited for its beautifully carved portal, although it has an attractive interior too, lined with Gothic columns, with frescoes in the right chapel.

An excursion can be made 12km (7 miles) south-east of Belluno to the resort of **Nevegal**. In the winter it functions as a well-equipped ski resort, while in the summer it is an ideal spot for hiking or horse-riding, and has an extensive park of pine forest, the Pineta. As well as picnic areas and a children's playground there is also a chair-lift to Col Faverghera, where there is the Giardino Botanico delle Alpe Orientale botanical gardens.

To continue the route, return to **Ponte nelle Alpi** and follow the SS51, or the new motorway, to Vittorio Veneto, 30km (19 miles) south. On the way the road passes three lakes. The first, Lake Santa Croce, is the largest and most attractive, and has a small resort at its southern tip.

Vittorio Veneto is named after the decisive battle fought against the Austro-Hungarians between 24 October and 3 November in 1918, and which achieved Italy's independence. The town is stretched along the Meschio river and is in two distinct parts, **Serravalle** and **Ceneda**. The SS51 enters Serravalle, which is the more interesting part of the town. There are parking spaces around Duomo di Santa Maria Nuovo, which lies close to the River Meschio. The Duomo and its tall, spired *campanile* date from the eighteenth century and the interior is Baroque in style.

From the Duomo, cross the river to Piazza Flaminio, the main square in Serravalle. It is a long and narrow *piazza*, surrounded by fine buildings, the most impressive being Loggia Serravallese at the western end. Built in 1462, it now houses the Museo Cenedese which has paintings and sculptures by local artists dating from medieval times, and a small collection of archaeological finds from the region. From Loggia Serravallese stroll along the main street, Via Martiri della Liberta, looking out for the arcaded, Gothic *palazzi* on either side.

Ceneda, the other part of the town, can be visited on the way out of Vittorio Veneto. Follow Via Petrarca south from the Duomo along the river bank, noticing the old town fortifications on the hill to the right. Continue south through the modern resort that has grown up between Serravalle and Ceneda, to Piazza Meschio, where the church of Santa Maria di Meschio contains a good painting by Previtali of the *Annunciation*. Those who wish to visit the centre of Ceneda should turn right along Via A. Diaz, and continue until reaching the main *piazza*. Loggia Cenedese, on the north side of the *piazza*, is attributed to the Renaissance architect Sansovino, and was built in 1538.

The next place of interest along the route is the wine-making town of **Conegliano**. It is reached by following the SS51 for 8km (5 miles) from Vittorio Veneto in the direction of Venezia. The Duomo, in the town centre, was built in the fourteenth century and has a fine Gothic portal, and an attractive *campanile*, which was erected in 1497. The interior contains an excellent altar painting (1492) by G. Cima, who was born in Conegliano, and his house, which now contains a small museum, is behind the Duomo at number 24 Via Cima. The neo-Classical façade of Oratorio di Sant'Orsola can be seen on the hill above the town. Next to it in the crenellated tower, which is all that remains of the medieval town castle, is a small wine-making museum, where there is also a collection of paintings and frescoes.

Those interested in Conegliano's wines should look out for Bianco di Conegliano, Prosecco, Cartizze and Bianco dei Colli in the town's shops. To buy directly from the local producers follow the *strada del vino bianco*, signposted to **Valdobbiadene**, which lies 42km (26 miles) west of Conegliano. Valdobbiadene produces Spumante wines and a festival is held here every September. Conegliano also has a grape festival, Festa dell'Uva, which is celebrated with folk displays and gastronomy stands, as well as the local wines, on the first Sunday in October.

Leave Conegliano on the SS13 to Treviso, which lies 27km (17 miles) south across the Venetian plain. On the way the road passes by numerous *ossario*, war memorials, which commemorate those who died in the battle of Veneto, which was fought along the banks of the River Piave.

Treviso, like every city on the Venetian plain, has large industrial outskirts. The centre, however, although it suffered bomb damage in World War II, is well worth visiting. Waterways, flanked by frescoed *palazzi*, course through the city giving it a whiff of Venice. This is not altogether surprising as the Venetians ruled Treviso from 1389 to 1796. The local tourist office suggests touring the city by bicycle and has drawn up a number of interesting itineraries.

Piazza dei Signori, in the middle of the city, is a good place from which to start a tour. The *piazza* is surrounded by medieval and Renaissance buildings and a sixteenth-century loggia on the east side supports Palazzo dei Trecento (1217). Palazzo del Podesta, which stands next to it, is also medieval, although it was entirely rebuilt in the nineteenth century, complete with its crenellations and tower, the Torre del Comune. Another loggia lies 200m (218yd) east of the *piazza* behind Palazzo dei Trecento. Built in 1195, Loggia della Cavalieri, has a wooden ceiling supported on a single central column.

Return to Piazza dei Signori and head north-west to the Duomo, along Calmaggiore, a porticoed street lined with frescoed buildings. The Duomo, with its seven large domes, was rebuilt during the fifteenth and sixteenth centuries and has a neo-Classical façade which was added in 1836. The vast but plain interior is filled by massive piers supporting the domes, and in the chapel on the right, which is decorated with frescoes by Paris Bordone, there is a painting by Titian of the *Annunciation* (1520). The twelfth-century columns from the earlier Duomo can be seen in the crypt, which is opened on request by the sacristan. To the left of the Duomo stands the baptistery and behind it the *campanile*; both date from the twelfth century.

Other places of interest in Treviso lie further afield and visitors may prefer to visit them by car. The Museo Civico lies just under 300m (328yd) north-west of the Duomo, close to the city walls. It is housed in a sixteenth-century cloister and on the ground floor there is a collection of archaeological finds, dredged from the River Sile, which includes attractive bronze artefacts dating from Roman Treviso, *Tarvisium*. Upstairs there is a *pinacoteca* which has a large collection of paintings by the Venetian school, including a fine painting of the *Madonna* by G. Bellini. Also of note is the portrait of a *Domenican* by Lorenzo Lotto, and a portrait of *Sperone Speroni* by Titian. Before leaving the museum, inquire at the desk about access to Santa Caterina dei Servi di Maria, a small fourteenth-century church on the east side of the city. It is worth visiting in order to see the fine fresco cycle of the *Life of St Ursula* by Tommaso da Modena.

The vast Domenican church of San Nicolo, which lies some 500m (547yd) south of the Museo Civico, also contains frescoes by Tommaso da Modena. The church was built during the thirteenth and fourteenth centuries, and was founded by Niccolo Boccassini, who later became Pope Benedict XI. Inside, each of the brick columns lining the nave is decorated with a fresco panel. At one time the frescoes were all believed to be the work of Tomasso da Modena, but now only the second column on the left is attributed to him. The colossal and rather naive fresco of St Christopher, on the right wall is by Antonio da Treviso (1410). Other fresco fragments dating from the fourteenth century cover the walls of the main apse and the chapels either side. The ex-seminary behind the church is also worth visiting as it contains portraits of Domenican monks studying in their cells by Tommaso da Modena (1352). Cardinal Hugh of Provence is shown wearing perhaps one of the first pairs of glasses ever to be painted.

Visitors with time can wander along the banks of the waterways, visiting sights such as the fish market on the islet of Peschiera in the

River Botteniga. During the summer it is possible to join one of the boat excursions which are made along the Sile river to Venice and the Venetian lagoon. This chapter ends at Treviso and visitors who wish to join chapter 8 should leave on the SS13 and follow it across the Venetian plain to Venice.

Additional Information

Places of Interest

ROUTE 7A
Trento
Museo Diocesano Tridentino
Palazzo Pretorio
18 Piazza del Duomo
38100 Trento (TN)
☎ (0461) 234419
Open: March to October Monday to Saturday 9.30am-12.30pm and 2.30-6pm.

Museo Provinciale d'Arte
Castello del Buonconsiglio
5 Via B. Clesio
38100 Trento (TN)
☎ (0461) 233770
Open: Tuesday to Sunday 9am-12noon and 2-5pm.

Museo Tridentino del Risorgimento
Castello del Buonconsiglio
3 Via B. Clesio
38100 Trento (TN)
☎ (0461) 230482
Open: Tuesday to Sunday 9am-12noon and 2-5.30pm.

San Michele all'Adige
Museo Provinciale degli Usi e
   Costumi d. Gente Trentina
38100 San Michele all'Adige (TN)
☎ (0461) 650314
Open: Tuesday to Saturday 9am-12noon and 2.30-5.30pm.

Appiano
Castel Ganda
39057 Appiano (BZ)
☎ (0471) 52141
Open: summer Tuesday to Sunday 10am, 11am, 3.30pm.

Bolzano
Museo Civico di Bolzano
14 Via Cassa di Risparmio
39100 Bolzano (BZ)
☎ (0471) 974625
Open: Tuesday to Saturday 9am-12noon and 2.30-5.30pm. Sunday 10am-1pm.

Castel Mareccio
Via Claudia de'Medici
39100 Bolzano (BZ)
☎ (0471) 976615
Open: daily except Sundays.

ROUTE 7B
Cortina d'Ampezzo
Pinacoteca e Museo
Casa de Ra Regoles
1 Viale Parco
32043 Cortina d'Ampezzo (BL)
Open: Monday to Saturday 4-7pm.

Pieve di Cadore
Casa di Tiziano
Via Arsenale
32044 Pieve di Cadore (BL)
☎ (0435) 32262
Open: summer Tuesday to Sunday 9am-12.30pm and 4-7.30pm.

Palazzo della Magnifica Comunita
Cadorina
Piazza Tiziano
32044 Pieve di Cadore (BL)
Open: summer Tuesday to Sunday 9am-12.30pm, 4-7.30pm.

ROUTE 7C
Belluno
Museo Civico
Piazza Duomo
32100 Belluno (BL)

☎ (0437) 24835
Open: April to October, Tuesday to
Sunday 10am-12noon and 3-6pm.

Vittorio Veneto
Museo del Cenedese
1 Piazza Flaminio
31029 Vittorio Veneto (TV)
☎ (0438) 57103
Open: winter daily except Tuesday
2-3pm. Summer daily except
Tuesday 3-4pm.

Museo della Battaglia
Piazza Giovanni Paolo I
31029 Vittorio Veneto (TV)
☎ (0438) 57695
Open: winter Tuesday to Sunday
10am-12noon and 2-5pm. Summer
Tuesday to Sunday 10am-12noon
and 4-6.30pm.

Conegliano
Museo Civico
Piazzale Castelvecchio
31015 Conegliano (TV)
☎ (0438) 22871
Open: winter Tuesday to Sunday
9am-12noon and 2-5.30pm.
Summer Tuesday to Sunday 9am-
12noon and 3.30-7pm.

Casa di Giambattista Cima
24 Via Cima
31015 Conegliano (TV)
☎ (0438) 21660
Open: winter Saturday and Sunday
3-5pm. Summer Saturday and
Sunday 4-6pm.

Treviso
Palzazzo dei Trecento
Piazza Indipendenza
31100 Treviso (TV)
Telo (0422) 541716
Open: Monday to Saturday
8.30am-12.30pm.

Museo Civico Luigi Bailo
22 Borgo Cavour
31100 Treviso (TV)
☎ (0422) 51337
Open: Tuesday to Saturday 9am-
12noon and 2-5pm. Holidays 9am-
12noon.

Tourist Information Centres

ROUTE 7A
Trento
Azienda Autonoma di Soggiorno e
 Turismo
4 Via Alfieri
38100 Trento (TN)
☎ (0461) 983880

Bolzano
Azienda di Soggiorno e Turismo
8 Piazza Walther
39100 Bolzano (BZ)
☎ (0471) 970660 or 975656

ROUTE 7B
Cortina d'Ampezzo
Azienda Autonoma di Soggiorno e
 Turismo
Piazza Roma
32043 Cortina d'Ampezzo (BL)
☎ (0436) 2711

ROUTE 7C
Belluno
Azienda di Promozione Turistica
21 Via R. Psaro
32100 Belluno (BL)
☎ (0437) 940083

Vittorio Veneto
Azienda di Soggiorno e Turismo
Piazza del Popolo
31029 Vittorio Veneto (TV)
☎ (0438) 57243

Treviso
Azienda di Promozione Turistica
 di Treviso
Palazzo Scotti
41 Via Toniolo
31100 Treviso (TV)
☎ (0422) 547632

8

VENICE AND THE VENETIAN PLAIN

Chapter 8 covers Venice and the cities of the Venetian plain. After visiting Venice it heads south through the lagoons to Pomposa, from where it heads inland, making a sweeping arch across the plain, from Ferrara to Verona, after which it returns to Venice via Vicenza and Padua. Each city on the route warrants a day at the very least and visitors short of time are advised to select only those that most take their interest. It is possible to leave chapter 8 at Pomposa to join chapter 9 at Ravenna, or chapter 10 at Pesaro. It is also possible to head to Lake Garda from Verona to join chapter 6.

Route 8a Venice

ITINERARY I

The city of Venice with its decayed splendour is beautiful and hovers almost like a mirage above the surface of the Venetian lagoon. It is built on an archipelago of over one hundred small islets, although much of it is supported on a mass of wooden piles driven into the clay bed of the lagoon.

The first inhabitants of Venice were probably Christians who took refuge here in the fifth century, from the onslaught of the Barbarians. They passed into the control of Constantinople and the Byzantine empire, and had achieved the status of an independent Byzantine Province by the ninth century. This was later to be known as the Republic of the 'Serenissima', which was ruled by a locally elected Doge. The burgeoning city expanded rapidly between the ninth and thirteenth centuries and soon became the capital of the most powerful republic in Italy. It profited from its links with the Byzantine empire in the east Mediterranean, but not content with this, it seized control of all eastern Mediterranean trade after leading the Fourth Crusade on a destructive rampage through Constantinople in 1202. Genoa, the other major maritime power in Italy, vied for control of Mediterranean trade, but was defeated in battle by the Venetian Republic in 1381, giving the Venetians undisputed supremacy of the region for almost another century.

The seeds of Venice's ultimate economic decline were sown at the Ottoman conquest of Constantinople in 1453, and by the opening of the sea-trading routes to the Far East by Vasco da Gama. However, the process was only gradual and during the Renaissance, Venice was of great cultural and artistic importance. The painter Giovanni Bellini (around 1435-1516) was at the forefront of the Venetian Renaissance and was followed by many notable artists.

After the Renaissance, even though the slow drying up of Venice's wealth continued, the city remained culturally important. During the eighteenth century Tiepolo painted his numerous frescoes and Canaletto his views of Venice, while Vivaldi enriched European music with his compositions. Economic recovery was only achieved in the twentieth century, after World War I, with the construction of a new commercial port and the oil refinery at Marghera, as well as the mainland town of Mestre. Venice itself, however, remained relatively neglected up until 1966, when a very high flood focused the attention of the world on the danger facing it. UNESCO, realising the situation was critical initiated a major restoration project.

In the 1970s, it was reported that Venice was sinking and many countries set up funds, such as 'Venice in Peril' in Britain. The situation now is less grave and many valuable art works and fine historical buildings have been restored, although no satisfactory solution has yet been found to prevent the periodic flooding of the city and the salt water continues to corrode brick and damage the porous stonework of the buildings.

At least 3 days should be allowed to visit Venice. There are four itineraries to cover: the first travels along the Grand Canal to St Mark's Square; the second explores the district surrounding St Mark's; the third covers the area to the west of the Grand Canal; and the fourth is made up of boat excursions to the outlying islands. The city is linked to the mainland by a 4km (2 mile) causeway which is crossed by rail and road. Those approaching by car must either park on Piazzale Roma at the city outskirts, or in the carparks on the man-made island just to the west, Isola del Tronchetto, which is linked to Venice by regular ferries. During the summer, extra parking facilities are provided on the mainland with special ferry services operating from San Giuliano, just to the north of the causeway, and Fusina 5km (3 miles) to the south. To avoid the parking problem altogether, particularly in peak season, visitors are well-advised either to approach Venice by boat from Padova, or take one of the trains from Mestre.

Getting around Venice itself is fun, easy and inexpensive as there is an excellent network of *vaporetti* (waterbuses). The Number 1 *vaporetti*, which departs regularly from both Piazzale Roma and Ferrovia (the railway station), follows the Grand Canal to San Marco. There is no more delightful approach to the city centre than this as the boat zig-zags along Venice's widest and busiest canal, which is over 3km (2 miles) long, passing over a hundred palaces, which date from the fourteenth to the eighteenth centuries. One of the first major

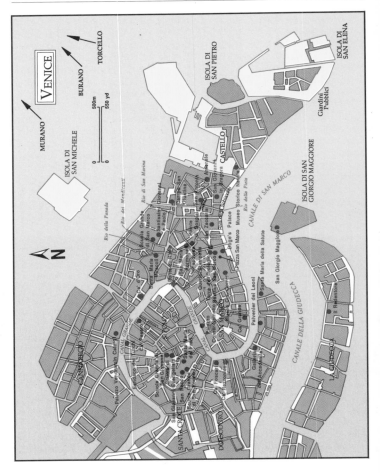

buildings to be passed on the right is the **Fondaco dei Turchi.**
Reconstructed in the original Veneto-Byzantine style of the thirteenth century, it was used as a Turkish warehouse from 1621 up
until 1838, and now houses the Museo di Storia Naturale (Natural
History Museum). Next on the left is the sixteenth-century **Palazzo
Vendramin Calergi** where R. Wagner died in 1883. It has a fine
Renaissance façade which was completed by T. Lombardo, and
contains the Casino Municipale. Roughly 300m (328yd) further on,
just past the San Stae landing stage on the right, which is named after
the Baroque church next to it, is **Ca'Pesaro.** This fine, seventeenth-

Carnival masks in a shop window, Venice

The Rialto Bridge, Venice

century *palazzo*, designed by B. Longhena, and decorated with grotesque masks, contains the Gallery of Modern Art and has a piece of modern sculpture at the waterfront. On the left side of the canal, 100m (110yd) or so further, is the striking Gothic façade of **Ca'd'Oro** which was built in 1425. It is one of the grandest palaces on the canal and houses the Franchetti private collection of art. The right bank of the canal up as far as the Rialto Bridge is filled by a busy market, and the Pescheria, an attractive loggia, is built on the site of the four-teenth-century fish market. The **Rialto Bridge** (Pointe di Rialto) built across a bend in the canal, was constructed in 1592 by A. da Ponte to replace an earlier wooden bridge. The attractive, Renaissance **Palazzo Corner Spinello** (not open to the public) is on the left, roughly 500m (547yd) beyond the bridge. After passing the landing stage at Sant'Angelo on the left, **Ca'Foscari** (not open to the public) is on the right, at the junction of Rio Ca'Foscari, where a large lantern projects from the corner. On the same side, a few blocks further on, is **Ca'Rezzonico**, which was built in the seventeenth century to a design by Longhena and now houses the Museum of Eighteenth-Century Venetian Art. On the right is the **Accademia**, which is the Academy and Gallery of Fine Arts. Shortly after, the canal passes beneath Ponte dell'Accademia, a wooden bridge, constructed in 1932. Some 200m (218yd) beyond the bridge, also on the right, the canal runs by the former home of Peggy Guggenheim, **Palazzo Venier dei Leoni**, which although started in 1749, was never com-pleted, and now houses the Guggenheim Collection of Modern Art. On the opposite side of the canal **Ca'Grande**, the seat of the *prefettura*, is a good example of Sansovino's work; he designed it in 1537. After passing the large Baroque church of Santa Maria della Salute on the right, the *vaporetto* draws up to the landing stage of San Marco.

Climb ashore and walk along the waterfront to **Piazzetta San Marco**, where the pair of granite columns, one surmounted by the winged lion of St Mark and the other a statue of St Theodore, mark, as they have done since the twelfth century, the entrance to the city. To the right, the magnificent pink and white Gothic façade of the Doge's Palace with its tracery balconies looks out over the water, while on the left stands the Libreria Marciana, which was designed by Sansovino (1553) and was praised by Palladio as the finest building erected since ancient times. Walk through the Piazzetta to St Mark's Square, which, even when it is crowded with tourists and souvenir stalls, is a breath-taking sight. Three sides of this vast square are enclosed by the uniform colonnades of the former law-courts which date from the sixteenth and seventeenth centuries, while the fourth side holds the famous **Basilica San Marco.**

The Basilica was built between 1063 and 1073 to house the relics of Mark the Evangelist, which had been taken by the Venetians, earlier in the ninth century, from a tomb in Alexandria. It is designed on a Greek cross ground plan and has five oriental style domes, which, along with the decorative mosaics, are strongly reminiscent of eastern Byzantine architecture.

The rich façade leads into an equally beautiful narthex, or hall, which extends along the front and left side of the basilica and is covered by numerous small domes, each of which holds outstanding, thirteenth-century mosaics. The walls of the narthex are faced with magnificent panels of matched marbles and the floors are covered by excellent, twelfth-century mosaic paving. The originals of the four bronze horses can be seen by climbing up from the narthex through the narrow door to the right of the main entrance. The horses, which date from the fourth century BC, are in the Sala Cavalli at the top of the stairs. From here it is also possible to climb up to a gallery which looks down on the magnificent interior of the Basilica, as well as to get outside onto the loggia where the copies of the horses are, and from where there are fine views over St Mark's Square.

The interior of the Basilica is sumptuously adorned with rare marbles, porphyrys and splendid mosaics on gold grounds. Numerous columns with beautifully-carved capitals support a gallery, formerly reserved for women, which runs right round the cross-shaped interior. There is a dome over each arm of the cross, and the one in the nave is filled by an early twelfth-century mosaic showing the Holy Ghost surrounded by the Apostles. The largest dome is the central one. It holds a mosaic dating from the thirteenth century of the *Ascension*. In the right transept is the dome of St Leonard with a mosaic of four saints, which dates from the early thirteenth century, while in the left transept the dome of St John has a mosaic depicting the *Life of St John the Evangelist*, which dates from the late twelfth century. The mosaic in the dome above the presbytery also dates from the twelfth century and shows *Christ and the Virgin among the Prophets*. The presbytery is divided from the rest of the interior by a colonnaded rood screen of dark marble. The pulpit on the left of the screen is made of precious marbles and is surmounted by a small oriental cupola. The entrance into the presbytery is at the far right end of the screen. It contains the famous **Pala d'Oro**, an extraordinary altarpiece made by goldsmiths in Constantinople in the tenth century and encrusted with precious stones, enamel and gold. The treasury, reached through a door in the right transept, contains other precious objects, made by Byzantine goldsmiths, which were mostly removed from Constantinople in the Fourth Crusade. The baptistery is next door and is entered from the right aisle. It contains a font designed by Sansovino who is also buried here, and fourteenth-century mosaics depicting the *Life of St John the Baptist*.

Outside the Basilica, turn left and enter the **Palazzo Ducale** (Doge's Palace) through the Gothic carved gate, Porta della Carta (1442). The gate leads into a courtyard which is surrounded by the palace on three sides with the Basilica, which was the Doge's private chapel, along the fourth. The palace was the seat of government and the residence of all 120 of Venice's Doges throughout the Republic's history. The present structure dates from the twelfth century, al-

The Basilica San Marco in Venice is adorned with splendid mosaics

The Bridge of Sighs gave prisoners a final chance to view the city of Venice

though it was continuously altered during the 500 years which followed. Cross the courtyard, passing by the Scala dei Giganti on the right,to the ticket office in the left corner. The Scala d'Oro, climbs up to the Atrio Quadrato, a small hall on the third floor with a wooden ceiling painted by Tintoretto. The hall leads into the Sala delle Quattro Porte, which was designed as an ambassador's waiting room by Palladio and contains numerous large paintings including a work by Titian on the right wall. The first door on the left leads through to the Anticollegio where there is a fine fireplace by Scamozzi, and on the wall opposite, Veronese's famous *Rape of Europa*. The room next door, the Sala del Collegio, has a magnificent ceiling also painted by Veronese (around 1577), as is the painting above the throne. Other paintings in this room are of mythological scenes, painted by Tintoretto, amongst others. The Sala del Senato, decorated with *The Triumph of Venice* by Tintoretto, is linked with one of the preceding rooms, the Sala delle Quattro Porte, so head for the door on the opposite side of the room, and enter the Sala del Consiglio. This was the seat of the Council of Ten, a notorious body which may be likened to the modern day secret police, which was responsible for state security. Some of the scenes decorating the ceiling here were painted by Veronese. Continue through to the small room, Sala della Bussola, where a box, the Bocca di Leone, set in the wall to the right of the door was used for secret denunciations. A flight of stairs lead up from here to the Council of Ten's private armoury, from where the Scala dei Censori, another staircase, descends to a vestibule. At the end of the hall on the right is the massive Sala del Maggiore Consiglio, the seat of the Great Council. The painting of *Paradise* by I. and D. Tintoretto (1587-90) on the wall above the throne is said to be the largest oil painting in the world and has impressive dimensions, 7mx22m (23ftx72ft). A passage leads into the basement from here to the prisons and the **Bridge of Sighs**, which was built in the seventeenth century, and offered prisoners their last glimpse of the city before being incarcerated, hence its name.

The vast **Campanile** which towers above St Mark's Square is 99m (325ft) high. Quite unexpectedly, in 1902, it collapsed, but due to public demand was re-erected in the same year. It stands opposite the Basilica and has a fine porch which was designed by Sansovino (1537-49). Pass through the porch to the interior of the tower and take the lift which climbs swiftly to the top, where there is an excellent panorama of the city.

At the far end of St Mark's Square, along the west side, is the **Museo Civico Correr**. The entrance is inside the archway, Sotto Portego San Geminian, on the right. The museum is on the first floor and contains fifty or so rooms filled with paintings by Venetian artists.

ITINERARY II

The second itinerary starts in St Mark's Square, to the left of the Basilica, at the **Torre dell'Orologio** This charming clock tower was built in 1496 and is topped by two brass Moors who strike a large bell on the hour. Pass beneath the tower and follow the Mercerie, a busy shopping street which leads in the direction of the **Rialto bridge**. At the church of San Giuliano, turn right and follow Calle delle Bande to **Santa Maria Formosa**. The church stands on the bank of the small canal of the same name and has an attractive fifteenth-century bell-tower, and a light, airy, cross-shaped interior. Leave the church through the door at the back on the right and cross over the canal to the small gallery, **Pinacoteca Querini Stampalia**, which contains a collection of Venetian paintings.

Return back past the church and cross the square, Campo Santa Maria Formosa, to Calle de Borgo Loco in the far corner. Follow this narrow street, crossing Rio di Paradiso, and passing through Campo Santa Marina. Cross over Rio di Santa Marina, which is lined with gracefully crumbling *palazzi*, before turning left to the beautiful, fifteenth-century church of **Santa Maria Miracoli**.

Head around the back of the church, and cross over the canal, Rio San Canciano, which runs directly beneath its north wall. Continue across the next canal, Rio della Panada, to the attractive bridge, Ponte Cavallo, which straddles Rio dei Mendicanti. The brick façade of Santissimi Giovanni e Paolo is directly ahead, and the **Scuola di San Marco** (not open to the public) with its outstanding Renaissance façade clad in *trompe l'oeil* scenes and relief statues by P. and T. Lombardo, is to the left. **Santissimi Giovanni e Paolo** was built by the Domenican Order between 1234 and 1430, and is one of the earliest Gothic churches in Venice. Its façade was never completed, but a nonetheless fine portal, which incorporates six ancient Greek marble columns, leads into a vast interior lit by rows of long windows that pierce the apse. Five large columns and numerous tombs and funerary monuments belonging to the many doges and patricians that are buried here, line either side of the nave. At the second altar in the right aisle there is a fine polyptych painted by Giovanni Bellini, while a door in the left aisle leads through to the sixteenth-century sacristy. The Cappella del Rosario, in the left transept, has a fine ceiling painted by Veronese of the *Annunciation, Assumption* and *Adoration of the Shepherds*.

Leave the church, and head along its right side, past the equestrian bronze statue of B. Colleoni by Verrochio (1481), and follow Salizada San Zanipolo. This narrow street leads past the magnificent Baroque façade of Santa Maria dei Derelitti, also known as the **Ospedaletto**, (closed to the public). From here follow Barbaria delle Tole, passing through the pleasant square of Campo di San Giustina detto de Barbaria, and crossing Rio di San Giustina to another fine square, Campo San Giustina. After crossing Ponte del Fontego, head south along the network of narrow walkways to **Scuola di San Giorgio**

degli Schiavoni. This small building was founded in 1451 for the
Dalmatian community that lived in Venice at the time. The interior
contains a series of paintings by Carpaccio (1502-8) depicting the
lives of the three Dalmatian patron saints, Jerome, Tryphon and
George.

Continue to head south alongside Rio della Pieta, and turn left past
the church of Sant'Antonin, which is attributed to Longhena, and
follow Saliz Sant'Antonin to Campo Bandiera e Moro. The small
church of **San Giovanni in Bragora**, in the left corner of this square,
was built in 1475 and contains a number of paintings by Cima da
Conegliano and A. Vivarini, as well as the font where Vivaldi was
baptised in 1678.

From the left of the church follow Calle dei Preti for a short way
before turning left along Calle del Pestrin to the Rio dell'Arco. Follow
this canal, past the church of San Martino, to the **Torri di Arsenale.**
The Arsenal is still in military use, but worth pausing to admire the
fine entrance, built in 1460, which is flanked by ancient lions:
Continue past the Arsenal, crossing the wooden bridge, where a pair
of brick towers guard the entrance from the lagoon, and follow the
Fondamenta de l'Arsenale to the **Museo Storico Navale**. The museum
houses a collection of Venetian boats dating from the sixteenth to the
eighteenth century, and a Turkish caique which was used by the Italian
ambassador in Istanbul to cross the Bosphorus up until 1920.

From the square in front of the museum, a pleasant walk can be
made along the waterfront to the attractive public gardens at the
western tip of Venice. Otherwise head back towards the centre along
the wide promenade, known as the Riva degli Schiavoni. It crosses
over three canals before passing by the grand, white stone church,
Chiesa della Pieta, where Vivaldi worked in the eighteenth century.

Continue across the next canal and then take the passage,
Sotoportego San Zaccaria, on the right. It leads into a square which
contains the church of **San Zaccaria** with its thirteenth-century
campanile. The church was built between 1444 and 1515 and contains
a number of fine paintings and frescoes.

Return to Riva degli Schiavoni, from where visitors may wish to
take one of the boat excursions suggested in itinerary IV from the
landing stage of San Zaccaria, which is opposite the passage. Otherwise continue along the promenade across Rio dei Vin. Pause at the
next canal, which runs alongside the Doge's Palace, to see the famous
Bridge of Sighs (Pointe di Sospiri) before reaching the Piazzetta of St
Mark's which is only a few steps further.

ITINERARY III

The third itinerary, which explores the area to the west of the Grand
Canal, starts at the landing stage of San Marco. Take *vaporetto*
Number 1 from here to the impressive church of **Santa Maria della
Salute**, which dominates the entrance to the Grand Canal. It was
built between 1631 and 1681 to a design by B. Longhena which was

based on an octagonal ground plan. The central dome is supported on a high drum which is decorated with giant volutes and statues. The interior has a circular aisle with chapels lining the walls and there is a fine polychrome marble pavement.

Return to the landing stage and continue up the Grand Canal on *vaporetto* Number 1 to Accademia. Those who wish to walk should cross over the canal that runs along the side of the church, Rio dei Salute, passing the church of San Gregorio on the left and continuing westwards behind the Guggenheim collection, before crossing an-

The domes of Basilica San Marco stand over the rooftops of Venice

other canal, Rio San Vio, to the back of the **Galleria dell'Accademia**. This important gallery houses the best collection of fourteenth– to eighteenth-century Venetian art in the world. The paintings are hung in a chronological order in the twenty-four rooms of the former convent and Scuola della Carita.

From the Accademia landing stage, continue up the Grand Canal either on *vaporetto* Number 1 or on foot as far as **Ca'Rezzonico**. This fine *palazzo* is where Robert Browning died in 1889 and is the seat of the Museo dei Settecento Veneziano. The entrance is at the side of the building along the small canal, Rio San Barnaba. The interior, has many fine ceilings frescoed by G.B. Tiepolo and a collection of paintings by other Venetian artists of the era.

Head north of Ca'Rezzonico, crossing over Rio Foscari and follow Calle Larga Foscari to Rio della Frescada. A small square, Campo San Rocco, is on the other side of this canal, behind the great apse of the Frari church. On the south-east side of the square, facing the apse, is the **Scuola Grande di San Rocco,** which was started for the Confraternity of St Roch in 1515, and was completed in 1549 by Scarpagnino who designed the façade. In 1564 Tintoretto began the decoration of its interior and did not finish until 23 years later by which time he had completed over fifty paintings, including some of his greatest works. *The Life of the Virgin*, on the ground floor, was one of the last paintings Tintoretto did at the school, while the *Crucifixion*, upstairs, was the first and is considered to be his masterpiece. There are paintings by other artists too, including the *Dead Christ* by Titian and *Christ Carrying the Cross* by Giorgione.

Before leaving Campo San Rocco, the church of San Rocco, which is next to the Scuola, can be visited to see other paintings by Tintoretto. Leave the square by passing around the apse of Frari and enter its side door. Properly named **Santa Maria Gloriosa dei Frari**, the church was founded by the Franciscans, and built between 1338 and 1443 in the Gothic style. The vast interior contains numerous works of art, amongst the most important of which is Titian's *Assumption* (1518) in the main apse. The third chapel on the left of the main apse contains a triptych of *St Mark Enthroned and Saints* by B. Vivarini (1474). A fine altar-piece by the same artist of the *Virgin with Child and Saints* can be seen in the third chapel on the right of the apse, while the sacristy, next door, contains an excellent triptych painted by Giovanni Bellini (1488). The nave, is divided by four vast columns on either side.

It is worth spending some time wandering about this charming quarter of the city, exploring its little-visited canals and quiet squares. Of particular interest is the attractive, fifteenth-century **Scuola di San Giovanni Evangelista**, on a tiny courtyard to the north of Frari, and Campo San Polo which is to the east of Frari. The Campo, a vast square surrounded by elegant *palazzi*, holds the brick-built church of San Polo and its free-standing *campanile*, which dates from 1362. A finely-carved Gothic portal, opposite the *campanile*, leads into the spacious interior, where the *Marriage of the Virgin* by Veronese can be seen in the left apse chapel, while the oratory (opened by the sacristan) contains the *Stations of the Cross* and has ceiling paintings by G.B. Tiepolo.

ITINERARY IV

A number of pleasant excursions can be made by boat from the landing stage at San Zaccaria which is 250m (264yd) west of Piazzetta San Marco along Riva degli Schiavoni. The shortest is to the island of **San Giorgio Maggiore**, which is reached on *vaporetto* Number 5 (circolare destra). It lies just across the basin of St Mark's and is dominated by the church of San Giorgio Maggiore with its towering *campanile*. The church was begun in 1566 by Palladio and finished in 1610 by S. Sorella. Its white marble, Palladian façade resembles the portico of a temple with four large columns. The simple interior is cruciform in shape and contains two paintings by Tintoretto. The former Benedictine monastery which extends behind the church dates from 1223 and now houses the Giorgio Cini Foundation which is only open when special exhibitions are on display.

Continue on *vaporetto* Number 5 (circolare destra) from San Giorgio Maggiore to **La Giudecca,** a long archipelago composed of eight small islets. A fine promenade skirts its north side from one end to the other and offers fine views across the water to Venice. Roughly midway along the promenade is one of Palladio's most successful churches, **Il Redentore.** It was built between 1575 and 1576 to give thanks for the deliverance of Venice from the plague.

The island of **Murano** is the nearest and most attractive of the islands in the lagoon. It is serviced by *vaporetto* Number 5 (circolare sinistra) which departs from the landing stage at San Zaccaria. On the way, the boat passes through the arsenal and docks, and skirts along the northern edge of the city before heading across the lagoon, past the cemetery which is built on its own island, to the island of Murano where glass has been made for well over 500 years. Get off at the first stop on the island and follow Fondamente dei Vetrai along the edge of a canal which is lined with *fornace*, glass-makers. Most establishments invite tourists in to watch demonstrations of glass-blowing and there is a wide selection of hand-made glass for sale, ranging from strings of beads to stylish modern vases. To see a collection of twentieth-century Murano glass cross the canal on the first bridge, Ponte Santa Chiara, to the Museo Vetrario. Keep your ticket as it is also valid for the other part of the museum, which is reached by continuing along Fondamente dei Vetrai to the main canal. At the junction cross over Ponte Vivarini and turn right along Fondamente Cavour. The museum is roughly 300m (324yd) beyond the bridge, and is housed in five rooms of a fine fifteenth-century *palazzo*. The exhibits include examples of Roman glass as well as locally-made glass dating from the fifteenth to the eighteenth centuries. It is possible to return to San Zaccaria on *vaporetto* Number 5 from the landing stage just outside the museum.

The two other main islands in the lagoon, Burano and Torcello, lie beyond Murano and are about a 45 minute boat-trip from Venice. They are only 10 minutes apart and are both serviced by *vaporetto* Number 12 which departs hourly from Fondamento Nuovo (on the north side of Venice, opposite the cemetery), or from the Faro landing stage on the south side of the island of Murano.

Burano has been a centre of lace-making since the sixteenth century and has numerous shops selling the locally-made lace along its attractive small canals which are lined with colourfully painted houses. While on the island it is also worth visiting the parish church of San Martino to see the painting by G.B. Tiepolo of the *Crucifixion*.

Torcello is the least populated of the lagoon islands and is rather bleak but the cathedral of Santa Maria Assunta, which was built in AD639 when the island had a population of over 20,000, is well-preserved. It is typical of the Veneto-Byzantine style and contains some excellent twelfth-and thirteenth-century mosaics. The nearby church of Santa Fosca is also built in the Veneto-Byzantine style and dates from the tenth century. It is built on an octagonal ground plan and contains beautiful marble columns with finely carved Byzantine capitals.

Route 8B — Venice to Mantua

Leave Venice on the SS309 Romea, following the shores of the Venetian lagoon south for 60km (37 miles) to **Chioggia**. It is built on an island dissected by narrow canals and this, as well as its Venetian style architecture, is why it is often called Little Venice. However, it does not have Venice's grandeur and is better described as an attractive fishing town. It is approached across an impressive causeway and is linked to the mainland by a bridge, Ponte Lungo. Once on the island head for the Duomo, which is a short distance beyond the bridge on the left. First built in the fourteenth century, it was reconstructed in the Baroque style in 1674 by B. Longhena and only the tall *campanile* survives from the original structure.

Follow the main road, Corso del Popolo, north of the Duomo, past the fourteenth-century church, Tempio di San Martino, to the town centre. Park on the large *piazza* opposite the church of San Giacomo, and explore the rest of the town on foot. Head north along Corso del Popolo, a fine pedestrianised street lined with Venetian buildings. Take any one of the narrow lanes off right to see the Canal Vera. Filled with colourful fishing boats and overlooked by attractive buildings, it is the most picturesque of Chioggia's canals.

Sottomarina, reached by a bridge from the east side of town, is Chioggia's beach resort. It has a long sandy beach, good leisure and sports facilities, and a wide promenade.

Return to the mainland and continue south along the SS309 Romea across the Po Delta. The flat land is intensively farmed, the fields being separated by tall poplars, and is criss-crossed by umpteen canals and rivers. The most important of the rivers the road bridges are the Brenta, the Adige, the Po, and the Po di Goro which forms the boundary between the Po Delta and Rovigo regions. After passing the town of **Mesola**, 33km (20 miles) south of Chioggia, look out for Castello Estense di Mesola on the right. It was built between 1578 and 1583 for Alfonso II, the last Este duke of Ferrara, but the lodge (Castello Estense) is open to the public during peak season only. The ducal hunting ground, Boscone di Mesola, lies to the left of the road. The forest, which stretches as far as the coast, covers over 1,000 hectares (2,470 acres), and is now a nature reserve.

The vast *campanile* of **Pomposa** abbey punctuates the horizon, 11km (7 miles) south of Mesola. Originally founded by Benedictine monks in the sixth century, the abbey was expanded in the eleventh century and reached the peak of its importance in the fourteenth. It was of short lived importance, for within the next hundred years the abbey fell into a decline as malaria from the surrounding marshes took its toll, the last monks retreating to Ferrara in 1496. The Palazzo della Ragione at the abbey gate was built in the eleventh century as the monks' court of justice. It has an attractive loggia and now contains an exhibition centre and information office. Continue along the path to the abbey, pausing to admire its fine Lombard *campanile*. Built in 1063 and having nine storeys, it stands to a height of 48m (157ft). The abbey façade, has an attractive tenth-century porch

Chioggia is often called Little Venice

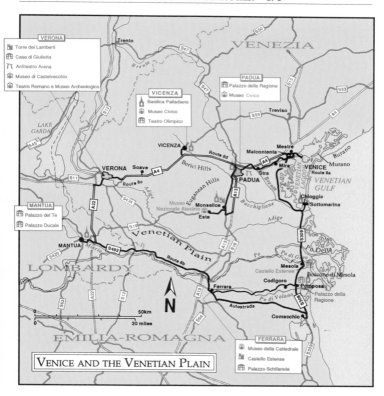

VENICE AND THE VENETIAN PLAIN

which is decorated with terracotta reliefs and carvings. The interior is made up of a large central nave lined with Roman and Byzantine columns and the walls are decorated with fourteenth-century frescoes by the Bolognese school. The best are by Vitale da Bologna (1351) in the apse.

The courtyard along the right side of the abbey also contains fine buildings. The Sala Capitolare at the far end has a fourteenth-century fresco of the *Crucifixion*, while the refectory on the right contains *La Cena di San Guido*. Musicians might be interested to note that San Guido d'Arezzo, who is remembered for inventing the musical scale, was a monk here in the eleventh century.

The next place of interest along the route is Ferrara. The quickest route there is along the SS309 Romea south to **Comacchio**, from where the motorway, a short *autostrada* link, can be joined. A more scenic, and also slightly shorter route (50km/31 miles), leads west from Pomposa through **Codigoro**, along the course of the Po di Volano river.

Ferrara, seat of the Este dukes for nearly 400 years, is a prosperous industrial and agricultural city, well known for its fruit market. Once through the inevitable modern developments which girth the city, either follow signposts to one of the small carparks in the centre where parking is restricted to 2 hours, or park outside the south city wall on Viale Kennedy, near Porta Reno.

The first place to visit is the Cattedrale at the heart of the city. Built in 1135, it has a beautiful façade of pink and white marble. The lower part is Romanesque and the upper Gothic, but the two styles are united by the vertical division of the façade into three parts. The loggia above the central porch dates from the fourteenth century and contains a statue of the *Madonna and Child* by C. da Firenze (1427). To its left is a statue of Alberto d'Este (1393), while above are the carved reliefs of the *Last Judgement*, which date from the thirteenth century. The porch, flanked by lions supporting columns, gives entrance to a narthex, or hall, from where steps climb up into the dark but richly decorated interior of the Cattedrale. The first chapel on the right contains a *Madonna and Child*, a fragment of a fifteenth-century fresco. Far more impressive is the fresco in the main apse, the *Last Judgement*, which dates from 1580 and is the work of Bastianino. In the chapel, to the right of the apse, is a large bronze *Crucifixion* (1678), flanked by statues of St George and San Maurelio which date from the fifteenth century, and are by D. Paris. Other works of art from the cathedral are housed in the Museo della Cattedrale, the entrance of which is in the narthex. It contains paintings, tapestries, statues and carvings, as well as a collection of illuminated manuscripts.

The Cattedrale is in a lovely part of the city. Do not miss Piazza Trento Trieste, to the right, a lively area of cafés and market stalls, and Piazza Municipio, opposite. It is also worth wandering around the medieval quarter to the south of the Cattedrale, especially along Via delle Volte, a street with well-preserved vaults and arches.

Castello Estense, Ferrara's other major monument, is north of the Cattedrale. Follow Corso Manzoni della Liberta, and turn left through the arches to Piazzetta del Castello. Surrounded by a moat and guarded by a tower at each of its four corners, the castle was built in 1385 for the Este dukes. Drawbridges on the north and south sides lead into a central courtyard, on the west side of which is the museum. In the basement are the medieval jails; above them the ducal apartments. The rooms of the apartments are frescoed, the most important being those in the Sala dell'Aurora (Room of Dawn), the Saletta and Salone dei Giochi (Games' Rooms). They date from the sixteenth century and are by Ferrarese artists, including Bastianino. The duchess' apartments include a small orangery and the Cappella di Renata di Francia. Renata di Francia was the daughter of the French king, Louis XII who married the Este duke Ercole II.

Other places of interest in Ferrara are further out from the centre and are perhaps best visited by car. Palazzo dei Diamanti is 450m (492yd) north of the *castello* along Corso Ercole d'Este. The *palazzo* was built in 1492 by Biagio Rossetti and derives its name from its façade, which is decorated with a diamond pattern, the Este emblem. The *palazzo* houses the Pinacoteca Nazionale, which has a fine collection of Ferrarese art, dating from the thirteenth to eighteenth centuries. The thirteenth-century frescoes taken from now demolished local churches are of particular interest, as is the collection of sixteenth-century paintings by Garofalo and Dosso Dossi.

Palazzo Schifanoia is at the opposite side of town, close to Piazzale Medaglie d'Oro. On foot it is best to head east from the Cattedrale along Via Voltapaletto, past the brick church of San Franceso. This church contains sixteenth-century frescoes. Continue east along Via Savonarola, past Casa Romei on the right. This typical fifteenth-century house is preserved as a museum. At the end of the street turn right along Via Madama before turning left at the Baroque church of Santa Maria in Vado.

Palazzo Schifanoia was built in 1385 for Alberto d'Este, but modified between 1466 and 1493 by Ferrara's prolific architect, B. Rossetti. It contains an interesting museum and numerous frescoes, the most important of which is the cycle in the Sala dei Mesi. They have deteriorated since they were first painted in the fifteenth century by Ferrarese artists, including F. del Cossa, but are still an important Renaissance work. It is just possible to distinguish the scenes; those of courtly life along the lower walls, representations of the twelve months above, and astrological and classical scenes around the top. Amongst the exhibits in the second room, are seven small alabaster panels, carved in Nottingham and presented by the British Embassy to the Este dukes in the fifteenth century. The third room contains a painting, made as a copy of the Sala dei Mesi frescoes, in 1901 by Mazzolano. Other rooms contain paintings, ceramics and glassware, mainly from the fifteenth century.

Another *palazzo* built by B. Rossetti, Palazzo di Ludovico il Moro, lies 300m (328yd) due south of Palazzo Schifanoia. It houses an archaeological museum, containing finds from the necropolis of *Spina*, near Comacchio. Those still left with time and energy may like to make the walk around the city walls which are 9km (6 miles) in length. The best section is through the park, between Porta Santa Maria degli Angeli and Porta Romana.

Take the SS482 from Ferrara to Mantua 89km (55 miles) to the north-west. It is an easy drive, through a flat cultivated landscape, following the north bank of the River Po for most of the way. The last part of the journey follows the River Mincio, a tributary of the Po, which widens into a string of lakes that almost surround the city. Ponte San Giorgio crosses Lago Inferiore, the easternmost of the lakes, to Castello di San Giorgio, where it is best to park.

Mantua's most impressive monuments date from the reign of the Gonzaga family, a dynasty that ruled the city from 1328 to 1708. At its heyday during the Renaissance, it was one of the greatest courts in Europe, and patronised artists such as G. Romano, a pupil of

Raphael, in the early part of the sixteenth century. Castello di San Giorgio, is part of the massive Gonzaga residence, Palazzo Ducale. It was built in the late fourteenth century by Bartolino da Novara and contains a notable Renaissance fresco by Mantegna in the Camera degli Sposi, which was painted between 1465 and 1474. The main part of Palazzo Ducale, just south, is built around no less than fifteen courtyards and has over 500 rooms. It dates from the sixteenth century when Isabella d'Este was the envy of court society. Guided tours, which last about 2 hours, can be made of the interior. The highlights are the Archers' Saloon with its works by Rubens, the Tapestry Room where some of the tapestries are to designs by Raphael, the Sala dei Principi with its red sinopia sketches by Pisanello and the Summer Apartment, decorated with frescoes by G. Romano, and containing a collection of ancient statues.

Piazza Sordello, along the north-west side of Palazzo Ducale, is the largest *piazza* in the city. The Duomo, at the northern end, is neo-Classical, although the massive *campanile* is a remnant of the Romanesque building that once stood here. Head south of Piazza Sordello to Piazza delle Erbe, where the arcades of the medieval buildings which surround it are filled with busy cafés. Head for the small brick rotunda in the south corner, which dates from 1082, and is decorated with columns, typical of the Romanesque style. Next to the rotunda stands the thirteenth-century Palazzo della Ragione. It has a fine façade of mullioned windows and fish-tailed crenellations, as well as a beautiful clock tower with the signs of the zodiac painted on its face. The medieval Broletto, which encloses a charming courtyard, is joined to the northern end of Palazzo della Ragione. It dates from the twelfth century, although it was largely rebuilt in the fifteenth.

In the small adjoining square, Piazza Mantegna, is the church of Sant'Andrea. It was designed for the Gonzaga family in 1472 by Leon Battista Alberti, although the vast dome was not added until 1782. The Baroque interior is cruciform in shape and is mainly of interest for the small chapel near the entrance which contains the tomb of Andrea Mantegna. This famous Renaissance painter, born in Mantua, died in 1606. His bust stands near the tomb.

The Gonzaga family built their summer palace, Palazzo del Te, at the south side of the city. It is clearly signposted and is best reached by car. It was built in the Mannerist style by G. Romano between 1525 and 1535, and encloses a series of courtyards. Set in magnificent gardens, the interior of the one-storey building adorned with frescoes by Romano. The finest are in the Sala dei Cavalli, Sala della Zodiaco, Sala dei Banchetti, Sala delle Aquile and the vaults of the Loggia d'Onore. The interior also houses a collection of local twentieth-century paintings in the Galleria Civica d'Arte Moderna.

Route 8C — Mantua to Vicenza

Leaving Mantua, head north on the A22 *autostrada* for 28km (17 miles) to **Verona**. Although it is one of the busiest inland ports in Italy and surrounded by industrial outskirts, Verona is a fine city and possesses a beautiful historic centre, contained within a fortified wall and a deep bend of the Adige river. Some of the city's monuments date back to the Romans who established a colony here in 89BC, but Verona is predominantly a medieval city and was the setting for the vendetta between the Capulets and Montagues in Shakespeare's *Romeo and Juliet* (1302). The city was dominated by rival families, such as the Scaliger, Visconti and Carrara, and there was never much stability until the Venetian empire put an end to family feuding and endowed the city with its fine Renaissance architecture, built with the pink Veronese stone.

The main parking areas are outside the city wall near Porta Nuova and Porta Palio, a 20-minute walk from the centre. Piazza Erbe has been the centre of the city since Roman times when it was the site of the forum, but there are no ancient remains to be seen and the *piazza* now holds a lively and colourful market. At the south-eastern end is the sixteenth-century rostrum which was used by the city governors to address the public. In the centre is the Fontana di Madonna Verona, an elegant fountain erected in 1386, while in the north-western end is the winged lion of Venice (1523), which looks down from the top of a fluted column. Behind it is the Baroque Palazzo Maffei and to the right the beautifully frescoed façade of Casa Mazzanti, which dates from the sixteenth century. In the corner to the left is Torre del Gardello, a brick tower which was built in 1370. Return to the rostrum, passing the Casa dei Mercanti, which can be identified by its crenellated top and arcaded basement, to the start of Via Cappello. Follow the street for 120m (131yd) to number 23, the Casa di Giulietta, Juliet's House. It is not difficult to identify as there is usually a crowd outside, gathered to see the lovers' balcony.

Return to the *piazza* and pass through Arco della Costa, an arch-way leading off to the right into another fine square, Piazza Signoria. The *piazza* has been the administrative centre of the city since the eleventh century and has preserved its medieval character. Palazzo della Ragione, on the right, dates from the twelfth century and its tower, Torre dei Lamberti, standing at a height of 84m (275ft) is the tallest in Verona. It can be ascended from a charming courtyard inside the *palazzo*. The building on the left side of the *piazza* is the fifteenth-century Loggia del Consiglio, built in the Venetian-Renaissance style, and the finely crenellated building on the far side is the Palazzo del Governo, where Dante, whose statue stands at the centre of the *piazza*, stayed as a guest.

Take Via Santa Maria Anticha, along the right side of Palazzo del Governo, to Arche Scaligere, the monumental tombs built for the Scaliger family. Surrounded by a fourteenth-century wrought iron screen, the tombs are carved in the Gothic style, the most elaborate being that of Cansignorio who died in 1375. It is adorned with statues and carvings by Bonino da Campione, one of the best fourteenth-century stone masons. Continue beyond the tombs to the end of the street and turn left along Via Duomo. After a short distance Sant'Anastasia is reached. It is a vast Gothic basilica, built for the Domenican order between 1290 and 1481, and has a fourteenth-century portal with carved reliefs and a tall *campanile*. The spacious interior, lit by stained-glass windows, is typically Domenican, having a deep apse with two chapels on either side. The first chapel on the right, Cappella Pellegrini contains twenty-four terracotta reliefs by Michele da Firenze (1435). The second chapel holds frescoes by Altichiero (1395).

Continue for 150m (164yd) along Via Duomo to the Duomo itself, which is set in a *piazza* at the end. Its distinctive *campanile* was designed by Sammicheli in the sixteenth century, but the Duomo itself dates from the twelfth century, although it was greatly altered in the fifteenth. Its attractive façade of pink and white stone is decorated with twelfth-century reliefs and has the original portal, which is flanked by griffins supporting columns. The massive interior is divided into three wide aisles by pink stone columns. Fresco fragments decorate the walls, the best of which are in the apse, behind Sammicheli's colonnaded screen, which was added in 1534.

Other places of interest in Verona lie at the opposite end of the city, some 500m (547yd) south of Piazza Erbe. The monuments are fairly spread out and visitors may wish to continue their tour by car. The focal point of this part of the city is Piazza Bra, the site of the Roman arena. Dating from the first century, the arena is the largest and best-preserved in Italy, and provides a dramatic venue for productions of Shakespeare, as well as opera, during the summer. Its massive exterior wall stands on 72 arches, while the interior contains 44 tiers of seating, with a capacity of 25,000 spectators. At the south end of the *piazza* there is a small public garden, to the left of which stands the Palazzo Municipale. Designed by Barbieri, it was built in 1838 during the Austrian occupation of the city.

The interesting church of San Fermo Maggiore can be visited by following Via dei Alpini, behind Palazzo Municipale and turning left down Strada San Fermo. Follow the street for 400m (437yd) to the church, which stands at the end on the right. It was originally founded by the Benedictine Order in the eleventh century, but is built in two distinct styles, Gothic and Romanesque. The main portal, patterned with pink and white stone, leads into a spacious interior made up of a single nave with a fine fourteenth-century wooden ceiling. The nave is beautifully decorated with frescoes dating from the fourteenth and fifteenth centuries and has a fine pulpit carved from pink marble. There is also a good painting by G.F. Caroto (1528) at the main altar. A door on the right leads down through the cloisters to the original church, the Chiesa Inferiore, which is filled with pillars. The walls of the church have the faint remains of eleventh- to thirteenth-century frescoes.

Return to Piazza Bra and cross it, passing the public gardens, to

Portoni di Bra, the fine double gate in the corner, which was originally built in 1389. Take Via Roma to the right of the gate, and follow it for 320m (350yd) to the walls of Castelvecchio. This well-preserved stronghold was built for the Scaliger family in 1354 and is situated on the banks of the river. It is defended by a moat, seven towers and row upon row of fish-tailed crenellations. Part of the castle houses the Museo Civico d'Arte, which contains paintings and sculptures by the Veronese school, dating from the twelfth to sixteenth centuries, and includes works by well-known Venetian artists such as Tintoretto and Tiepolo. Walk around the back of the castle to the fortified bridge which spans the river. It has high crenellated walls on either side, but there are excellent views from the sentry posts. The basilica of San Zeno Maggiore is visible on the left.

San Zeno Maggiore lies 800m (850yd) east of Castelvecchio. It is best reached by following Rigaste San Zeno, the road along the river bank, before turning left along Via Barbarani to Piazza San Zeno. The basilica is one of the finest of the Lombard-Romanesque churches in Northern Italy and has a beautiful twelfth-century rose window in its façade. The tall, striped *campanile* which stands to the right side was built in the eleventh century, while the reliefs on either side of the main portal date from 1138. The bronze doors, cast in the eleventh century, but enlarged in the twelfth, have scenes depicting the life of St Zeno and stories from the Old and New Testaments. The interior, divided into three naves with a raised presbytery in the apse, is decorated with the remains of frescoes dating from the thirteenth to fifteenth centuries. It also has a decorated ceiling which was put up in 1386. The most outstanding work of art, however, is the altar painting on the left side of the presbytery. This extraordinarily beautiful triptych by Mantegna depicts the *Madonna and Saints* and dates from 1459. A door in the left aisle leads into the cloisters, which, dating from the twelfth to fourteenth centuries, surround a courtyard with a row of double columns, and have a loggia on one side.

Visitors who have the time can visit Castel San Pietro and the Roman theatre on the north bank of the Adige river, opposite Sant'Anastasia. The theatre, built into the hillside in the first century, and still used for theatrical performances during the summer festival, overlooks the river. A lift climbs the hill above the theatre to San Girolamo, a former monastery which now houses the local archaeological museum. Castel San Pietro, built for the Visconti family, is at the top of the hill and has excellent views of the city.

Leave Verona on the A4 *autostrada* to Vicenza, 51km (32 miles) to the east, passing by the attractive hill town of **Soave**, 23km (14 miles) east of Verona, which gives its name to a well-known white wine. **Vicenza** lies at the confluence of two rivers, the Retrone and Bacchiglione, at the edge of the Venetian plain, on the gentle slopes of the Berici hills. The Romans, who established a settlement here in 49BC, called the town *Vicetia* and in the Middle Ages it was the seat of the Lombard dukes. Vicenza as it stands today, however, is the foundling of the Venetian empire. The great Renaissance architect, Palladio, was born in Vicenza in 1508 and went on to endow his city with a wealth of outstanding architecture. When in 1603 Inigo Jones visited Vicenza he was so taken with the appearance of the city that he used it as a model for a new architectural style that was to spread throughout Europe and America, the Palladian style.

The city centre is pedestrianised and there are several small carparks dotted around its small squares. The largest parking area, however, is near the stadium, just under a kilometre south-east of the city centre. It is linked to the centre by a shuttle bus service, which leaves every 5 to 10 minutes. The first place to head for is Basilica Palladiano on Piazza dei Signori, which is considered by many to be Palladio's masterpiece. This vast basilica has a high green roof, and is more reminiscent of a town hall than a church, which is exactly what it was in the fifteenth century before Palladio re-designed it. The basilica, built between 1549 and 1614, is on the first floor, above an arcaded basement containing shops and market stalls. Climb up the steps at the south end, and enter the basilica from the loggia. The interior is vast, with a tall wooden ceiling shaped like the hull of a boat. The loggia, which runs right round the basilica, looks down on Piazza delle Erbe, with its colourful flower market, on the south side, and offers a fine view of Piazza dei Signori on the north.

The tower at the northern corner of the basilica is the Torre di Piazza. It was constructed during the twelfth century, but only reached its present height of 82m (269ft) during the fifteenth. Close to it at one end of Piazza dei Signori stand a pair of Venetian columns, one of which bears the lion of St Mark (1473). Also on the *piazza*, but opposite the basilica, is the sixteenth-century Palazzo del Monte di Pieta with the small Baroque church of San Vincenzo (1617) built into its façade. At the west end of the *piazza* is the Loggia del Capitanio, designed by Palladio in 1571, but never completed.

Leave Piazza dei Signori from the west side, and head for the Duomo, which is 150m (164yd) due west. It has an attractive façade, patterned with pink and white stone, which was designed by Domenico da Venezia in 1467. The *campanile* is Romanesque and dates from the eleventh century, while the apse is a Renaissance addition. The interior, with its single nave and high vaulted ceiling is lined with chapels on either side. In the third chapel on the left is a painting by B. Montagna, and in the fifth on the right, a polyptych by Lorenzo Veneziano (1356).

About 150m (164yd) further west from the Duomo stands a tall, crenellated tower which guards the city gate, Porta Castello. From here return in the direction of the city centre along Corso Palladio, turning left after 200m (218yd) down Corso Fogazzaro. Continue down it for roughly 200m (218yd) to the church of San Lorenzo, which was founded by the Franciscan order in the thirteenth century. It has a richly carved portal dating from 1344 and ancient sarcophagi are set into the wall on either side. The interior is crowded with columns and contains numerous altars and funerary monuments dating from the fourteenth to sixteenth centuries. In the chapel to the left of the apse there is a fresco by B. Montagna.

Return to Corso Palladio and continue along it, past Palazzo del Comune at number 98, which was designed by Scamozzi in 1592. A little further along the street, Contra Porti, a fine street of medieval and Renaissance houses leads off to the left. Head down it to see Palazzo Porto Barbaran (1570) and Palazzo Iseppo da Porto (1552), both designed by Palladio. Return to Corso Palladio and continue past the fifteenth-century Palazzo da Schio, which has a collection of ancient inscription stones in its hallway. Take the next left turn, Contra Santa Corona to the church of Santa Corona. Originally founded by the Domenican order in 1261, it contains many notable works of art. In the third chapel on the right is an excellent *Adoration of the Magi* painted by Veronese in 1573, and in the fourth, Cappella del Rosano, there is a magnificent ceiling covered with 34 panels, which were painted between 1556 and 1630, by artists from the Maganza school. At the fifth altar on the left is a fine painting by G. Bellini of the *Baptism of Christ*, while to the left of the main apse is another good painting, the *Crown of Thorns* by Fentorello, which

Teatro Olimpico courtyard at Vicenza is lined with statues

dates from the fifteenth century. The main altar, in the raised presbytery, dates from 1670 and is decorated with intricately inlaid stone panels. The three statues adorning the altar date from the sixteenth century. Behind the altar are the choir stalls, which date from 1482 and are also handsomely inlaid. Steps lead beneath the apse to a large chapel, designed by Palladio in 1481.

Return to Corso Palladio and continue to Piazza Matteoti at the end of the street. Palazzo Chiericati, on the right, was designed by Palladio between 1550 and 1557, and is now the seat of the Museo Civico. Pass through the grand classical façade into a hallway hung with portraits, off which is the Sala Marchese with its fine ceiling by Antonio Roi. The museum has twelve spacious rooms and surrounds a courtyard. It contains a well-displayed collection of works of art dating from the fourteenth to eighteenth centuries, many by the Venetian school. Look out for the *Crucifixion* by H. Memling in room 5, and the excellent collection of paintings by B. Montagna in rooms 7 and 8. Room 9, the Palladian room, is a recent addition and contains fine frescoes as well as paintings by G. Fasolo and Fontana. Room 11 contains later Venetian paintings, including works by Tintoretto and Veronese. Room 12 has paintings by Vicenzan painters, such as the Bassano family. On the ground floor, Sala del Firmamento, with a fine frescoed ceiling (1516-67), is passed on the way to the exit.

Cross over the road from the museum to the Teatro Olimpico. A gate leads into a gravel courtyard lined with statues, at the far side of which is the entrance to the theatre. Designed by Palladio in 1580, it was his last major work. The architect died, aged 72, before it was completed, leaving the project in the hands of V. Scamozzi. It mimics the style of a classical theatre, but is constructed of wood and stucco rather than stone. The stage set has a triumphal arch at the centre, with streets painted in perspective on either side. The busts adorning the middle level of the façade are portraits of members of the Accademia Olimpica, the founding body of the theatre. It is still used for performances today, and sitting in the cavea beneath a *trompe l'oeil* painted sky, it is easy to imagine that one is really sitting in an ancient Greek or Roman theatre.

Before leaving Vicenza a short excursion can be made to the Santuario di Monte Berico, on a hilltop to the south of the city. It is reached along Viale X Giugno which is lined with porticoes and chapels dating from the eighteenth century. The basilica with its distinctive dome was founded in 1426, but largely rebuilt between 1688 and 1703. In the former refectory, the Sala di Quadro, is a magnificent fresco by Veronese of the *Supper of St Gregory the Great*.

It is also worth making the excursion 2km (1 mile) south of Vicenza along the SS247, to Villa Valmarana, which was built in 1668 and contains frescoes by G. Tiepolo. Villa Rotonda nearby was designed by Palladio in 1550 and finished by V. Scamozzi. Unfortunately only the grounds of the Rotonda are open to the public, nonetheless the classical exterior of this, one of Palladio's finest villas is worth seeing.

Route 8D — Vicenza to Venice

Take the A4 *autostrada* from Vicenza to **Padua** (known as Padova in Italian), which lies 30km (19 miles) to the east. The ever-expanding industrial suburbs which surround the city have brought it wealth, but it is also a city of great historical importance and has many fine monuments. The earliest settlement dates back to the fourth century BC, when it was settled by an Iron Age people, the Veneti, also known as the Atestines. It was a Roman municipality from as early as 45BC, and remained under their control until AD602 when it was burnt down by the Lombards. During medieval times, Padua was dominated by a succession of feuding families, such as the La Scala, Carrara and Visconti, but nonetheless passed through a period of great artistic and cultural florescence. Padua university, one of the earliest and most famous in Europe, was founded in 1222 and had soon employed Galileo, Dante and Petrarch as lecturers.

The modern day city is well organised. Large carparks are clearly signposted around the outskirts, and are linked by regular bus services to the centre. Carparks 2 and 3, to the north of the city, are the most convenient for visiting the centre. Start a tour of the city in the centre, on Piazza Erbe, which like so many of the squares in the city contains a daily market. On the north side of the *piazza* stands Palazzo della Ragione, originally built as the law court in 1218. It was enlarged by the addition of a loggia and a high roof, by Giovanni degli Eremitani in 1306. On the first floor the vast hall, Il Salone, is decorated with frescoes, generally attributed to Giotto and school. The originals were, however, destroyed by fire in 1420 and those seen today are fifteenth-century copies. In the arcaded basement beneath the *palazzo* is a covered market with a wide passage passing through it that links Piazza Erbe to Piazza Frutta.

Head left across Piazza Frutta to Piazza dei Signori, which is surrounded by numerous fine buildings. The Palazzo del Capitanio on the left is the most outstanding. It dates from the sixteenth century and has an attractive porch designed by G. Falconetto. There is a beautifully painted clock face on its sturdy tower, the Torre dell'Orologio, which dates from 1427.

Follow Via Dante south out of Piazza dei Signori for 100m (110yd) to the Duomo, passing Loggia della Gran Guardia (1496-1523) and the seventeenth-century façade of Palazzo del Monte di Pieta on the way. The Duomo itself is rather unimpressive with its plain brick façade, but standing next to it in Piazza Duomo is a circular baptistery which dates from the twelfth century and contains a fresco cycle by Guisto de Manabuoi (1376-8).

The next major place of interest, the Cappella degli Scrovegni, is a 10-minute walk north of the city centre and some visitors may prefer to take their cars. To reach it on foot return to Piazza Frutta and head past the *municipio* to Corso Garibaldi. Turn left up Corso Garibaldi to Piazza Cavour. It is worth pausing briefly here as on Piazzetta

Pedrochi, off one side of Piazza Cavour, is the Caffe Pedrocchi, famous for the student uprisings that were started here in 1848. Continue north from Piazza Cavour to Piazza Garibaldi, crossing straight over it to Chiesa degli Eremitani, which is a short distance further on the right. The church, almost flattened by allied bombs in 1944, has been excellently restored, although few of the original frescoes have survived. It was first built in 1276, but the church was not finished until Fra Giovanni degli Eremitani took over the works in 1306. The massive interior, made up of a single nave, is lined with fourteenth- to sixteenth-century tombs and altars. Fresco remnants decorate the three chapels on the right, while in the Ovetari chapel, there are detached frescoes by A. Mantegna (1448-57) of the *Assumption* and the *Lives of St Christopher and St James*. The main apse contains the best of the frescoes, which were painted in the Giottesque style by Guariento and Guisto in the fourteenth century.

Next to the church, the cloisters of the former Eremitani monastery now house the Museo Civico and the Cappella degli Scrovegni. The museum is arranged around a courtyard on three floors. The ground floor contains a collection of archaeological finds from various locations, which range from Egyptian to early Venetian artefacts. On the first floor is Museo Bottacin, a private collection of Roman coins and nineteenth-century Venetian paintings, which was donated by Nicolo Bottacin in 1865. The second floor houses the Museo d'Arte Mediovale e Moderna. Most of the collection is made up of Venetian paintings dating from the fourteenth to nineteenth centuries, but there are also a number of Renaissance bronzes.

A footpath leads from the museum foyer to the Cappella degli Scrovegni. This small chapel, originally built in 1303 as part of the Scrovegni family estate, is entirely covered by one of Italy's most hotly disputed fresco cycles. Who was it painted by? It has long been attributed to Giotto, but scholars have pointed out the discrepancies in style between it and the other major fresco cycle attributed to Giotto at Assisi. Painted between 1303 and 1305, the frescoes in the chapel are nonetheless remarkable. There are thirty-six panels, arranged in three layers, depicting scenes from the life of Mary and Christ, with the *Last Judgement* above the main door.

Outside the museum, on the *piazza* in front of the chapel are the remains of the Roman amphitheatre. It was originally built in AD60 and today the ruins are incorporated into the public gardens, the Giardini dell'Arena.

Padua's other major monument, the Basilica of Sant'Antonio, lies just over a kilometre to the south of the museum. Visitors may wish to go there by car, parking on Prato della Valle, near the basilica. Visitors on foot should retrace their steps along Corso Garibaldi, and turn left down Via San Francesco, a short distance past the *municipio*. The street leads through Piazza Sant'Antenore, where a thirteenth-century sarcophagus, commemorates Antenore, the mythical founder of Padua. Shortly after passing the tomb, turn right down Via del Santo, a porticoed street, lined with shops selling religious souvenirs. The street ends at Piazza del Santo, opposite Donatello's bronze equestrian statue, the Erasmo da Narni (1453), which is dedicated to Gattamelata. Rising from the *piazza* behind the statue, the high bulbous domes of the basilica are reminiscent of eastern architecture, and the tall, spindly bell towers have more than a passing resemblance to the minarets of a mosque. Built between 1232 and 1307 to house the mortal remains of St Anthony, the basilica attracts a steady stream of pilgrims as well as tourists. The façade of brick and stone leads into a richly decorated interior. Divided by massive pillars into three naves, galleries encircle the upper walls, and shallow transepts extend on either side of the walled presbytery. Gattamelata's tomb, seen in the first chapel on the right, dates from the fifteenth century. Further along, the transept on the right, has pointed arches, around its upper walls, each containing a frescoed scene from the *Legend of San Giacomo*, by Jacopo Avanzo (1397), while the end wall of the transept holds a large fresco of the *Crucifixion*. The doorway on the right leads to the cloisters. The apse, behind the presbytery, contains five chapels which are connected by an ambulatory. The central chapel contains the basilica treasury and relics of St Anthony. In the left transept is the Cappella di Sant'Antonio, added between 1500 and 1549, with an ornate gilded stucco ceiling

In Italy, market squares are not the only place where people buy and sell

by Falconetto (1533). The chapel contains St Anthony's well-attended tomb, and the walls are decorated with nine stone reliefs depicting the life of the saint, all of which date from the sixteenth century. The presbytery, contained within its wall of red marble, has bronzes by Donatello (1443-50) and stone reliefs depicting the miracle of St Anthony.

On the *piazza* to the right of Sant'Antonio is the Scuola di Sant'Antonio. It was built in 1427 for the brotherhood of St Anthony, and the chapterhouse on the first floor contains an impressive cycle of frescoes, by various sixteenth-century artists including Titian, Filippo da Verona and B. Montagna. On the same side of the *piazza* is the Museo Civico. The permanent collection has mostly been moved to the new premises on Piazza Eremitani but a good collection of eighteenth-century Venetian paintings and sculptures remain.

From the corner of the *piazza*, next to the museum, take Via Belludi to Prato Della Valle. Originally the site of the Roman theatre, this vast area was left as marshland until 1775 when it was reclaimed and made into a park. The gardens are encircled by a canal which is lined with 78 statues of Paduan nobles. At the south side of the park is the sixteenth-century basilica of Santa Giustina, which is similar in style to Sant-Antonio, while on the west side is the Loggia Amulea, an elegant nineteenth-century arcade, built in the Venetian style.

An easy excursion can be made from Padua to the Venetian castles of Monselice and Este. Leave Padua on the A13 *autostrada* and head south for 22km (14 miles) to **Monselice**. On a slope of the Euganean hills, above the town, lie the *castello*, the Duomo Vecchio, and Villa Duodo. Park at the bottom of the hill on Piazza Mazzini and walk up to the *castello* on the left, which can only be visited by taking a guided tour. It contains a collection of medieval and Renaissance art work, and is in two parts: the thirteenth-century Palazzo di Ezzelino, and the fifteenth-century Palazzo del Marcello. From the *castello* continue up the cobbled hillside to the Duomo Vecchio on the right. Built in 1256 in the Romanesque style, the interior contains fifteenth-century frescoes by the Venetian school. Continuing still further uphill, through a gateway flanked by lions, the road is lined with seven small chapels, known as the Santuario Sette Chiese. They were designed by V. Scamozzi between 1593 and 1611, and represent the stages of the cross. Villa Duodo, at the top of the road is not open to the public, but offers good views of the surrounding countryside from its well-kept terrace.

To reach **Este**, follow the SS10 east from Monselice for 9km (6 miles). The town is named after the Este family, the Dukes of Ferrara, who ruled one of the largest north Italian principalities until the Venetian empire gained the upper hand. The main attractions of the town are its excellent fortified wall and Museo Nazionale Atestino, which are both at the western end of town. The museum is housed in the sixteenth-century Palazzo Mocenigo and contains an excellent collection of local archaeological finds from pre-historic Atestine settlements, as well as Roman relics and a small collection of medieval art. The gardens spread behind the museum are enclosed by the fortified wall and contain the remains of a tower, which was built in 1339 as part of the Castello di Umbertino de Carrara.

Visitors have the option from Este either to return on the motorway past Padua to Venice, or to continue south to Bologna to join chapter 9. Visitors planning to return to Venice may consider taking the attractive route along the Brenta canal. To do this leave the motorway at Padua and follow the SS11 to Venice, a total of 34km (21 miles) east. Stop briefly at **Stra** to visit the eighteenth-century Villa Nazionale, and at **Mira**, where the post office is housed in the eighteenth-century Palazzo Foscarini. Also be sure not to miss the Palladian villa of **Malcontenta** on the outskirts of Venice itself.

Additional Information

Places of Interest in Venice

ROUTE 8A
Museo di Storia Naturale
Santa Croce 1730
30100 Venezia (VE)
☎ (041) 5240885
Open: Tuesday to Saturday 9am-1.30pm. Sunday and holidays 9am-1pm.

Museo d'Arte Moderne Ca'Pesaro
San Stae
Santa Croce
30100 Venezia (VE)
☎ (041) 721127

Ca'd'Oro
Galleria Franchetti
Cannaregio
30100 Venezia (VE)
☎ (041) 5238790
Open: Monday to Saturday 9am-1.30pm. Holidays 9am-12.30pm.

Museo del'700 Veneziano
Ca'Rezzonico
San Barnaba
30100 Venezia (VE)
☎ (041) 5224543
Open: Tuesday to Saturday 10am-4pm. Holidays 9am-12.30pm.

Galleria dell'Accademia
Dorsoduro
30100 Venezia (VE)

☎ (041) 5222247
Open: Monday to Saturday 9am-2pm. Holidays 9am-1pm.

Collezione Peggy Guggenheim
701 San Gregorio
Dorsoduro
30100 Venezia (VE)
☎ (041) 5206288
Open: daily 11am-6pm. Saturday 11am-9pm.

Loggia dei Cavalli
Basilica San Marco
Piazza San Marco
30100 Venezia (VE)
☎ (041) 5225205
Open: daily 9.45am-4pm.

Pala d'Oro e Tesoro
Basilica San Marco
Piazza San Marco
30100 Venezia (VE)
☎ (041) 5225697
Open: Monday to Saturday 10am-4pm. Sunday 1.30-4pm.

Palazzo Ducale (Doge's Palace)
Piazzetta San Marco
30100 Venezia (VE)
☎ (041) 5224951
Open: winter daily 9am-4pm. Summer daily 9am-7pm.

Museo Civico Correr
Piazza San Marco
30100 Venezia (VE)

☎ (041) 5225625
Open: Monday, Wednesday,
Thursday, Friday and Saturday
10am–4pm. Sunday and holidays
9am–12.30pm.

Campanile di San Marco
Piazza San Marco
30100 Venezia (VE)
☎ (041) 5224064
Open: daily 10am-4pm.

**Museo della Fondazione
Scientifica** Querini Stampalia
4778 Castello
30100 Venezia (VE)
☎ (041) 5225235
Open: Tuesday to Sunday 10am-
12.30pm.

Scuola di San Giorgio degli Schiavoni
Ponte dei Greci
Castello
30100 Venezia (VE)
Open: Tuesday to Saturday 10am-
12.30pm and 3.30-6pm. Holidays
10.30am-12.30pm.

Museo Storico Navale
Arsenale
2148 Castello
30100 Venezia (VE)
☎ (041) 5200276
Open: Monday to Saturday 9am-1pm.

Scuola Grande di San Rocco
Campo San Rocco
Frari
30100 Venezia (VE)
☎ (041) 5234864
Open: Monday to Friday 10am-1pm.
Saturday and Sunday 10am-4pm.

Chiesa dei Frari
Campo dei Frari
San Polo
30100 Venezia (VE)
☎ (041) 5222637
Open: Monday to Saturday 9-
11.45am and 2.30-6pm. Holidays
3-5.30pm.

Museo Vetrario di Murano
Isola di Murano
30100 Venezia (VE)
☎ (041) 739586
Open: daily 9am-4pm.

Venice: Useful Information

Tourist Information Centres
Ufficio Informazioni
Piazzale Roma
30100 Venezia (VE)
☎ (041) 27402

Uffici Informazioni
71C Piazza San Marco
30100 Venezia (VE)
☎ (041) 5226356

Emergency Telephone Numbers
Emergencies (Soccorso Pubblico di
Emergenza) 113
Police (Carabinieri Pronto
Intervento) 112
Fire (Vigili del Fuoco) 115
Ambulance (Ambulanza) 118
Car Breakdown (Soccorso Stradale) 116

Medical
Ospedale Civile (First Aid)
☎ (041) 5294111

Croce Azzura (Blue Cross Ambulance)
☎ (041) 5230000
Croce Rossa (Red Cross)
Piazza San Marco
Open: Monday to Saturday 8am-8pm.

Dial 192 to find out which
pharmacies are open outside
regular working hours. The local
newspaper, Il Gazzettino, publishes
a list of pharmacies on night duty
in the column under *farmacia di
turno*. Every pharmacy also hangs a
notice in their window with the
pharmacist on duty that night.

Postal Services
Central Post Office
Fontego dei Tedeschi
Rialto
Open: Monday to Saturday 9am-
8pm, Sunday 9am-12noon.
Services: current accounts,
telegraphic money orders, postal,
poste restante, telegrams.

General Post Office
Bocca di Piazza
San Marco
Open: Monday to Friday 8.15am-
2pm, Saturday 8am-12noon.

General Post Office
Piazzale Roma
Fondamenta Gaffaro

Lost Property Offices
Ufficio Oggetti Rinvenuti (General
    Lost Property Office)
Palazzo Farsetti-Loredan Riva del
    Carbon San Marco
☎ (041) 5224063/5236010
Open: Monday to Friday 8am-2pm.

**Ufficio Oggetti Rinvenuti
    (Railway Lost Property Office)**
Ferrovie dello Stato
☎ (041) 5289600
Open: daily 8am-12noon, 3-6pm.

**Ufficio Oggetti Rinvenuti (Public
    Transport Lost Property Office)**
Corte dell'Albero
3380 San Marco
☎ (041) 780111
Open: Monday to Friday 8.30am-
12.30pm.

Shopping
The main shopping street in
Venice, the Mercerie, runs from
Piazza San Marco to the Rialto
Bridge. There is a wide selection of
exclusive boutiques along here
selling fashions, jewellery and
antiques, as well as souvenirs such
as masks which are sculpted from
leather, Venetian glass, marbled
paper and lace. Other smart
shopping streets include Calle
Vallereso, Calle Frezzeria and Calle
Largo 22 Marzo. Shopping for food
around these areas can be
expensive, and it is probably better
to head away from the main tourist
attractions. A fruit and vegetable
market is held every afternoon near
the Rialto bridge with the goods
sold from boats at the waterside.
However, less-frequented by
tourists, are the local markets on
Campo Santa Margherita, Rio Terra
San Leonardo and Campo Santa
Maria Formosa.

Travel
Aeroporto Marco Polo (Airport)
☎ (041) 661262

Ferrovie dello Stato (Railway)
☎ (041) 715555

Stazione Marittima (Seaport Station)
☎ (041) 5289820

**Azienda del Consorzio Trasporti
    Veneziano (Vaporetti)**
3880 Corte dell'Albero
30124 Venezia (VE)
☎ (041) 780111
The Vaporetti are the main form of
public transport in Venice. A map
of the Vaporetti routes, times and
fares is available free of charge
from the above address. Standard
fares are charged for each line,
although visitors may wish to
purchase the fare-saving 24 hour or
3-day tickets. Tickets are purchased
at the main boat stations and
should be stamped at the automatic
dispensers before boarding.

Motoscafi (Water Taxis)
Water taxis should have a list of
tariffs on display and a taxi meter.
The principal taxi stands are as
below:
Piazzale Roma
Rialto
San Marco Giardinetti
San Marco Molo
Fondamente Nuove

Gondola
As with water taxis, all gondolas
should have a list of tariffs on
display. The principal gondola
stations are as below:
Bacino Orseolo
Calle Vellereso
Riva del Carbon
Riva degli Schiavoni
San Marco Molo
Campo San Moise
San Toma
Santa Maria del Giglio
Ferrovia
Tronchetto
Piazzale Roma

Traghetti
Traghetti are boats similar to
gondolas which ferry passengers
from one side of the canal to the

other. The service, which is both cheap and convenient, is mainly used by local residents. The principal crossing points are as follows:
Calle Vallaresso — Punta Dogana
San Marcuola — Fondaco dei Turchi
San Samuele — San Barnabas
Santa Maria del Giglio — San Gregorio
Ca'Garzoni — San Toma
Riva del Carbon — Riva del Vin
Santa Sofia — Pescheria
Ferrovia — Fondamenta San Simeon Piccolo

Other Places of Interest

ROUTE 8B
Mesola
Castello Estense
Mesola (FE)
☎ (0533) 993483
Open: summer only.

Pomposa
Abbazia di Pomposa
44021 Comune di Codigoro (Fe)
Open: daily 8am-12noon and 1.30-5pm.

Abbazia di Pomposa Palazzo della Ragione
44021 Comune di Codigoro (FE)
☎ (0533) 710100
Open: summer only.

Ferrara
Museo della Cattedrale
Piazza della Cattedrale
44100 Ferrara (FE)
Open: daily except public holidays 10am-12noon and 3-5pm.

Castello Estense
Piazza della Repubblica
44100 Ferrara (FE)
☎ (0532) 399234 or 299275
Open: Tuesday to Sunday 10am-1pm and 2-5pm.

Pinacoteca Nazionale
Palazzo Diamante
21 Corso Ercole d'Este
44100 Ferrara (FR)

☎ (0532) 205844
Open: Tuesday to Sunday 9am-1pm or 2pm.

Palazzo Schifanoia e Civico Lapidario
23 Via Scandiana
44100 Ferrara (FE)
☎ (0532) 64178
Open: daily 9am-2pm.
Card and bookshop.

Casa Romei
30 Via Savonarola
44100 Ferrara (FE)
☎ (0532) 40341
Open: Tuesday to Sunday 8.30am-2pm.

Museo Archeologico Nazionale
Palazzo di Ludovico il Moro
124 Via XX Settembre
44100 Ferrara (FE)
☎ (0352) 66299
Open: Tuesday to Saturday 9am-2pm. Holidays 9am-1pm.

Mantua
Palazzo Ducale
Piazza Sordello
46100 Mantova (MN)
☎ (0376) 320283 or 320586
Open: Tuesday to Saturday 9am-1pm and 2.30-4pm. Sunday and Monday 9am-1pm.

Palazzo del Te
Viale Te
46100 Mantova (MN)
☎ (0376) 323266 or 365886
Open: winter Tuesday to Sunday 9.30am-12.30pm and 2.30-5.30pm. Summer Tuesday to Sunday 9am-12noon and 3.30-6.30pm.

ROUTE 8C
Verona
Torre dei Lamberti
Piazza delle Erbe
27100 Verona (VR)
☎ (045) 32726
Open: winter Tuesday to Sunday 8am-1.30pm. Summer Tuesday to Sunday 8am-6.45pm.

Casa di Giulietta
23 Via Cappello
27100 Verona (VR)
☎ (045) 38303
Open: Tuesday to Sunday 8am-
6.45pm.

Anfiteatro Arena
Piazza Bra
27100 Verona (VR)
☎ (045) 8003204
Open: Tuesday to Friday 8.40am-
12.20pm and 3-5.50pm. Saturday
8.40am-12.20pm.

Museo di Castelvecchio
Corso Castelvecchio
27100 Verona (VR)
☎ (045) 594734
Open: Tuesday to Sunday 8am-
6.45pm.

Teatro Romano e Museo Archeologico
Via Redentore
27100 Verona (VR)
☎ (045) 33974
Open: winter Tuesday to Sunday
8am-1.30pm. Summer Tuesday to
Sunday 8am-8.30pm.

Vicenza
Basilica Palladiano
Piazza dei Signori
36100 Vicenza (VI)
Open: Tuesday to Saturday
9.30am-12noon and 2.30-5pm.
Sunday 10am-12noon.

San Lorenzo
Corso A. Fogazzaro
36100 Vicenza (VI)
☎ (0444) 323644
Open: daily 9am-12noon and 3.30-
7pm.

Santa Corona
Corso Palladio
36100 Vicenza (VI)
☎ (0444) 323644
Open: daily except Monday
morning 9am-12.15pm and 3.30-
6pm.

Museo Civico
Palazzo Chiericati
Piazza Matteoti
36100 Vicenza (VI)
☎ (0444) 321348

Open: Tuesday to Saturday
9.30am-12noon and 2.30-5pm.
Sunday 10am-12noon.

Teatro Olimpico
Piazza Matteoti
36100 Vicenza (VI)
☎ (0444) 323781
Open: winter Monday to Saturday
9.30am-12noon and 2-4.30pm,
Sunday 9.30am-12noon. Summer
Monday to Saturday 9.30am-
12.30pm and 3-5.30pm, Sunday
9.30am-12noon.

Santuario di Monte Berico
36100 Vicenza (VI)
☎ (0444) 320999
Open: daily
7am-12noon and 2.30-6pm.

Villa Valmarana 'Al Narni'
Palazzina e Forestia
36100 Vicenza (VI)
☎ (0444) 321803
Open: summer only, Monday,
Tuesday, Wednesday and Friday 3-
6pm. Thursday, Saturday and
Sunday 10am-12noon and 3-6pm.

Villa Rotonda
36100 Vicenza (VI)
☎ (0444) 321793
Open: summer only Tuesday,
Wednesday and Thursday 10am-
12noon and 3-6pm.

ROUTE 8D
Padua
Palazzo della Ragione
Piazza Erbe
35100 Padova (PD)
☎ (049) 8205006
Open: winter Tuesday to Sunday
9am-1pm and 3-6pm. Summer
Tuesday to Sunday 9am-7pm.

Battistero
Piazza del Duomo
35100 Padova (PD)
☎ (049) 662814
Open: winter Tuesday to Friday
9.30am-12.30pm and 2.30-5.30pm,
Saturday and Sunday 9.30am-
12.30pm. Summer Tuesday to
Sunday 9.30am-12.30pm and 3-7pm.

Chiesa degli Eremitani
9 Piazza Eremitani
35100 Padova (PD)
☎ (049) 31410
Open: Monday to Saturday
8.15am-12noon and 3.30-5.30pm.
Holidays 9am-12noon, 3.30-5.30pm.

Musei Civici Eremitani
Piazza Eremitani
35100 Padova (PD)
☎ (049) 8751153 or 8752321
Open: winter Tuesday to Sunday
9am-6pm. Summer daily 9am-7pm.

Pinacoteca del Museo Civico
12 Piazza del Santo
35100 Padova (PD)
☎ (049) 650125
Open: Tuesday to Saturday 9am-
1.20pm. Holidays 9.30am-1pm.

Monselice
Castello
35043 Monselice (PD)
Open: April to November Tuesday,
Thursday and Saturday. Guided
tours 9am, 10.30am, 2.30pm and 4pm.

Este
Museo Nazionale Atestino
Via Guido Negri
35042 Este (PD)
☎ (0429) 2085
Open: Tuesday to Sunday 9am-
1pm and 3-6pm.

Tourist Information Centres

ROUTE 8B
Chioggia
Azienda Autonoma di Soggiorno e
   Turismo
32 Viale Veneto
Sottomarina
30015 Chioggia (VE)
☎ (041) 400621

Ferrara
Informazione Azienda Turistica
19 Piazzetta Municipale
44100 Ferrara (FE)
☎ (0532) 209370 or 419269

Mantua
Azienda Promozione Turistica
6 Piazza Mantegna
46100 Mantova (MN)
☎ (0376) 350681

ROUTE 8C
Verona
Azienda di Promozione Turistica
38 Piazza delle Erbe
27100 Verona (VR)
☎ (045) 8000065 or 8006997

Ufficio Informazione
6 Via Dietro Anfiteatro
27100 Verona (VR)
☎ (045) 592828

Vicenza
Uffici Informazioni
12 Piazza Matteoti
36100 Vicenza (VI)
☎ (0444) 320854

ROUTE 8D
Padua
Azienda di Promozione
8 Riviera dei Mugnai
35100 Padova (PD)
☎ (049) 8750655

Bookshop, information office
Scuola del Sant'Antonio
L'Arciconfraternita di Sant'Antonio
11 Piazza del Santo
35100 Padova (PD)
☎ (049) 8755235
Open: December and January 9am-
12.30pm. February and March
9am-12.30pm and 2.30-6.30pm.
October and November 9am-
12.30pm and 2.30-4.30pm.

9

EMILIA-ROMAGNA AND MILAN

Chapter 9 carves through the centre of Emilia-Romagna, a wealthy agricultural region, south of the River Po. The route starts at Rimini on the Adriatic coast, heading north-west to Cremona, and continuing through Lombardy to its capital, Milan. The chief attraction of the route is the wealth of art and architecture contained in the cities, which spans the Byzantine, Renaissance, Lombard and Baroque periods. Many of the cities were founded as staging posts along Via Emilia, the great Roman road from Rimini to Piacenza, and developed as independent communes during the medieval era. Today, linked by motorway and surrounded by industry, the scene is quite different, but at the heart of every city there is a well-preserved historic centre.

Route 9A — Rimini to Ravenna

Rimini has been one of the most popular holiday venues on the Adriatic coast since it was first established as a bathing resort in 1843, and wide sandy beaches, plush hotels, bingo halls, discoes and bars, line the coast for 20km (12 miles) on either side. It also has a well-restored historic centre about a kilometre inland from the coast. A number of carparks are signposted around the centre, the largest of which is on Piazza Malatesta, beneath the walls of Castel Sigismondo (1446), the Malatesta castle.

The Malatesta were the dominant family in the region during the fourteenth and fifteenth centuries. Sigismondo (1417-68), the most forthright of the Malatesta dynasty, was known for his violent temper and was punished by Pope Pius II, who canonised him to hell. Despite his notoriety he was a great patron of the Renaissance arts, and commissioned Rimini's most prestigious monument, Tempio Malatestiano. To visit it, start from Piazza Cavour in the middle of the pedestrianised city centre, and head along Corso di Augusto. At Piazza Tre Martiri, take the busy main road, Via IV Novembre left for 150m (164yd) to Tempio Malatestiano, which is on the right.

Originally a thirteenth-century Gothic church, Sigismondo commissioned Leon Battista Alberti, the great Florentine Renaissance architect, to remodel it in the form of a classical temple. Construction took place between 1447 and 1460. However, Sigismundo's funds ran dry and the upper part was never completed, although the lower façade with its triumphal arch is considered to be Alberti's masterwork. The interior contains a quantity of fine stone work, lined as it is with balustraded chapels on either side of its single nave. The balustrades are decorated with cherubic statues by Agostino di Duccio. In addition to this, each chapel is decorated with sculptural reliefs based on different themes: the third on the right has symbols of the zodiac, while the third on the left represents learning. The initials of Sigismondo, intertwined with those of his wife Isotta, are carved throughout the building, as is the Malatesta rose. The largest chapel, the first on the right, contains a fresco by Piero della Francesca (1451), showing Sigismondo kneeling before his patron saint, St Sigismund of Burgundy. Also of note is the crucifix painted by Duccio around 1310 in the second chapel on the right.

Return to Piazza Tre Martiri, once the site of a Roman forum, and head in a southerly direction down Corso di Augusto for 300m (328yd) to the Arco di Augusto. This huge gate is the best remaining structure of Roman *Ariminum*, which was established as a colony in 268BC. It was erected in honour of Augustus in AD27 at the end of Via Emilia.

An excursion can be made from Rimini to the Republic of San Marino, 23km (14 miles) inland, along the SS72. Covering an area of 62sq km (24sq miles), it is the smallest and oldest republic in the world. It has been independent since the ninth century and has its own coins and stamps, which along with tourism and a mass of other souvenirs, provide the capital, **San Marino**, with its main source of income. The town clings to the steep western slope of Monte Titiano (739m/2,424ft) and is visible from a great distance. It is best to park either in the carpark below the town and take the *funivia* up, or park along the western walls and walk up. The town, strung out along the slope, has no real centre apart from the area around the Palazzo Publicco, in Piazza della Liberta. This building is not as old as it looks; it was built in the style of a medieval *palazzo* in 1894. Climb up above the *piazza* along the steeply terraced streets packed with souvenir shops, to the top of the town. A footpath, with extensive views on either side, leads along the ridge to the thirteenth-century citadel, with its three large towers. From here there is an impressive view of the Republic, the Adriatic to the east, and the Appenines to the west.

Return along the SS72 to the outskirts of Rimini and head north along the SS16 to Ravenna. The road follows a part of the coast known as the Riviera Romagnola, and passes through a chain of popular beach resorts where leisure facilities, watersports and amusements abound. Just outside Rimini there is a scale model of Italy, Italia in Miniatura. On a more serious note, 13km (8 miles) north of Rimini, the road crosses the River Rubicon. In the days of the

Roman Republic, the river formed the boundary between Italy and Gaul, so that when Caesar, the then Governor of Gaul crossed the Rubicon with his army in 49BC, it was in effect a declaration of war against Pompey in Rome. The road continues north past **Cesenatico**, an attractive resort with a busy canal, and crosses several more waterways before reaching the basilica of **Sant'Apollinare in Classe**, 5km (3 miles) south of Ravenna.

The basilica was built in AD549 at Ravenna's ancient port, *Classis*. Today, it stands near a busy main road and the sea is some 5km (3 miles) away, but the basilica is nonetheless awe-inspiring, particularly the interior, which contains fine Byzantine columns and some beautiful mosaics. Do not miss the marvellous *Transfiguration* in the apse.

Mosaics are the first and foremost reason for visiting **Ravenna**, as the city's modest brick architecture contains some of the greatest mosaics in Western Europe. Visitors should make sure, therefore, of visiting the city when the museums and monuments are open. Carparks are scattered around the city centre and next to the major monuments, but be warned, most have a 2-hour time-limit. Getting about the city on foot involves a fair amount of walking, and despite the flat terrain, some visitors might prefer to visit the major sights by car.

Start on the north side of the city at one of Ravenna's greatest monuments, the Basilica of San Vitale. The entrance is at the west end of Via San Vitale, through the Museo Nazionale, which houses a collection of Byzantine relics as well as paintings dating from the fourteenth to the eighteenth centuries. The basilica was begun in AD525 by the Ostrogothic king, Theodoric, who unfortunately died the following year, leaving his Ostrogothic kingdom to fall into a state of decline. Justinian, the eastern Byzantine emperor, seeing the power vacuum, took the opportunity to invade, and with his general Belisarius fought a bloody path up the peninsula to Ravenna in AD540. This led to the basilica being finally consecrated in AD547.

It has an octagonal ground plan with a dome at the centre supported on eight fine columns. Small chapels decorated with beautiful marbles and connected by an ambulatory surround the central space, but the focus of the interior is on the exquisite mosaics which cover the main apse. In the choir the right wall shows the *Sacrifice of Abraham*, and the left wall, the *Last Supper*. In the apse itself, Justinian and his empress Theodora are depicted with their court and the Bishop Maximian, who consecrated the basilica. From the semi-dome of the apse, Christ looks down between St Vitalis, on the left, and Bishop Ecclesius, who is depicted offering a model of the basilica, on the right.

From the door in the north side of the basilica, follow the footpath to the small cruciform mausoleum, Mausoleo di Galla Placidia. Turn on the lights before entering the small tomb, which is decorated inside with charming mosaics. Galla Placidia was the sister of

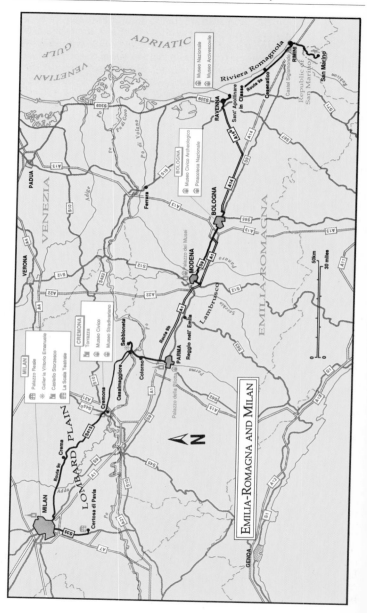

Honorius, who ruled the crumbling remains of the western Roman empire from Ravenna in AD402 and the mosaics, which date from the fifth century, are amongst the oldest in Ravenna. A dark hallway, spangled with stars and flowers, leads into the main chamber where San Lorenzo is depicted with his flaming gridiron on the end wall. Stags intertwine with foliage on the side walls.

Follow the footpath to the exit, past the attractive circular *campanile* of the basilica, back onto Via San Vitale. Head east towards the city centre along Via San Vitale until reaching Piazza A. Costa where there is a covered food market. The main square, Piazza del Popolo, is pedestrianised and lies a short distance south along Via IV Novembre. It is surrounded by elegant buildings, including the fifteenth-century Palazzo Veneziano, and is best admired from one of the numerous cafés. Leave the *piazza* from the eastern end and follow Via A. Diaz for 150m (164yd) before turning left to visit the Battistero Ariani, next to the church of Spirito Santo. This simple octagonal baptistery has a beautiful domed interior covered by fifth-century mosaics. The *Baptism* fills the centre of the dome, surrounded by portraits of the twelve Apostles. From the back of the church, follow Via di Roma, the main thoroughfare through the city centre, south for 200m (218yd) to Sant'Apollinare Nuovo, on the left. The basilica was founded by Theodoric in AD519, but the façade was added in the sixteenth century and the great *campanile* dates from the eleventh. Inside are excellent, original sixth-century mosaics. They line the central aisle on either side, high up above the rows of columns which support the upper walls. The left side shows a procession of saints and virgins, headed by three magi offering gifts, leaving the port of *Classis*. The right side depicts a procession of twenty-six martyrs leaving Theodoric's palace.

Visitors with time may wish to continue south of Sant'Apollinare Nuovo, along Via di Roma to the *pinacoteca*, which is housed in the Accademia di Belle Arti. Others should turn right off Via di Roma and follow Via Guaccimanni for 250m (273yd) to the church of San Franceso. The church dates from the tenth century, although it was largely rebuilt after bomb damage in World War II. The interior is divided by antique columns into three aisles.

The small *piazza* in front of the church has an attractive portico down the left side, through which is a mausoleum, built in 1780 to contain Dante's tomb. The poet died, an exile of Florence, in 1321. Return to the *piazza* and follow Via Ricci, in which Byron lived for 2 years, to Piazza Caduti Della Liberta. Cross over the busy *piazza*, and head for Piazza Arcivescovile, just to the west. In the south corner of Piazza Arcivescovile follow signs to the entrance to the Museo Arcivescovile at the back of the Duomo. The showpiece of the museum is the exquisite ivory pulpit, presented by Justinian to the Bishop Maximian in the sixth century. Also of interest is the tiny chapel, built by Bishop Peter II (AD494-519) which is clad with beautiful mosaics.

Head from the museum down the side of the Duomo to the Battistero Neoniano on the right. Built by Bishop Neoni in the sixth century, it contains yet more breathtaking mosaics. The dome, similar to that of Battistero Ariani, contains the *Baptism* at the centre, which is encircled by the twelve Apostles. The lower walls are beautifully patterned with gold intertwining foliage on a dark ground. The font in the middle of the room was added in the twelfth to thirteenth centuries. The Duomo dates from the eighteenth century and holds little of interest, except for its fine sixth-century marble ambo, a type of pulpit, on the right of the main aisle. It is attractively carved with whimsical animals and birds.

Route 9B — Ravenna to Parma

Leaving Ravenna, follow signs for the A14 *autostrada* to **Bologna**. Head along the motorway in a westerly direction for 68km (42 miles) to the outskirts of Bologna following signs to the city centre. Parking in the centre can be difficult as there are few metered spaces and the only large carpark, which is on Piazza Roosevelt, is usually full. There are a number of private underground carparks, but they tend to be costly and being unsignposted are hard to find. It is easiest therefore to park on the northern side of the city, either on Largo Respighi, or near the coach station on Piazza XX Settembre.

Bologna is a large and crowded city, in which the very modern is blended with the traditional and the historic. Bologna is known for its cuisine, its left-wing politics and its nightclubs and is the centre of new wave music in Italy, yet the streets, laid out roughly as they were in Roman times, are lined with some 35km (22 miles) of old brick porticoes. The earliest to be built date back to the twelfth century when Bologna was an independent commune and had already established its university, one of the earliest to be founded in Europe. There seem to be more restaurants in Bologna, tucked away under its porticoes, than in many other Italian cities, and although Bolognese sauce is perhaps the best known of its culinary inventions it has a wealth of other dishes to offer, not least its own salami, which is flavoured with garlic and is very good.

Start a tour of the city in the grand central square, Piazza Maggiore, where the largest church in Bologna, San Petronio, stands on a stepped platform along the south side. The church was started in 1390, but was still being constructed in the seventeenth century and has never really been completed. The top half of the façade is devoid of the pretty pink and white marble that decorates the lower half. The attractive carvings around the main portal are by the famous Sienese sculptor, Jacopo della Quercia (1425-38), while those adorning the side portals date from the sixteenth century. The massive vaulted interior, divided into three aisles by vast brick columns, is lined either side with chapels, a number of which hold frescoes dating from the early fifteenth century. The second chapel on the right also has a good polyptych of the fifteenth century, and in the eighth chapel on the same side there are beautifully inlaid stalls dating from 1521. The small museum at the back of the church contains the original plans that were projected for the façade and a sixteenth-century model of the church.

The *piazza* is surrounded by a number of other impressive buildings. Palazzo del Podesta, opposite the church, has a Renaissance façade which was built in 1484. The thirteenth-century Palazzo Comunale to its left has a fine clock tower (1444) and houses an art collection on the second floor, comprised of paintings by artists of the Bolognese school, dating from the fourteenth to sixteenth centuries.

The small Piazza Nettuno, to the north of Palazzo Comunale, holds a fine bronze statue of Pope Gregory XIII. The *piazza* is named, however, after the decorative fountain at its centre which, adorned with bronze sculptures (including that of Neptune), was designed by Giambologna in 1566. On the right side of the *piazza*, joined to the back of Palazzo del Podesta, is Palazzo di Re Enzo. This attractive building, surrounding a charming inner courtyard was built in 1246, although it was a prison for Enzo, King of Sardinia and illegitimate son of Emperor Frederick II. He was imprisoned here for the last 22 years of his life after he had been taken captive in the battle of Fossalta (1249) when Bologna, who fought on the side of the papal Guelphs, defeated the Emperor's Ghibelline army.

Head north of Palazzo di Re Enzo and turn right along Via Rizzoli. This wide porticoed street, lined with fashionable shops and cafés, leads to Piazza di Porta Ravegnana which is dominated by two impressive towers. They are the only two left standing of some 180 towers that once punctuated Bologna's skyline during medieval times, when local feuding families erected them as symbols of their power. Both towers lean slightly: the tallest, Torre Asinelli is out by 1m (3ft); while Torre Garisenda, which was shortened to its present height of 48m (157ft) in 1351, is 3m (10ft) off true. Those with energy to climb to the top of Torre Asinelli, which is 97m (318ft) high, will be rewarded by a fine panorama.

Head past the right side of Torre Asinelli to the north-east corner of the *piazza* and follow Via Zamboni, which has some of Bologna's finest sixteenth- to eighteenth-century *palazzi*, for just over 150m (164yd) to the church of San Giacomo Maggiore. This thirteenth-century, brick-built church has a spacious interior with an attractive ambulatory in its apse. The last chapel on the left, reached by the ambulatory, was built for the Bentivoglio family who ruled Bologna in the fifteenth century. Covered by a small cupola, the walls of the chapel are decorated with fine frescoes by L. Costa and there is a brightly coloured altar painting, dating from 1494, by F. Francia.

Continue for a further 400m (492yd) along Via Zamboni to the Pinacoteca Nazionale which is on the left. The fine gallery houses an excellent collection of paintings by the Bolognese school, ranging from fourteenth-century altar-pieces to Ba-

Parma is famous for its smoked ham

Salami is a favourite with those who enjoy traditional Italian cuisine

roque paintings by famousartists such as G. Reni.

Return to Piazza Maggiore and head along the east side of San Petronio to Bologna's other major museum, the Museo Civico Archeologico, which contains a good collection of prehistoric and Etruscan finds from the local area. Continue past the museum to the Archigennasio which was part of Bologna's famous university when it was founded in 1119. It is now a library but it is worth stepping inside to see its fine inner courtyard, which has shields and plaques covering its walls.

Heading south, cross over Via Farini and follow Via Garibaldi for 200m (218yd) to the church of San Domenico. The church was built in 1221 by the Domenican order, and overlooks a pleasant cobbled piazza which is surrounded by obelisks surmounted by seventeenth-century statues, and canopied tombs supported on columns dating from the late thirteenth century. The interior holds a number of interesting art works, amongst the most important of which is the sarcophagus of St Dominic which is in the sixth chapel on the right. The beautifully-carved relief scenes depicting the life of the saint are by N. Pisano and his workshop, while the statues of an angel and Saints Petronius and Proculus are by Michelangelo (1495).

The large sanctuary, Madonna di San Luca, which looks down on Bologna from the Guardia hill (291m/954ft), to the south-west of the city, is linked by Via San Luca from Porta Saragozza. The road is $3^1/_2$km (2 miles) long and is lined with 665 porticoes which were built between 1674 and 1793. The sanctuary, erected between 1723 and 1757, contains a precious painting of the Madonna which was removed from Constantinople in the twelfth century and is attributed to St Luke.

Head west out of Bologna on the A1 *autostrada* to **Modena**, which is only 25km ($15^1/_2$ miles) away. Follow signs in towards the centre and either park near the stadium, where there is a large carpark serviced by regular mini-buses, or try to find a metered space inside the city wall. The city, which was originally built by the Romans, lies between two rivers, the Secchio and Panaro. It was ruled by the Este Dukes from 1284 up until the French invaded in 1797. The Dukes endowed Modena with much of the fine architecture seen in the city today, and had their seat here for nearly 200 years.

The city is centred around the Duomo, which stands on a vast cobbled square, Piazza Grande. Designed in 1099 by Lanfranco, it has a classic façade of pink and white stone, and with its large rose window in the centre, is a fine example of Lombard-Romanesque architecture. The attractive sculptural reliefs around the window, and also the portal, were added in the twelfth century, by Willigelmo. The *campanile*, Torre Ghirlandina, leaning jauntily to one side just behind, has a slender Gothic spire, which was added in 1319. The whole structure stands to an impressive height of 88m (289ft). The Duomo's interior is lit by a myriad of windows and contains many pieces of finely carved stone. The relief at the altar, depicting the *Passion*, dates from 1180, while the finely carved pulpit is from the early fourteenth century. The Duomo also has a large crypt, which can be reached by steps from the apse. It is filled by a mass of sixty columns, each with a beautifully carved capital, and contains the sarcophagus of San Geminiano.

Modena's museums are conveniently contained under one large roof, the Palazzo dei Musei. It is 400m (437yd) west of Piazza Grande, along Via Emilia, on the left. On the first floor is the Biblioteca Estense, one of the best libraries in Italy, with around 600,000 books. Some of the rare manuscripts are on permanent display, including the Borso d'Este Bible, which was illuminated by the Ferrara School. The second floor holds the Museo Civico Archeologico, Medioevale e Moderno, which has a wide collection of artefacts ranging from prehistoric flints to medieval folk costumes. On the top floor, the Galleria Estense houses the Este collection of paintings, which date from the fourteenth to eighteenth centuries, and are by the Emilian and Venetian schools.

The Este residence of 1629, Palazzo Ducale, now houses a military academy and only the exterior can be viewed. To see it, return back up Via Emilia, passing Piazza Grande, to Via Farini on the left. The *palazzo* lies at the far end of the street on Piazza Roma.

Leave Modena by following signs to the A1 *autostrada* in the direction of Milano. Continuing alongside Via Emilia, the motorway passes through the wine-making region of Lambrusco. This sweet, slightly fizzy, red wine is drunk in copious amounts throughout Emilia-Romagna, as well as being widely exported. The industrial town of **Reggio nell'Emilia** is passed 24km (15 miles) west of Modena, but there is little of interest there and it is far better to press on to the beautiful city of Parma, which is a further 28km (17 miles).

Parma, a famous centre of smoked ham, parmesan cheese and sugared violets amongst other products, is also a great historical city with many fine monuments. The Etruscans were the first to settle on this site, which is situated on the fertile banks of a tributary of the Po. They dwelt here from 525BC up until the Roman conquest in 183BC. During medieval times, the city was ruled by a succession of powerful families, including the Visconti, Sforza, Este and La Scala, but in 1545 Pope Paul III made Parma into a duchy, which was then ruled by his son, Pier Luigi Farnese. The city remained in the hands of the Farnese family up until 1815 when Maria Louisa, Napoleon's widow, took power.

The main carpark is in what is known as the episcopal centre, around the rambling walls of Palazzo della Pilotta, on Piazzale Marconi. Start a tour of the city from Piazza del Duomo, which is a grand cobbled square, surrounded by a wealth of fine buildings. The most important is the Duomo, which was built in 1090 by the bishop-counts who ruled the city at the time. It was consecrated in 1106 and is a unique example of the Padana-Romanesque style, which is typified by rows of dainty columns and arcades. The main portal, flanked by lions and decorated with reliefs, was added by Giambino da Bissone in 1281. The elegant *campanile* is also a later addition, and dates from 1294. The interior, decorated with sixteenth-century frescoes by the Parmese school, has a large dome which is pierced by a row of windows. The dome contains a fresco of the *Assumption*, painted by Correggio (1522-30), the leading artist of the Parmese school. His use of perspective and foreshortening of figures, typical of the Renaissance style, successfully give the illusion of looking up to the heavens. One of the few remnants of the original interior is the carved relief of the *Deposition*, in the right transept. It is by B. Antelami and dates from 1178.

The octagonal baptistery, on the *piazza*, to the right of the Duomo is also attributed to B. Antelami. Constructed in 1196, it is built of Veronese marble and has five layers of arcades. The interior, encircled by a series of attractive galleries, contains sculptures by B. Antelami and remains of thirteenth-century frescoes.

To see other frescoes by Correggio, follow Via Cardinal Ferrari, between the baptistery and Duomo, to the Renaissance church of San Giovanni Evangelista. The church was built in 1510, and less than a decade later Correggio frescoed the interior of the dome, which contains the *Vision of St John*.

Return to Piazza del Duomo and head for the Camera del Correggio, in the former convent of San Paolo, 150m (164yd) east of the Duomo, on Via Melloni. The small dining room in the convent, has an attractive vaulted ceiling, frescoed by Correggio.

Continue to the end of Via Melloni and turn left along Strada Garibaldi. Follow the street for 200m (218yd) to the church of Madonna della Steccata on the right. This grand domed church, built between 1521 and 1539, by B. and G. Zaccagni, contains further Renaissance frescoes, although this time not by Correggio, but other artists of the Parmese school, most notably, F. Parmigianino. The crypt of the church houses the Farnese tombs.

Return back up Strada Garibaldi and turn left to Palazzo della Pilotta, the Farnese residence. Built between 1583 and 1622, it is a rambling construction of brick that was never really completed. Today, it houses two museums. On the first floor is the Museo Archeologico, which contains the Farnese, and also the Gonzaga, private collection of classical antiquities, as well as locally excavated artefacts. On the second floor is the Galleria Nazionale and the entrance to the Farnese theatre. The gallery has an important collection of paintings by the Emilian, Venetian, Tuscan and Parmese schools, dating from the fourteenth to eighteenth centuries, and includes works by Correggio. The theatre, built in 1618, was the largest in Europe at the time, and has been excellently restored to its former grandeur.

Route 9C — Parma to Milan

The route to Milan dawdles through the Lombard plain, north of the River Po, and visitors short of time may prefer to take the A1 *autostrada*. Others should leave Parma in the direction of Mantova on the SS343. It reaches the small town of **Colorno** after 15km (9 miles) which is clustered around the eighteenth-century Farnese Palace. The interior is only open when the palace is hosting an exhibition, but there are extensive gardens, which are open to the public, behind it. The route continues, crossing the River Parma behind the *palazzo*, and heading north on the SS343 across the flood plain of the River Po. The massive expanse of the Po itself forms the regional boundary between Emilia-Romagna and Lombardy. On the Lombard shore, where the road forks, take the SS420 for 5km (3 miles) to visit the *centro storico* of **Sabbioneta**. Parking is available in the centre on Piazza Castello.

In 1577 this small village woke up one day to find that it had been transformed into an independent duchy. Soon fine Renaissance buildings that would befit a city were erected within a hexagonal defensive wall. The ruler of this short lived Duchy was Vespasiano Gonzaga, and although the Duchy expired after his death, the grand architecture which he created remains. To visit the duke's palace, which was built in 1554, it is necessary to take a guided tour from the tourist office on Piazza Castello. The richly decorated interior houses a collection of antique and equestrian statues and twenty-one plaster busts of the Gonzaga family. The summer palace, completed in 1588, is connected by a vast, arcaded corridor, Corridor Grande, which lies along one side of Piazza Castello. The duke's theatre, Teatro Olimpico, designed in 1588 by V. Scamozzi, is on the main street, Via Vespasiano Gonzaga, while in the fine square at the back of the theatre, Piazza Ducale, is the sixteenth-century parish church of Santa Maria Assunta. Built in 1581, it has an attractive façade of pink and white marble. The duke is buried in Santa Maria Assunta Coronata, the small church near Porta Vittoria in the north-west wall of the town. The mausoleum, designed by G.B. Della Porta in 1592, has a bronze statue in front of it by L. Leoni, which dates from 1588.

Return back up the SS420 from Sabbioneta to **Casalmaggiore**, a wine-making town on the banks of the River Po. Turn right through the town and follow the SS343 to **Cremona**, 40km (25 miles) to the west. Park, either along the city walls, or follow signs to the small carparks which are dotted around the centre. Cremona, one of Lombardy's finest cities, has made violins since the sixteenth century. The tradition was started in 1530 when Andrea Amati made the first violin, and was perpetuated by his and then the Guarneri family. However, it was A. Stradivarius in the eighteenth century who achieved worldwide acclaim. Today, with over sixty workshops, as well as an international school of violin-making, the city has a well-earned and prestigious reputation.

Start a tour of Cremona at Piazza del Comune, the hub of the historic centre. The *piazza* was built during early medieval times when Cremona was an independent *comune*. Surrounded by medieval porticoes, it contains numerous fine monuments, including, on the north side, the Torrazza, the tallest tower in Italy. Built between 1250 and 1284, it stands to a height of 112m (367ft), and offers a remarkable panorama to anyone prepared to climb to the top. The Duomo, joined to the Torrazza by a loggia, is an attractive Lombard-Romanesque building, which dates from 1107. The white marble façade, ornamented with rows of arcades, has a fine rose window of 1274. Carved reliefs, by the Antelami school decorate the portal, while the three statues above are Tuscan and date from 1310. The interior has a high vaulted central aisle decorated with frescoes, which date from 1506 and are of the Venetian-Lombard school. The bas-relief on the right of the main aisle, and also the two pulpits, were carved by the Renaissance sculptor, G. Amadeo.

On the *piazza*, to the right of the Duomo, is the baptistery, a charming octagonal building topped by a green cupola. It was built in 1167 in the Lombard style, although the baptismal font inside is

A mass of towering pinnacles adorn the cathedral in Milan

sixteenth century. The Loggia dei Militi (1292), with its wide arches and mullioned windows, stands on the *piazza*, opposite the Duomo. The Palazzo del Comune, joined to the back of the loggia, dates from 1206 and houses the *municipio*. It is worth visiting in order to see the Saletta dei Violini, where there are four of the world's most famous violins; two by the Amati family, one by A. Stradivarius and another by G. Guarneri. Those interested in seeing more violins can wander around the back streets and visit the workshops as well as Museo Stradivariano at the north end of town. To reach it from Palazzo del Comune, cross over Piazza Cavour and follow Corso Campi for 500m (547yd). The museum documents the history of violin making in Cremona and has a large collection of Cremonese violins. The Museo Civico is next door, housed in the sixteenth-century Palazzo Affaitati. It contains Cremonese art objects and paintings from medieval times to the present day, as well as the treasury from the Duomo.

Leave Cremona on the SS415 to Milano, which is 83km (51 miles) to the north-west. The road passes the attractive, walled town of **Crema**, before heading through Milan's industrial outskirts onto the *tangenziale*, the ring road around the city. Follow signs to *centro* through the vast suburban sprawl and look for an *autosilo*. Trying to park elsewhere is fairly hopeless; most streets are lined with cars double and triple parked. Alternatively park outside the city and take public transport to the centre. Milan has a good public transport network and it is usually possible to get almost anywhere if all the forms of transport are considered. The choices are the *metro*, trams or buses. It is not a bad idea to get one of the Tourist day-passes which are issued for all city transport.

Milan is the second largest city in Italy. It leads the way in fashion and design, and is the throbbing pulse of Italy's industry, commerce, banking and finance. Renowned for its opera house, Milan is an innovative centre of art and culture, and on top of all this the city has an outstanding wealth of great historical monuments. To forgo a visit to Milan would be to miss the third largest Gothic cathedral in the world, and Leonardo da Vinci's priceless *Last Supper*. It would also mean missing the great art collections which were collected and commissioned over the centuries by Milan's ruling dynastic families, the Visconti and the Sforza.

At least 2 days are required to get around Milan's main sights, by which time the visitor will either be lured to stay longer or be frantic to escape. The tour can be divided into three areas: central, northern and western. Start at the centre, on Piazza del Duomo. Whether emerging from the underground *metro*, or approaching along one of the elegant surrounding shopping streets, the first sight of the Duomo is breathtaking. It is a mass of towering pinnacles, no less than 135 in all, decorated with over 2,000 statues. This Gothic masterpiece was started in 1386 under the most notorious of the Visconti dukes, Gian Galleazo, but its construction took a very long time, and it was not consecrated until 1577. The final pinnacles were only completed in 1958. To get a closer look at the pinnacles which top the structure take the lift or climb the stairs up from the left side of the Duomo. The view from the top takes in the entire city and on a clear day the Alps are visible. The façade of the Duomo, which was completed in 1805, gives way to the massive interior. It is divided by vast pillars topped by richly carved capitals, into five aisles, while coloured light pours in through fine stained-glass windows. The first six windows on the right are the oldest and date from the fifteenth century. The bronze ciborium at the altar dates from the sixteenth century and the candelabra on the left, the thirteenth. Behind it are the beautifully inlaid walnut stalls of the choir, which were made between 1572 and 1629. The Duomo treasury is in the crypt, along with the Cappella delle Sante Masse.

Other works of art from the Duomo can be seen in Palazzo Reale, on the *piazza*, to the right of the Duomo. The *palazzo*, which dates from the eighteenth century, has over twenty rooms of religious vestments, sculptures, tapestries and stained-glass, dating from the fourteenth up to the twentieth centuries. The *palazzo* also houses the Museo d'Arte Contemporanea, a collection of twentieth-century art.

Back on the *piazza*, cross to the opposite side and walk through Italy's most famous shopping arcade, Galleria Vittorio Emanuele. Built of glass, it is four storeys high and has a fine dome at its centre. It was constructed in the nineteenth century, and has been one of Milan's social hotspots ever since, with as many cafés and restaurants as there are shops. The arcade leads to another of Milan's social venues, the La Scala opera house. Named after B. Visconti's wife, Regina della Scala, the opera house was built in 1776. The history of the theatre, punctuated with all the greatest names in opera, from Verdi to Toscanini, is documented in the adjoining museum. If no performances or rehearsals are in progress, the auditorium, complete with its 1830s decor, can be visited too.

The next stage of the tour concentrates on the northern city, around Castello Sforzesca. Either take the red line *metro* from the Duomo to Cairoli, or some other form of transport, or be prepared for a walk of about a kilometre. By foot, leave Piazza del Duomo from the west corner, along Via Mercanti. After 200m (218yd) cross straight over Piazza Cordusio onto Via Dante, which leads to the *castello* walls. First built as the Visconti stronghold in 1386, the massive fortress seen today, was constructed in 1450 by Francesco Sforza. The fine clock tower above the south door was built in 1452 to a design by the Tuscan architect, Il Filarete, while the two great round towers at either corner were designed by the imperial architect B. Gadio in 1455. A park covering some 47 hectares (116 acres) stretches behind the castle and contains the Palazzo d'Arte exhibition centre, an arena and a triumphal arch, L'Arco della Pace. Inside the walls of the fortress is a vast central courtyard. The well-restored buildings around the courtyard house a massive collection of art, as well as libraries, archives, and an art school. The Musei Civiche houses the main collections. Arranged in thirty-seven rooms of the Corte Ducale, the ducal apartments, the exhibits range from early medieval masonry to eighteenth-century antique furniture, and include a good collection of paintings dating from the fifteenth to eighteenth centuries. Not to be missed is Michelangelo's *Pieta Rondanini*, his last major work, in Sala degli Scarlioni.

An even greater collection of art, amongst the best in Italy, is housed in Pinacoteca di Brera, just over 500m (547yd) east of the *castello*. Head through the attractive pedestrianised back streets of the Brera district rather than walking along the main roads, Via Tivoli and Via Pontaccio. The gallery is housed in Palazzo Brera which was first built in 1651 by F. Richini. Displayed in thirty-eight rooms, the collection is made up of some of the finest paintings produced by Northern Italian artists, particularly of the Lombard and Venetian schools. It covers the period from the fourteenth to the nineteenth centuries and amongst the most important works are the *Marriage of the Virgin* by Raphael, the *Dead Christ* by A. Mantegna, the *Supper at Emmaus* by Caravaggio and the *Madonna with Saints* by Piero della Francesca. There are also numerous other fine works by very famous artists such as Tintoretto, Veronese,

People and pigeons vie for space on the Piazza del Duomo, Milan

Titian, Correggio, Rubens, Rembrandt and Van Dyck.

The tour continues in the western part of the city. Return to the *castello* and either take a tram, or head west along Via Boccaccio. After some 300m (328yd) turn left down Via Caradosso. The church of Santa Maria delle Grazie is a further 150m (164yd) on the right.

The church was started in 1463 and enlarged during the Renaissance by Bramante. However, the main reason for visiting this church is to see the Cenacolo, the *Last Supper*, painted by Leonardo da Vinci. It covers the end wall of the refectory in the former Domenican monastery next door. Painted between 1494 and 1497, it has been excellently restored and is one of the high points of the city. Those interested in seeing Leonardo da Vinci's models and drawings should head for the Museo Nazionale delle Scienze e della Technica. Cross the *piazza* in front of the church and head south along Via Zenale. At the end of the street turn left along Via San Vittore. The museum entrance is a short distance further on the right, housed in a former Benedictine monastery. The Leonardo gallery is the most popularly visited, but the museum contains many other exhibits, ranging from metallurgy to typewriters.

Continue along Via San Vittore to the church of Sant'Ambrogio, just over 300m (328yd) east. St Ambrose was the Bishop of Milan in AD374 and the church was founded in AD386, although the present structure dates from the ninth to eleventh centuries. It is built in the Romanesque style and has an attractive façade, flanked by two towers. The tallest one dates from the twelfth century, the other remains from a ninth-century Benedictine monastery that once stood here. The interior contains excellent mosaics. Those in the apse date from the eighth to eleventh centuries, while those in the Cappella di San Vittore in Ciel d'Oro, on the right, date from the fifth century. The chapel also has a portrait of St Ambrose, who is buried in the crypt.

Those with time and energy can continue along the main road, Via Edmondo, to the church of San Lorenzo Maggiore, 800m (850yd) south-east of Sant'Ambrogio, which has an octagonal ground plan, taken from a temple that stood on the site in the second century. A row of sixteen columns, the only remains of Roman *Mediolanum*, stand in front of the church. They were erected in their present position in the fourth century. The city wall lies at the end of the street, pierced by the thirteenth-century Porta Ticinese which is decorated with attractive reliefs dating from the fourteenth century.

A worthwhile excursion from Milan is to **Certosa di Pavia**, 26km (16 miles) south on the SS35. It was the Lombard capital between the sixth and eighth centuries, but the famous charterhouse seen today dates from 1396. The Lombard-Renaissance façade, intricately decorated with coloured marbles and sculptural reliefs, is one of the finest in Italy. The complex also holds the original cloisters of the Carthusian monastery and a palace built for the Dukes of Milan in 1625.

Additional Information

Places of Interest

ROUTE 9A
Ravenna
Basilica di San Vitale
17 Via San Vitale
48100 Ravenna (RA)
☎ (0544) 33696
Open: winter daily 9.30am-4.30pm.
Summer daily 8.30am-7.30pm.

Museo Nazionale
17 Via San Vitale
48100 Ravenna (RA)
☎ (0544) 34424 Open: Tuesday to
Sunday 8.30am-1.30pm.

Basilica di Sant'Apollinare Nuovo
Via di Roma
48100 Ravenna (RA)
☎ (0544) 336961
Open: daily 9.30am-4.30pm.
Card and souvenir shop.

Battistero degli Ariani
Via degli Ariani
48100 Ravenna (RA)
Open: daily 8.30am-12.30pm and 2-
5.30pm.

*Museo Arcivescovile e Cappella
    Sant'Andrea*
Piazza Arcivescovile
48100 Ravenna (RA)
☎ (0544) 33696
Open: daily 9.30am-4.30pm.

Tomba di Dante
Piazza San Francesco
48100 Ravenna (RA)
☎ (0544) 482208
Open: daily 9am-12noon and 2-5pm.

Battistero Neoniano
Via Battistero
48100 Ravenna (RA)
☎ (0544) 33696
Open: daily 9.30am-4.30pm.

ROUTE 9B
Bologna
Museo di San Petronio
Basilica di San Petronio

Piazza Maggiore
40122 Bologna (BO)
☎ (051) 234264
Open: Monday, Wednesday and
Friday 10am-12noon and 4-6pm.
Saturday 10am-12noon.

Museo Civico Archeologico
2 Via dell'Archiginnasio
40122 Bologna (BO)
☎ (051) 233849
Open: Tuesday to Saturday 9am-
2pm. Sunday 9am-12.30pm.

Collezioni Comunali d'Arte
Palazzo d'Accursio
6 Piazza Maggiore
40122 Bologna (BO)
☎ (051) 203526
Open: daily except Tuesday 9am-
2pm. Sundays 9am-12.30pm.

Museo di San Stefano
Basilica di San Stefano
24 Via San Stefano
40122 Bologna (BO)
☎ (051) 223256
Open: daily 9am-12noon and 3-
6pm.

Pinacoteca Nazionale
56 Via delle Belle Arti
40122 Bologna (BO)
☎ (051) 243249
Open: Tuesday to Saturday 9am-
2pm. Holidays 9am-1pm.

Modena
Museo d'Arte Medioevale e Moderna
Palazzo dei Musei
Palazzo Estense
41100 Modena (MO)
☎ (059) 223892
Open: Tuesday to Saturday 9am-
1pm.

Museo Archeologie ed Ethnologi
(address as above)
Open: Tuesday and Thursday 3-
6pm. Sunday 10am-12.30pm and 3-
6pm.

Mostra Bibliografica
(address as above)
Open: Monday to Saturday 9am-1pm.

Galleria Estense
(address as above)
Open: Tuesday, Wednesday and
Friday 9am-2pm. Thursday and
Saturday 9am-7.30pm. Sunday
9am-1pm.

Parma
Battistero
Piazza del Duomo
43100 Parma (PR)
☎ (0521) 235886
Open: daily 9am-12noon and 3-7pm.

Camera di San Paolo
Via Melloni
43100 Parma (PR)
☎ (0521) 233309
Open: Tuesday to Sunday 9am-
7.15pm.

Galleria Nazionale e Teatro Farnese
Palazzo Pilotta
43100 Parma (PR)
☎ (0521) 233718
Open: Tuesday to Sunday 9am-
7.15pm.

Museo Archeologico Nazionale
Palazzo Pilotta
43100 Parma (PR)
☎ (0521) 233718
Open: Tuesday to Sunday 9am-2pm.

ROUTE 9C
Cremona
Torrazza
Piazza del Comune
26100 Cremona (CR)
Open: winter Saturday and Sunday
10am-12.30pm and 3-6pm.
Summer Monday to Saturday
10am-12noon and 3-6.30pm.
Holidays 10am-12.30pm and 3-7pm.

Palazzo del Comunale
Piazza del Comune
26100 Cremona (CR)
Open: Monday to Saturday 9am-
12noon and 3-7pm. Holidays 9am-
12noon.

Museo Stradivariano
Via Palestro 17
26100 Cremona (CR)
☎ (0372) 29349

Open: Tuesday to Saturday
9.30am-12.15pm, 3-5.45pm. Sunday
and holidays 9.30am-12.15pm.

Museo Civico
4 Via V. Dati
26100 Cremona (CR)
☎ (0372) 29349
Open: Tuesday to Saturday
9.30am-12.15pm and 3-5.45pm.
Holidays 9.30am-12.15pm.

Museo del Duomo
14 Piazza del Duomo
20100 Milano (MI)
☎ (02) 860358
Open: Tuesday to Sunday 9am-
12.30pm and 3-6pm.

Milan
Museo d'Arte Contemporanea
Palazzo Reale
9 Piazza del Duomo
20100 Milano (MI)
☎ (02) 6236
Open: Tuesday to Sunday 9.30am-
12.15pm and 2.30-5.15pm.

La Scala Museo Teatrale
2 Piazza della Scala
20100 Milano (MI)
☎ (02) 8053418
Open: Monday to Saturday 9am-
12noon, 2-6pm. Holidays (summer
only) 9.30am-12noon and 2.30-6pm.

Musei Civiche
Castello Sforzesco
Piazza del Castello
20100 Milano (MI)
☎ (02) 875851
Open: Tuesday to Sunday 9.30am-
12.15pm and 2.30-5.15pm.

Pinacoteca di Brera
28 Via Brera
20100 Milano (MI)
☎ (02) 808387
Open: Tuesday to Sunday 9am-
1.45pm. Holidays 9am-12.45pm.

Cenacolo Vinciano
Piazza Santa Maria delle Grazie
20100 Milano (MI)
☎ (02) 4987588
Open: Tuesday to Friday 9am-
1.15pm and 2-6.15pm. Saturday to
Monday 9am-1.15pm.

*Museo Nazionale della Scienza e della
   Technica*
21 Via San Vittore
20100 Milano (MI)
☎ (02) 48010040
Open: Tuesday to Sunday 9.30am-
4.50pm.

Certosa di Pavia
26km (16 miles) south of Milan on
SS35.
Open: winter Tuesday to Sunday 9-
11.30am, 2.30-6pm.

Tourist Information Centres

ROUTE 9A
Rimini
Ente Provinciale Turismo
Piazzale C. Battisti
47037 Rimini (FO)
☎ (0541) 27927

San Marino
Ufficio Statale per il Turismo
Palazzo del Turismo
47031 San Marino
☎ (0541) 992102

Ravenna
Informazione Azienda Turismo
8-12 Via Salara
48100 Ravenna (RA)
☎ (0544) 35404

Azienda Promozione Turistica
2 Via San Vitale
48100 Ravenna (RA)
☎ (0544) 35755

ROUTE 9B
Bologna
Azienda di Promozione Turistica
Bologna e Provincia
45 Via Marconi
40122 Bologna (BO)
☎ (051) 237413

Municipio Centro d'Informazioni
Palazzo d'Accursio
Piazza Maggiore
40122 Bologna (BO)
☎ (051) 203040

Modena
Ente Provinciale per il Turismo
1A Corso Canal Grande
41100 Modena (MO)
☎ (059) 222482

Parma
Ente Provinciale per il Turismo
5 Piazzale Duomo
43100 Parma (PR)
☎ (0521) 34735

ROUTE 9C
Sabbioneta
Pro Loco
31 Via Vespasiano Gonzaga
46018 Sabbioneta (MN)
☎ (0375) 52039
Open: Tuesday to Saturday 9-
11.30am and 2.30-5pm. Holidays 9-
11.30am and 2.30-6pm.

Cremona
Ente Provinciale Turismo
5 Piazza del Comune
26100 Cremona (CR)
☎ (0372) 23233

Milan
Ente Provinciale Turismo
Palazzo del Turismo
1 Via Marconi
20100 Milano (MI)
☎ (02) 809662

10

UMBRIA

The land-locked region of Umbria, often described as Italy's 'green heart', is predominantly hilly and covered in a patchwork of neat vineyards and olive groves. It is sleepier and much less visited than neighbouring Tuscany, even though the various clans and duchies which ruled here from the eleventh to the sixteenth centuries, left the region with a wealth of fine art and architecture. Umbria is dotted with monasteries, hermitages and churches, many containing fine frescoes depicting the lives of saints, a great number of whom were born in Umbria, including St Francis of Assisi.

The route starts at the Adriatic coast, and heads inland to Umbria, through the northern part of the Marche, and gradually wends it way south to the fine Umbrian town of Todi. From here visitors who wish to join chapter 2 can do so at Orvieto, which is 34km (21 miles) to the west, while those returning to Rome can join the A1 motorway just south of Orvieto. Alternatively visitors can join the start of chapter 4 at Perugia by heading north of Todi for 35km (22 miles) on the SS3bis.

Route 10A — Pesaro to Gubbio

Pesaro is a large seaside town with a 4km (2 miles) stretch of sandy beach, good sport and leisure facilities, and a fine *centro storico*. The town was founded by the Romans and was known as *Pisaurum*, but its historic centre dates from the medieval period, when Pesaro was ruled by a succession of aristocratic families, such as the Malatesta, Sforza and Della Rovere.

Follow signs to one of the carparks around the centre, and head on foot to Piazza del Popolo, the main square. The *piazza* is surrounded by fine brick buildings, the grandest of which is Palazzo Ducale. Originally built in the fifteenth century for the Sforza dukes, it was enlarged by the Della Rovere family in the sixteenth. The *piazza* also contains an attractive fountain, Fontana dei Tritoni, which dates from the seventeenth century.

Leave the *piazza* from the north corner on Via Rossini. Rossini, who was born in Pesaro in 1792, lived at number 34, which is now a small museum. The Cattedrale, which dates from the thirteenth century and has an attractive brick façade, is a short distance further along the street, on the right. Take the street opposite the Cattedrale to Musei Civici, which contains a *pinacoteca* with paintings by the Venetian, Tuscan and Bolognese schools, including work by G. Bellini. It also houses one of the best collections of fifteenth- to seventeenth-century majolica ceramics in Italy.

Return to Via Rossini and head along the side of the Cattedrale to Piazzale Matteoti. Rocca Costanza, a stands at one end of the square, surrounded by a moat and guarded by four round towers. It was built for Costanza Sforza in 1474. From the opposite end of the square take Via San Francesco back towards the town centre. Look out for the finely carved Gothic portal of Madonna delle Grazie on the right as it has a number of attractive reliefs and sculptures dating from the mid-fourteenth century.

Visitors may wish to make the excursion 14km (9 miles) west of Pesaro to the impressive castle of **Gradara**. To do so, take the SS16 for 12km (7 miles) before reaching the left turn, which is signposted to Castello. The road crosses under the motorway, past a British military cemetery to the left, and then climbs up to the carpark at the foot of the castle walls. The castle has an advantageous position at the top of the hill and is surrounded by a small village enclosed within strongly fortified walls. It was built in the thirteenth century by the Malatesta, a family whose tragic tale is recounted by Dante in his *Divine Comedy*. Francesca da Rimini was married to Giovanni Malatesta but loved her brother-in-law, Paolo. Giovanni put an end to this embarrassing situation by murdering the pair of them, in the late thirteenth century, at Gradara. A small museum in the village has a collection of medieval weaponry and instruments of torture. The castle as it stands today dates from 1494, as it was rebuilt by G. Sforza. The interior is complete with its fifteenth- and sixteenth-century furnishings and frescoes, while the basement houses a prison and torture chamber. The castle turrets offer fine views to the coast, but good views can also be had by climbing the Torre di Porta from the main gate, and walking along the sentry walk.

Return to Pesaro and head right at the town's outskirts down the SS243 to Urbino. The road is flat and fast for the first 18km (11 miles), but after Cappone it leaves the Foglia river and follows the River Apsa, which carves a narrow valley through the hills for the remaining 17km (11 miles) to Urbino.

Urbino, spread along the top of two hills, is one of the finest towns in the Marche. Its architecture is the legacy of the Montefeltro family, which held power from the twelfth to the fifteenth centuries. The last of the Montefeltro dukes, Federico (1422-82), was a patron of the arts during the Renaissance and filled his court with artists and scholars. He has left the town a remarkable collection of art. The Renaissance in Urbino saw the birth of two great men: the architect Bramante and the painter Raphael.

Park outside the walls north of the town and take the elevator from the carpark, to the foot of Palazzo Ducale, the vast Renaissance palace which was built for Duke Federico in 1444. The entrance to the *palazzo*, now the seat of the Galleria Nazionale delle Marche, is in the corner of Piazza Duca Federico. The ground floor contains local archaeological finds. The main gallery is on the first floor and is spread through twenty-five elegant rooms decorated with fifteenth-century frescoes, marquetry and carvings. The first room contains a Della Robbia lunette, taken from San Domenico and a collection of medieval bas-reliefs. Fifteenth-century frescoes by G. Boccati, and paintings and furniture of the period, decorate rooms 2 through to 4, while room 5 contains frescoes from the church of San Biagio in Caprille. Other works of art from local churches fill rooms 6 and 7, the most notable of which is the *Crucifixion* by Pietro da Rimini. Renaissance paintings by the Rimini and Marche schools, are hung in rooms 8 through to 12. Two of the gallery's masterpieces, the *Flagellation*, and the *Madonna di Senigallia*, by Piero della Francesca, are hung in room 13. Room 14 is Duke Federico's study. It is clad in outstanding marquetry, the lower panels being attributed to Botticelli. Other exhibits of note in the museum are the Flemish and Gobelin tapestries, and the painting by Raphael, *La Muta*, in room 20. It is the only work by Raphael here, but it clearly demonstrates his immense talent. The most eye-dazzling ceiling in the *palazzo* is that of room 23, a magnificent work in stucco by F. Brandone (1522-75). The ten rooms on the top floor, added in 1536 by G. Genga, contain paintings and a collection of ceramics.

Back on Piazza Duca Federico, wander uphill past the Egyptian obelisk to the fourteenth-century church of San Domenico on the left. The buildings at the top of the hill are part of Urbino university, which is one of the oldest and has one of the best reputations in Italy. Return back downhill as far as the Duomo, which stands along the bottom edge of Piazza Duca Federico. The neo-Classical façade, dates from 1802, and was designed by C. Morigia. The gaunt interior contains Museo del Duomo Albani.

Continue downhill from the Duomo to Piazza della Repubblica, the town centre. Cross over to Via G. Mazzini, which leads from the west corner and climb the steps on the right, following Via Poste Vecchia for a short distance before turning left along Via Barocci. Follow this narrow street to the small church, Oratorio di San Giovanni Battista, which stands at the far end. On the same street, to the right, another tiny church, Oratorio di San Giuseppe, contains a stucco scene, dating from 1522 by F. Brandam.

Return to Piazza della Repubblica and cross over it to the fine loggia of San Francesco, which stands on the opposite corner. Head along Via Rafaello, which climbs uphill to Casa di Rafaello, the house where Raphael lived. This small museum is attractively restored in the style of the sixteenth century and contains paintings of the period, including works by Raphael's father, G. Santi, and a *Madonna and Child*, attributed to the young Raphael.

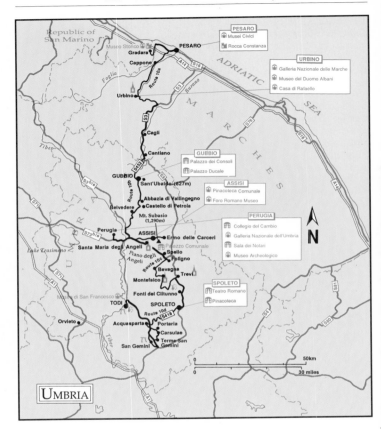

After Urbino the next place of interest is Gubbio, which lies just inside the Umbrian border, 70km (43 miles) to the south. From Urbino, follow the SS73bis for 18km (11 miles) to **Calmazzo** and turn right onto the SS3, which is signposted to Roma. The road passes through the Furlo tunnel, which is over 3km (2 miles) long, and follows the Burano river valley to **Cagli**, soon after which the valley narrows, and a Roman bridge, the Ponte di Epoca, is passed on the left. **Cantiano**, 11km (7 miles) south of Cagli, is a centre of Amaro, a sweet, herbal liqueur, which is popular in both the Marches and Umbria. Just after Cantiano turn right down the SS452, which winds for a further 15km (9 miles) to Gubbio.

Gubbio was first settled by the ancient Umbrian people in the third century BC and flourished during the medieval period, when it was an independent *comune*. In 1383 Antonio da Montefeltro

The Palazzo Ducale and attractive Fontana dei Tritoni, Pesaro

Market day in Gubbio

annexed Gubbio to the Urbino fiefdom and it remained in their hands throughout the Renaissance, a period that spawned Gubbio's famous ceramicist, Maestro Giorgio, as well as a good deal of fine architecture. Today Gubbio continues to make pottery, reproducing the flowery majolica ware, with its irridescent red glaze, of the sixteenth century. The town has also retained its medieval and Renaissance architecture.

Built on a hill and surrounded by a wall, the historic town centre, *vecchia citta*, is pedestrianised. The main carpark (except during the Tuesday market) is just inside the lower town walls, on Piazza Quaranta Martiri, near the church of San Francesco. The church, which dates from the thirteenth century, is worth popping into briefly as it contains a major fresco cycle, the *Life of the Virgin*, by O. Nelli, a leading artist of the Umbrian school. On the opposite side of the oval-shaped *piazza*, is an attractive weaver's loggia, where back in the fourteenth century wool was stretched out to dry. On market days in the summer, the cool shade beneath the arches is filled with a colourful fruit and vegetable market. Head uphill from the *piazza* to the most prominent building in Gubbio, Palazzo dei Consoli. Its crenellated walls and elegant belfry, rise above the town on Piazza della Signoria, the main square. Built between 1332 and 1337, it now houses the Museo Civico and Pinacoteca. A fine Gothic portal, reached by a flight of steps, leads into a great hall, the Salone dell'Arengo. The hall contains fragments of Roman masonry and a collection of medieval weapons. The most important exhibits, however, the Eugubine tablets, are in one of the two small adjoining rooms. These famous bronze tablets, seven in all, record events from the third to the first centuries BC. They are one of the best extant examples of Umbrian script and are written in both Etruscan and Latin. A grand stairway leads up from one end of the hall to the *pinacoteca* on the first floor. The collection is made up of religious paintings, dating from the fourteenth to the eighteenth centuries, by the Eugubian school, including works by T. and O. Nelli and F. Signorelli. The attractive loggia at the top of the building is reached from the last room. It overlooks the town, and in the plain below the excellently-preserved, first-century Roman theatre is clearly visible.

Back on Piazza della Signoria, spend some time browsing in the ceramic shops along Via dei Consoli, which runs along one side of the *piazza*. Many of the houses here, as well as in other streets, have unusual small arched doorways alongside the main door. Known as *porte della morte*, they were the door through which the occupants left their houses for the last time, and are typical of the region. A passage is signposted uphill to the Duomo and Palazzo Ducale from the street, as it leaves Piazza della Signoria. It is a steep 5-minute climb to the foot of the Duomo, from where a short flight of steps leads up to its fine Romanesque façade. It was built towards the end of the twelfth century and there are attractive carvings which symbolically represent the four Evangelists around its central window. The interior is a vast single nave with ten Gothic arches, the side walls of which are lined with sixteenth-century paintings by the Marches and Umbrian schools. A door on the right leads to an attractive cloistered presbytery, housing the Museo Diocesano.

Palazzo Ducale is directly opposite the Duomo. A modest façade leads into a fine inner courtyard surrounded by columns on three sides and attractive buttressing along the fourth. It was built for Federico da Montefeltro in 1476.

Return to Piazza della Signoria and head east along Via Savelli della Porta, which leaves the *piazza* from the back of the *municipio*. After some 400m (437yd) turn right along Via O. Nelli to the Gothic church of Santa Maria Nuova. Built in the fourteenth century, it contains a notable fresco by O. Nelli, the *Madonna del Belvedere*, which dates from 1413. Return to Via Savelli della Porta and continue to Porta Romana, the east gate of the town. Just outside the gate is the large church and convent of Sant'Agostino which was erected in the thirteenth century, although its rather unprepossessing façade was added in the eighteenth. The interior has excellent frescoes and should not be missed. Those in the presbytery are by O. Nelli and depict the *Last Judgement* (1420), while the walls are lined with a cycle showing the *Life of St Augustine*.

From the hillside above Sant'Agostino, a *cabinovia* climbs the steep slopes of Monte Ingino to **Basilica Sant'Ubaldo** (827m/2,712ft). The basilica, which dates from the sixteenth century, contains the mortal remains of the twelfth-century saint, Sant'Ubaldo. On 15 May an extraordinary race takes place, the Corsa dei Ceri, in honour of this saint, *Ceri*, cumbersome wooden obelisks, 8m (26ft) long, are carried by each of the three competing teams, who race from Piazza della Signoria up to the basilica.

Route 10B — Gubbio to Assisi

Leave Gubbio on the SS298, which heads south for 48km (30 miles) to Perugia. After 12km (7 miles) the road passes a fine abbey, the Abbazia di Valinengro, and the Castello di Petroia. **Belvedere**, 4km (2 miles) beyond the abbey is, as its name suggests, situated high up on a hilltop (662m/2,171ft) from where Perugia is visible in the distance on a clear day. From Belvedere the next 15km (9 miles) is all downhill, the road eventually reaching the junction with the SS3bis. This busy dual carriageway carves through Perugia's extensive industrial outskirts to the base of the hill on which the city is built. Follow signs to *centro* from here, climbing up a steep road past the Etruscan necropolis, the Ipogeo dei Volumni, on the right. At the top of the hill, follow signs to *scala mobili* and the main carpark on Piazza dei Partigiani. It is conveniently connected to the centre by a series of subterranean escalators.

Perugia, the capital of Umbria, has long been the most important settlement in the region. It first rose to prominence as far back as

500BC, when it was Etruscan, and over the years managed to side-step many of the bloody feuds which dogged the region, maintaining its political independence throughout the medieval period. However, as with most towns in Umbria in the sixteenth century, it was incorporated into the Papal States. Today, although the city is prosperous and is surrounded by modern industrial developments, nothing has been allowed to detract from or encroach on Perugia's very fine *centro storico*.

Visitors approaching the historic centre via the *scala mobili* will have the exciting experience of being escalated up through the vast underground palace, Rocca Paolina, which was designed by Sangallo for Pope Paul III in the sixteenth century. The escalator emerges on the nineteenth-century Piazza Italia, seat of the *prefettura*, from where the main artery of the city, Corso Vannuci, a wide pedestrian thoroughfare lined with elegant shops and cafés, heads north to the Cattedrale at the city centre.

The main places of interest in the city lie along Corso Vannuci. The first is reached by passing through one end of Palazzo dei Priori to the Collegio del Cambio (1452-7), the city exchange. The large hall inside, Sala dell'Udienza, is decorated with excellent frescoes, as is the small but attractive chapel. Those in the hall are by Perugino, while those in the chapel are by B. Bonfigli (1496) and G. di Paolo (1519), a pupil of Perugino. The Collegio della Mercanzia is next

The Guelph lion and Griffin are the symbol of Perugia

door. Built in the early fourteenth century, it was used as a meeting hall for the city guilds, and has a finely panelled interior.

Next on the left is the main entrance to Palazzo dei Priori. Its façade, pierced by a multitude of mullioned windows, was built between 1429 and 1443. The top floor houses the Galleria Nazionale dell'Umbria. It contains an unrivalled collection of paintings by the Umbrian School, which date from the twelfth to the seventeenth centuries. Many of the paintings are by well-known artists such as Duccio, Piero della Francesca, Fra Angelico and Pietro da Cortona to name but a few.

The oldest section of Palazzo dei Priori dates from 1293 and faces onto Piazza IV Novembre at the end of Corso Vanucci. A monumental staircase leads up from the *piazza* to its fine Gothic portal, which is decorated with a Guelph lion and a griffin, the symbol of Perugia. The council chamber, Sala dei Notari, inside is covered by frescoes dating from the thirteenth century and has the original fifteenth-century benches and stalls.

At the centre of Piazza IV Novembre stands the beautiful Gothic ✷ fountain, Fontana Maggiore, which dates from the thirteenth century. It is decorated with excellent reliefs by N. and G. Pisano, the originals of which are in the Galleria Nazionale dell'Umbria.

Palazzo del Capitano, Gubbio

Cattedrale di San Lorenzo dominates the opposite side of the *piazza*. Constructed between 1345 and 1490, this fine Gothic cathedral has a bronze statue of Pope Julius III (1555) to the left of the door, and an inlaid exterior pulpit to the right. The spacious interior is divided into three naves, lined with chapels along either side. The Cappella San Bernardino on the right contains an impressive painting by Baraccio, the *Descent from the Cross* (1569), while the Cappella Sant'Anello on the left, houses the wedding ring of the Virgin, which is made of a solid lump of white onyx. The treasury and other art works are kept in the Museo Capitolare, at the back of the cathedral, in the cloisters.

Return to Palazzo dei Priori and follow the narrow medieval street, Via dei Priori, which leads from the back of the *palazzo*. After a pleasant walk of 400m (437yd), which passes numerous small churches and one of Perugia's few remaining towers, Torre degli Scirri, the street opens out into a grassy *piazza* in front of the Oratorio di San Bernardino. This small church, peacefully set, just inside the west city wall, is remarkable for its façade of coloured marbles, which is by Agostino di Duccio (1457-61). The plain interior contains a fourth-century sarcophagus at the altar which originally stood in the church of San Francesco al Prato, next door to the right. Sadly only the shell of this building now remains standing.

To visit the monuments in the south part of the city, including an excellent archaeological museum, return to Piazza Italia, where the escalator from the carpark first emerged, and head down, from the left side of the *piazza*, to the Etruscan gate, Porta Marzia, which is built into the walls of Rocca Paolino. This gate, which dates from the third century BC, leads into the maze of underground streets inside the palace. Continue down the hill to the street below, Corso Cavour, and follow it south for 250m (273yd) to the church of San Domenico. The church was originally built in 1305 to a design by G. Pisano, but the vast interior is rather gaunt, and dates mainly from the seventeenth century. However, the tomb of Pope Benedict XI (1324) in the chapel to the right of the main altar, is worth more than a passing mention as it is richly sculpted from Roman marble in the Gothic style to a design which is commonly attributed to G. Pisano.

The archaeological museum is to the left of the church, and is housed in its massive cloisters. It contains an important collection of archaeological finds dating from prehistoric, Etruscan and Roman eras, as well as some early Umbrian pottery and bronze. One of the highlights of the collection is the *cippo Perugino* a tablet covered by one of the longest Etruscan inscriptions yet to be found. Looking out over the landscape from the cloisters, visitors will notice the fine Benedictine church of San Pietro, with its pointed *campanile*.

Leaving Perugia on the SS75, the route heads south for 20km (12 miles) to **Santa Maria degli Angeli**, which is just below Assisi. This vast Baroque basilica gives its name to the town, and was built in 1569 to a design by Alessi over a thirteenth-century church, the

Porziuncola. This tiny church played an important part in Franciscan history as it was here that the order originated (1209) and that St Francis died (1226), making the present day basilica a major pilgrimage site. The Porziuncola, set beneath the massive dome of the interior, is covered in fourteenth- and fifteenth-century frescoes. Its façade, which was painted by a German, F. Overbeck in 1829, leads into an intimate interior. The fine polyptych at the altar depicts the life of St Francis and was painted in 1393 by Ilario di Viterbo.

The Cappella del Transito, the chapel in the right transept, commemorates the spot where St Francis died. Decorated with frescoes of Franciscan monks by Lo Spagna (around 1520), the chapel contains a terracotta statue of St Francis by A. Della Robbia (1490). A door on the right leads through the sacristy, past a bed of roses, which have been thornless ever since St Francis is said to have wrestled with temptation in them, to the Cappella del Roseto. This chapel, built over a grotto, is beautifully frescoed by Tiberio d'Assisi (1518). Next to it is the tiny Cappello del Pianto, and nearby is the old pharmacy, as well as a souvenir shop.

Assisi, just 5km (3 miles) north-east, stands raised above the Piano degli Angeli plain, on the slopes of Mount Subasio. The road winds up in the shadow of the massive buttresses which support the great Franciscan basilica at the north-east end of the town. Follow signs to one of the carparks outside the town walls and proceed to the basilica, Assisi's chief attraction, on foot as the centre is pedestrianised.

St Francis, the son of a wealthy cloth merchant, was born in Assisi in 1182. He was 25 years old when, after serving a jail sentence in Perugia and recovering from a serious illness, he renounced worldly possessions, saying that they were the root of all evil. He carried out his mission to 'repair the Church' by founding the Franciscan Mendicant Friars, an order based on poverty, chastity and obedience. By the year of his death in 1226 the Franciscans had a widespread following, which is no less diminished today.

The basilica was built to house the saint's remains and is now the world's most important Franciscan sanctuary, as well as being a treasure house of frescoes, which attracts a constant stream of monks, pilgrims, and tourists alike. It was built in two stages: the lower basilica was constructed in 1228, while the upper basilica, although started in 1230, was not completed until 1253. It is best to start with the lower basilica which is entered from Piazza Inferiore through a finely carved Gothic portal. The vaulted interior, dark and atmospheric, contains an overwhelming wealth of frescoes. If at all possible visitors should come equipped with a strong flashlight as the frescoes are very poorly lit, even though they are some of the greatest Italian fresco works of the thirteenth and fourteenth centuries. Cappella della Maddalena, the third chapel on the right, is frescoed by Giotto or his pupils and includes what is believed to be one of the first portraits ever to be painted. It is of the Bishop of Assisi (1296-1329) and is known as *Brebaldo Pontano protected by San Rufino*.

The right transept contains a fresco by Cimabue, the *Madonna, Angels and St Francis,* as well as frescoes by Giotto, his school, and Simone Martini. The left transept is frescoed by P. Lorenzetti and assistants, and contains an exceptional *Crucifixion* and *Madonna and Child with St Francis and St Clare.* Stairs wind down from either side of the nave into St Francis' crypt, which was discovered, only recently, in 1818.

The upper basilica is a complete contrast, being both larger and lighter, but has equally remarkable frescoes. The walls of the vast single nave are covered by twenty-eight massive paintings depicting the *Life of St Francis.* They were started in 1296, which means that if they are by Giotto, as most people believe, he would have been just 29 years old. They are poised stylistically at the very birth of Renaissance painting, and their naturalism seemed revolutionary at the time. Their subject, however, is a familiar one and similar episodes can be seen in almost every fresco cycle dedicated to St Francis. Amongst the most popular scenes are: the saint offering his cloak to a beggar, the saint chasing the devils from Arezzo, the saint trying to convert the Sultan and the saint preaching to birds.

Both the left and right transepts contain the sadly faded remains of large frescoes by Cimabue, Giotto's master and one of the most influential early Italian artists. The outlines of what must have been a powerful *Crucifixion* can be discerned quite easily. The fine thirteenth-century stained-glass windows and the inlaid stalls in the choir are also worthy of attention.

Leave the upper basilica through the main portal and head across Piazza Superiore to the town centre, which lies roughly 800m (850yd) to the east. Those on foot should head along Via San Francesco, which is a lively pedestrian thoroughfare lined with medieval buildings. About 400m (437yd) from the basilica, the street passes the Oratorio dei Pellegrini on the right, a tiny church which is decorated with fifteenth-century frescoes by M. da Gualdo. From here continue straight ahead, along Via di Seminario and then Via Portica to the main square, Piazza del Comune. At the corner of the *piazza,* to the left of Via Portica, stands the Foro Romano Museo, which contains the remains of the Roman forum. On the left side of the *piazza* stands the façade of a Roman temple, with six impressive, first-century columns. It is one of the best-preserved in Italy even though only the façade has survived. Behind the columns, doors lead into the little church of Maria di Minerva which occupies the site of the rest of the temple. The Palazzo dei Priori, on the right side of the *piazza,* dates from 1337 and contains the Pinacoteca Comunale, a collection of paintings and frescoes from local churches.

Leave Piazza del Comune from the north-east corner and head uphill for 200m (218yd) along Via San Rufino to Duomo San Rufino. Built in the twelfth century, it has a fine Romanesque façade with three richly carved portals, which is pierced by three rose windows. The squat *campanile* on the left is built over the remains of a Roman cistern, while inside the Duomo there is a museum, the Museo

Capitolare. It contains a small but notable collection of religious paintings and frescoes, dating from the thirteenth to fifteenth centuries, including an excellent triptych, *Madonna, Child and Four Saints*, by N. Alunno. St Rufino's third-century sarcophagus lies beneath the Duomo in the crypt, which is entered from the small piazza in front of the Duomo. St Rufino was martyred in AD238 and is the patron saint of Assisi.

The evocative ruins of Rocca Maggiore stand high above the *piazza* on the slopes of Mount Subasio. It is a stiff walk, especially if the weather is hot, and visitors might prefer to go by car. A small road leads up to the castle walls from the site of the Roman amphitheatre at the east end of town. The castle was built in 1367 for Cardinal Albornoz, but has been ruined since the eighteenth century. The interior is open to the public and the site offers fine views down over Assisi. One of the churches visible is that of Santa Chiara, which is almost due south of the Duomo. Built between 1257 and 1265, it stands in a small square, and has a simple façade that is decorated with bands of pink and white stone. Set into the façade is a fine rose window and an elegant portal, with lions on either side. The church contains the remains of St Clare, companion of St Francis and founder of the Franciscan order of the Poor Clares (1212). Relics associated with St Clare are kept in the first chapel on the right, Cappella San Giorgio, while her remains are in the crypt below.

Visitors not yet exhausted with the cult of St Francis may wish to visit **Eremo delle Carceri**. This picturesque monastery lies at the edge of a gorge on the slopes of Monte Subasio, 3km (2 miles) above the town. The road to it is clearly marked by yellow signs from the town. The monastery was built in the thirteenth century on the site where St Francis came to pray and meditate. A path leads from the carpark to a courtyard which contains a well and a small fifteenth-century church, Chiesina di San Bernardino. It continues past another tiny church, partly hewn from rock, Chiesina dell'Eremo, which dates from the thirteenth century to a narrow passage that leads past a grotto to the edge of the gorge. The footpath makes a circuit back to the carpark via Cappella della Maddalena, another small chapel which was built in the fifteenth century.

Another excursion on the St Francis itinerary is that of San Damiano. This convent, which is also clearly signposted, lies $2^1/_2$km ($1^1/_2$ miles) below the town amidst a grove of olive trees. It was here that St Francis is said to have first received his message to 'repair the Church', and also where the order of the Poor Clares was established in 1253. The main church Chiesa Santuario, its walls blackened with age, leads into the convent through a door at the back on the right. Stairs lead up to a frescoed chapel, from where another flight of steps climbs up to the dormitory. A door to the right leads into the cloisters, at the far side of which is the Refettorio di Santa Chiara, the refectory. It contains what are believed to be the original tables and chairs.

Route 10C — Assisi to Trevi

The small medieval town of **Spello**, 12km (7 miles) south-east of Assisi along the SS75, is built on the site of Roman *Hispellum*. The scant remains of its Roman theatre, which date from the Augustan era when Spello was a Roman colony, are passed on the right just outside the town. The town has never expanded much beyond its Roman walls, which are 2km (1 mile) in length, and have five gates in all. As the walls come into sight, look for Porto Venere, a Roman gate flanked by towers, above the road to the left. A little further on, Porta Urbica is passed before reaching Piazza Kennedy. Enter the town walls from Piazza Kennedy through Porta Consolare, another grand gate, adorned with three statues from the Roman theatre. Follow Via Consolare up the hill and look for a parking space near the church of Santa Maria Maggiore, on the right.

Built in the twelfth century, this church is the highlight of Spello. It contains three outstanding frescoes by Pinturicchio, which are considered to be the artist's best work. The frescoes, dating from 1501, cover the walls of the small chapel on the left of the nave, Cappella Baglioni. The right wall holds the *Dispute in the Temple*, the left wall the *Annunciation*, while the back wall depicts the *Coming of the Magi* and the *Adoration of the Shepherds*.

The thirteenth-century church of Sant'Andrea, a short distance further up Via Cavour, also contains work by Pinturicchio. The most outstanding is the excellent *Madonna, Child and Saints*, which is hung in the right transept. Also of note is the wooden crucifix, which is painted in the style of Giotto and dates from the thirteenth century.

Continue up Via Cavour to the main square, Piazza della Repubblica. The Palazzo Comunale has a collection of Roman stones embedded in the walls of the ground floor, while on the first floor, Sala Emilia Greco, contains a small *pinacoteca*. Continue up the hill from Piazza della Repubblica, along Via Garibaldi to Via Belvedere. The street ends at a panoramic terrace, which offers fine views across the plain to Santa Maria degli Angeli, and on a clear day, Perugia.

Follow the SS75 south-east of Spello to the outskirts of the modern town of Foligno. Turn right to **Bevagna**, a charming but little-visited town, which is just 7km (4 miles) across the plain. It has fine medieval ramparts, built between 1249 and 1377, on Roman foundations. Drive along the walls to the main gate, Porta Foligno and look for a parking space inside the walls near the main square, Piazza Silvestri.

The *piazza* is surrounded by excellently-preserved medieval buildings, the oldest of which is the oddly truncated San Silvestro, a small Romanesque church dating from 1195. The Gothic Palazzo dei Consoli in the corner to the left of the church was built in 1275 and has four deep arches supporting an attractive façade of double-arch windows. The interior, entered up a monumental staircase, contains one of the finest theatres in the region. The church of San Michele, on the opposite side of the *piazza*, also dates from the thirteenth century and its Romanesque façade is decorated with Cosmati mosaic work. The gaping hole in the façade was left by a rose window which was added in the eighteenth century but subsequently removed.

Follow Corso Matteoti, the main thoroughfare in the town, from the *piazza* to Palazzo Comunale on the left. The first floor of the *palazzo* holds the Pinacoteca Comunale; a collection made up of paintings dating from the fourteenth to seventeenth centuries, and featuring work by the sixteenth-century Umbrian artist, Dono Doni. Continue to wander along Corso Matteoti, past the numerous small Baroque churches which line the street, to Piazza Garibaldi. On the right is a small church built on the foundations of a second-century Roman temple. Follow signs from here, left to the Roma Mosaica which are housed at number two Via di Porta Guelfo. The mosaics used to decorate the second-century Roman baths and are executed in black and white stone. They depict Triton surrounded by sea creatures and are in very good condition.

Leave Bevagna on the SS316 and fork left to **Montefalco** which is 6km (4 miles) to the south. The road passes through vineyards of the small black Sagrantino grape, which is used in the unusual sweet red wine, *passito*, for which Montefalco is well known. The town has a panoramic setting along the top of a ridge, earning it the title 'the balcony of Umbria', *ringhiera dell'Umbria*. Surrounded by a medieval wall, the town contains an extraordinary wealth of art, as well as many picturesque winding streets. Park at the top of the town on the circular main square, Piazza del Comune. Lined with mulberry trees, the square is dominated by the medieval Palazzo Comunale and its tall tower, from where there are superb views of the town.

Montefalco's most impressive attraction is the church of San Francesco and its museum. It is 50m (55yd) from the *piazza*, down Via Ringhiera Umbra, on the right. The church was originally built by the Franciscans between 1334 and 1340, but is now deconsecrated. It has recently been restored and contains magnificent frescoes, the most notable being those by the Florentine artist, Benozzo Gozzoli (1421-91). The apse contains Gozzoli's greatest fresco work, a radiant cycle, in fourteen parts, of the *Life of St Francis*. The Cappella San Gerolamon, the first side chapel on the left, is also covered in frescoes by Gozzoli, which date from 1450. The first chapel on the right is by Perugino (1515), while the second chapel, next to it, contains an excellent painting, *Madonna and Child with Saints*, by Tiberio d'Assisi (1510). Other chapels are frescoed by lesser-known, Umbrian artists, dating from the fifteenth and sixteenth centuries.

The museum consists of the Museo Lapidario on the ground floor, a collection of carved masonry dating from Roman to medieval times, and a *pinacoteca* upstairs. Arranged around five rooms, the gallery contains an excellent collection of Umbrian paintings dating from the fourteenth to seventeenth centuries, mostly removed from local churches. An entire room is devoted to the work of Montefalco's local artist, F. Melanzio (1481-1524). Other painters of note in the collection include G. Corraduccio, also from Montefalco, and the Renaissance artists Perugino and Tiberio d'Assisi.

Return to Piazza del Comune and cross over to Vicolo degli Operai, a narrow lane which heads downhill from the opposite side. It leads through a picturesque quarter of the town to a number of attractive churches, each clearly signposted. The first church, Santa Lucia, is on the left, a short distance along a charming street of rustic houses. Built in the thirteenth century, this tiny church is constructed from pink stone, and contains a sole fresco fragment of the saint, Lucia, in the back left corner. Continue down the hill and bear right along Viale Federico II to the much larger church of Santa Chiara.

Santa Chiara (St Clare), not to be confused with Santa Chiara of Assisi, was born in Montefalco in 1268. She became a nun at the early age of 6, and carried out her life's mission 'to carry the cross in her heart' in the Augustinian convent, still in use today, behind the church. The church itself dates from the eighteenth century and is of little interest, apart from containing the mummified body of St Clare herself. However, the chapel at the back of the church on the left, Cappella di Santa Croce, contains remarkable frescoes. Ring the bell for the door to be opened. The chapel, built in 1303, was frescoed by artists of the Umbrian school in 1333. The cycle depicts the *Life of St Clare*. On the right wall is a representation of the saint aged 6 and her first vision of the Pilgrim Christ.

Continue downhill, along Via Verdi, for 150m (164yd) to Sant'Illuminata on the left. Built in the sixteenth century this small church contains interesting frescoes by F. Melanzio. Head back up the hill, past Santa Chiara, and continue right along Viale Federico II to the church of San Bartolomeo. The church is built into the town walls, next to the thirteenth-century gate, Porto Federico II, and there are fine views from the walls across the Umbrian countryside.

Yet another interesting church, San Fortunato, lies just outside the town, $1^1/_2$km (1 mile) from the south walls. It is probably best to drive there, but be careful not to pass the entrance on the left, which is not clearly signposted. Set amongst olive groves and vineyards it was built in the fifteenth century on the site of a Roman basilica that dated from the fifth century. The main attraction is the courtyard in front of the church, which is decorated with frescoes by Tiberio d'Assisi. The Cappella delle Rose, on the left side of the courtyard, also frescoed by Tiberio d'Assisi, dates from 1512 and contains the *Life and History of St Francis*. Inside the church there are a few fragments of frescoes by B. Gozzoli.

Trevi, 14km (9 miles) east of Montefalco, is another of Umbria's small but pleasant towns. Steeply stacked on a hill above the main road to Spoleto, most people pass by it without stopping, even though the 3km (2 miles) ascent is well worth the effort. As the road winds up through the olive groves, look out for Madonna delle Lacrime, on the right. This attractive church was built in 1487 and contains sixteenth-century frescoes and an *Epiphany* painted by

Perugino (1521). Park on Piazza Garibaldi, just inside the eastern town walls and head for the town centre, Piazza Mazzini, which is 150m (164yd) west along Via Roma. The Palazzo Comunale is the main building on the *piazza*. It has a fine arcaded façade and contains a *pinacoteca* on the first floor. Amongst the most important works in the collection are a large painting by Lo Spagna, the *Coronation of the Virgin* (1522) and *Madonna* by Pinturicchio.

From the *piazza* follow signs through the maze of pretty cobbled streets up to Duomo Sant'Emiliano. It has a fine Romanesque façade dating from the twelfth century, and contains frescoes attributed to F. Melanzio (1510-12). To visit Trevi's Franciscan church return down the hill to Piazza Mazzini and head north along Via San Francesco for 100m (110yd). This thirteenth-century church has a severe Gothic façade and a sombre interior with recently restored frescoes dating from the fourteenth and fifteenth centuries.

Route 10D — Trevi to Todi

Follow the SS3 south of Trevi along the Clitunno river valley, through gentle hills covered with olive groves. After 9km (6 miles) the road passes **Fonti del Clitunno**, one of Italy's most famous springs. In Roman times it was a spa, and a temple to Clittunus stood here. Since then it has provided inspiration for any number of poets and artists, from Virgil to Byron, although today the tranquillity of this sacred spot is somewhat marred by the souvenir shops and restaurants.

Continue south for 12km (7 miles) to **Spoleto** which stands on a hill just to the right of the road. Do not attempt to drive into the historic centre as the streets are very narrow and many are pedestrianised, instead look for a parking space around the stadium, south of the centre, or along Viale Martiri on the east side of town.

Spoleto, originally an ancient Umbrian settlement, was known as *Spoletium* during Roman times, when it was a prosperous colony. It was destroyed by the Goth Totila in AD545 but subsequently rebuilt by the Lombards who made it the capital of the Duchy of Spoleto. Its power grew until it was razed to the ground again by F. Barbarossa in 1155. Almost 200 years later it fell under the protection of the papacy and managed, during a period of comparative peace, to once again become one of the most important towns in the region. Today, it is a centre of art and culture, and hosts one of Europe's major international festivals, the Festival dei Due Mondi.

Start a tour of the town at the Duomo. It is one of the most beautiful in Umbria and is pleasingly set on a gently sloping *piazza* with a backdrop of wooded hills. Constructed in 1067 on the site of a seventh-century church, the upper tier and rose windows were added during the thirteenth century. Carved reliefs of the Evangelists surround the largest window, while the arch above contains a Byzantine style mosaic, *Christ Between the Virgin and St John*, which dates from 1207. The *campanile*, on the left of the façade dates from the twelfth century, while the portico is a Renaissance addition and was built between 1491 and 1504.

The interior, with its original Romanesque mosaic floor, is enlivened by the rich colours of the recently restored frescoes by Fra Lippo Lippi in the presbytery. They were painted between 1467 and 1469 and were the artist's last work. From left to right the frescoes are: the *Annunciation*, the *Passage of the Virgin*, and the *Nativity*. The ceiling of the apse has a fresco which depicts the *Coronation of the Virgin*. Other frescoes, not restored but nonetheless impressive, cover the Cappella di Constantino Erioli, in the right nave. The chapel is composed of two small rooms, the first of which contains a *Madonna and Saints* by Pinturicchio, while the frescoes covering the walls of the second room are attributed to a sixteenth-century Sicilian artist, J. Santori.

Climb back up to the top of the *piazza*, passing the small Romanesque church of Sant'Eufemia on the right. Turn left up Via Saffi, a picturesque street lined with small galleries, and continue along it to Piazza F. Campello. At the top of the *piazza* there is a finely sculpted fountain, Fontana dei Mascherone, which dates from 1642. On the hillside above the *piazza* stands the massive Rocca del Albornoz. Construction was started on the orders of Cardinal Albornoz in 1359 and was finished in 1362. Up until 1984 it was used as a prison, but a massive restoration project since then has brought to light the original frescoes and carvings which decorate its interior.

To visit the Rocca and also to make a circuit around the base of its walls, take Via del Ponte from the top of Piazza F. Campello. The turning to the Rocca is on the left, while the road on the right leads to an impressive bridge before continuing in a circle beneath the castle walls. The bridge, the Ponte delle Torri, was originally a Roman aqueduct, and spans the Tessino river gorge which is 230m (754ft) wide. Reconstructed at the end of the thirteenth century to a design by Gattapone, it has ten slender arches, each 80m (262ft) high. A walkway leads across the bridge, offering excellent views midway, to the ruined tower house at the other side. From here visitors may wish to follow the footpath along the foot of Monteluco to the church of San Pietro (see below), which is roughly 2km (1 mile) to the south.

To continue a tour of the town, return to Piazza Campello, either by completing the circuit around the Rocca, a walk of about 20 minutes in all, or by returning back along Via del Ponte. Head back along Via Saffi, past Sant'Eufemia and take the first left to Piazza Mercato. The Palazzo Comunale which overlooks this lively market place houses a small but notable *pinacoteca*, on the first floor. The collection, which can only be visited in the company of a custodian, is made up of paintings dating from the twelfth to the eighteenth centuries. Amongst the most prominent works in the collection are those by the sixteenth-century painter Lo Spagna.

Head south across the *piazza*, which was once the site of the Roman forum, to Arco di Druso, the original forum gate, which was built in

AD23 to commemorate Drusus' victories in Germany. Pass through the gate and turn right at the bottom of the road, down Via Brignone. Follow the street for 100m (110yd) to Piazza della Liberta. On the west side of the *piazza* it is possible to look down over the Roman theatre, which dates from the first century. It is rather hemmed in by later buildings, particularly the church of Sant'Agate, which occupies most of the stage area, but has been restored and is still used during the summer festival.

A sight not to be missed in Spoleto is the church of San Pietro. It is just south of the town, off the main road to Terni. It is remarkable for its beautifully carved façade, which is decorated with a wealth of medieval bas reliefs. The reliefs carved in panels depict scenes from the Gospels as well as medieval legends. There is also an attractive scrolled pattern surrounding the door, which represents the tree of life, while the carved figures surrounding the rose window are of the Evangelists.

The SS418 from Spoleto to **Acquasparta**, 25km ($15^1/_2$ miles) to the west, passes through the Umbrian hills and is quite picturesque. Acquasparta lies directly above the SS3bis on the slopes of the Naia river valley and is best known for being a spa centre. Small resorts are built around the natural springs, the Sorgente dell'Amerino, at the north end of town, and the Sorgente Furapane which are 2km (1 mile) to the south. Contained within a fine wall, the town holds little of particular interest apart from the fine sixteenth-century Palazzo Cesi on the main *piazza*, and the maze of medieval streets which course through the south end of town.

An excursion 9km (6 miles) south can be taken along the SS3bis to visit another spa town, **San Gemini**. This old hill town with its attractive *piazza* and Gothic church of San Francesco, is the bottling centre of the famous San Gemini water, which is distributed all over Italy. The springs are at **Terme San Gemini** $3^1/_2$km (2 miles) north of the town. The spa has a fine, 8 hectare (20 acres) park and two springs, the Fabia, recommended for kidney and liver complaints, and the San Gemini. Just 2km (1 mile) further up the road are the remains of *Carsulae*, the best Roman ruins in Umbria. They are set in lovely wooded countryside and are reached by following the road up the hill above the spa, turning left at the junction. Follow the narrow road signposted on the left until it peters out into a track, at which point the ruins come into view.

Founded as a Roman colony, it rose to prominence with the construction of Via Flaminia, around 220BC. The city, once likened in grandeur to *Pompeii*, was sacked in the ninth century and never recovered from the shock. Start a tour at the medieval church of San Damiano to the left of the track, which is constructed of Roman stones taken from the forum. From the church, head up the paved way, the former Via Flaminia, passing the scant remains of a temple at the edge of the forum on the left. To the right of the road lie the foundations of a basilica, which was originally the law courts. The road, rutted by centuries of passing carts and carriages, leads to Arco di San Damiano, the Roman city gate. Continue past the gate to see the remains of two large Roman mausoleums, before returning back up the Roman road to the amphitheatre, which lies on the opposite side of the modern road. The Roman amphitheatre is just visible in a natural depression, although the theatre behind is better preserved.

Return to Acquasparta by following the track north of the ruins. Shortly after passing the village of **Portaria**, which is straggled along the hillside on the right, the track meets the SS3. Pass under the SS3 and head towards Acquasparta from where the SS3 itself can be joined. Follow the road north for 21km (13 miles) to **Todi** and look for a parking space outside the town walls near Porta Romana.

The town occupies an excellent position, on a hilltop with a commanding view over the Naia and Tiber river valleys. The history of Todi is almost visible, like the strata of a rock. Etruscan foundations lie beneath Roman ruins, which in turn support the prosperous town that developed here during the medieval era. After a period of decline in the fourteenth and fifteenth centuries the town became prosperous once more in the sixteenth, and a number of Renaissance monuments were erected.

The most interesting approach to the town centre is through the

The best Roman ruins in Umbria can be seen at Carsulae

Etruscan gate, Porta Marzia, which stands on the main street, Corso Cavour. Head up the hill from the gate for just over 100m (110yd), before taking the right turn to Piazza di Mercato Vecchio, a small market place which stands on the site of the former Roman forum. Four massive arches support the remains of a Doric frieze along the back of the *piazza*.

π

Santa Maria della Consolazione at Todi, is one of the finest Renaissance churches in Italy

Return to Corso Cavour and continue up the hill, past Palazzo Atti (1552) on the right, to Piazza del Popolo. This fine medieval *piazza* has been the centre of the town since Roman times. On the right is Palazzo del Capitano, which is joined to Palazzo del Popolo by a grand external staircase. Palazzo del Capitano was built in 1290 and has a fine façade pierced by triplets of Gothic windows, while Palazzo del Popolo, with its crenellated top, is one of the oldest civic palaces in Italy and was built between 1213 and 1233. At the southernmost end of the *piazza* stands the Palazzo dei Priori, which, distinguished by its large trapezoidal tower of 1514, dates from between 1293 and 1337.

The Duomo, built during the twelfth century on the site of a Roman temple, fills the northern end of the *piazza*. Its Romanesque façade of pink and white marble leads into a plain interior, divided into three naves by attractive Gothic columns. The most outstanding feature of the interior are the beautifully inlaid stalls of the choir, which date from 1530, but also of note is the thirteenth-century crucifix at the altar and the large sixteenth-century fresco of the *Last Judgement* by Ferrau da Faenza which covers the entrance wall. Also look out for the three carved figures to the left of the main door which are by the famous sculptor A. Pisano. The crypt, reached by a door at the back of the church on the left contains the Lapidario Museo, which consists of a collection of masonry fragments.

Leave Piazza del Popolo from the south side and head down to Piazza della Repubblica. Raised above the south side of the *piazza* is the church of San Fortunato. A striking Gothic portal, flanked by statues, leads into a large interior. Four massive piers divide the church into three naves, and there are chapels on either side. The fourth chapel on the right contains the *Madonna and Child*, by Masolino da Panicale (1432). Also worth seeing are the fresco fragments in the sixth chapel on the right, which depict the *Life of St Francis*. The crypt, seen through a grill beneath the altar, and reached by a door on the left, contains the tomb of the Franciscan poet, Fra Iacopone (1230-1306).

Outside San Fortunato, turn left and walk up the hill to the charming cloisters of Liceo-Ginnasio. Follow the track on the right to the remains of the Rocca, which was built by Cardinal Albornoz in 1376. The ruins are set in shady public gardens overlooking the town and the surrounding countryside.

Santa Maria della Consolazione, one of the finest Renaissance churches in Italy, lies at the bottom of the hill, south of the gardens. It is a 10-minute walk from the gardens or a short drive along the lower city wall. Construction started on the church in 1504 to a design by Bramante but was only completed in 1617. It has a symmetrical quatrefoil shape with a vast dome at its centre. The light and airy interior is lined with statues of the Apostles and has decorative altars in each of its four niches.

Additional Information

Places of Interest

ROUTE 10A
Pesaro
Casa di Rossini
Via Rossini 34
61100 Pesaro (PS)
Open: winter Monday to Saturday
10am-12noon, 2-4pm, holidays
10am-12noon. Summer Monday to
Saturday 10am-12noon, 4-6pm,
holidays 10am-12noon.

Musei Civici
29 Piazza Toschi Mosca
61100 Pesaro (PS)
Open: winter Tuesday to Sunday
8.30am-1.30pm. Summer Tuesday
to Sunday 9.30am-12.30pm and 4-
6.45pm.

Gradara
Castello
61012 Gradara (PS)
☎ (054) 964181
Open: Tuesday to Saturday 9am-
2pm. Holidays 9am-1pm.

Museo Storico
Piazza 5 Novembre
61012 Gradara (PS)
☎ (054) 964154
Open: Monday to Saturday 9am-
2pm. Holidays 9am-1pm.

Urbino
Galleria Nazionale delle Marche
Palazzo Ducale
61029 Urbino (PS)
☎ (0722) 2760
Open: winter Tuesday to Saturday
9am-2pm, holidays 9am-1pm.
Summer Tuesday to Saturday 9am-
7pm, Monday 9am-2pm, holidays
9am-1pm.

Museo del Duomo Albani
Duomo
61029 Urbino (PS)
Open: daily 9am-12.30pm and 3-7pm.

Oratorio di San Giovanni Battista
Via Barocci
61029 Urbino (PS)
Open: Monday to Saturday 10am-
12noon and 3-5pm. Holidays 10am-
12.30pm.

Casa di Rafaello
Via Rafaello
61029 Urbino (PS)
Open: winter Monday to Saturday
9am-1pm and 2.30-5pm. Holidays
9am-1pm. Summer Monday to
Saturday 9am-1pm and 3-7pm.
Holidays 9am-1pm.

Gubbio
Palazzo dei Consoli
Piazza della Signoria
06024 Gubbio (PG)
Open: winter daily 9am-1pm and
3-5pm. Summer daily 9am-12.30pm
and 3.30-6pm.

Palazzo Ducale
06024 Gubbio (PG)
Open: Tuesday to Sunday 9am-1pm.

ROUTE 10B
Perugia
Ipogeo dei Volumni
Viale Roma
06100 Perugia (PG)
Open: Tuesday to Saturday 9am-5
or 6.30pm. Holidays 9am-1pm.

Collegio del Cambio
Palazzo dei Priori
Corso Vanucci
06100 Perugia (PG)
☎ (075) 61379
Open: Tuesday to Saturday 9am-
12.30pm and 2.30-5.30pm.
Holidays 9am-12.30pm.

Collegio del Mercanzia
(address as above)
☎ (075) 24836
Open: Tuesday to Saturday 9am-
12.30pm and 3-6pm. Holidays 9am-
12.30pm.

Galleria Nazionale dell'Umbria
(address as above)
☎ (075) 20316
Open: Tuesday to Saturday
8.45am-1.45pm and 3-7pm.
Holidays 9am-1pm.

Sala dei Notari
Palazzo dei Priori
Piazza IV Novembre
06100 Perugia (PG)
Open: Tuesday to Saturday 9am-
1pm and 3-7pm. Holidays 9am-
12noon and 3-7pm.

*Museo Archeologico Nazionale
   dell'Umbria*
San Domenico
Piazza G. Bruno
06100 Perugia (PG)
☎ (075) 27141
Open: daily 9am-1.30pm and 3-
6.30pm. Holidays 9am-1pm.

Antico Convento e Museo
Santa Maria degli Angeli
06081 Perugia (PG)
☎ (075) 819220
Open: daily 9am-12noon and 2.30-
6.30pm.

Assisi
San Francesco
Piazza San Francesco
06081 Assisi (PG)
Open: daily 9am-12noon and 2-5pm.

Foro Romano Museo
Via Portica
06081 Assisi (PG)
Open: winter Tuesday to Sunday
9.30am-12noon and 3-7pm.
Summer Tuesday to Sunday
9.30am-8pm.

Pinacoteca Comunale
Piazza del Comune
06081 Assisi (PG)
☎ (075) 812219
Open: Tuesday to Sunday 9.30am-
12noon and 3-7pm.

Museo Cripto Chiostro
Piazza San Rufino
06081 Assisi (PG)
Open: daily 9am-12noon and 2-7pm.

Eremo delle Carceri
06081 Assisi (PG)
Open: daily 8.30am-12noon and
2.30-7pm.

Convento di San Damiano
06081 Assisi (PG)
Open: winter daily 10am-12.30pm
and 2-4.45pm. Summer daily 10am-
12.30pm and 2-6pm.

ROUTE 10C
Spello
Santa Maria Maggiore
Via Cavour
06038 Spello (PG)
Open: winter daily 8am-12noon
and 3-5pm. Summer daily 8am-
12noon and 4-8pm.

Palazzo Comunale
Piazza della Repubblica
06038 Spello (PG)
☎ (0742) 65250
Open: Monday to Friday 8am-2pm.

Montefalco
Museo di San Francesco
Via Ringhiera Umbra
06036 Montefalco (PG)
☎ (0742) 79598
Open: Tuesday to Sunday 10am-
1pm and 3-6pm.

ROUTE 10D
Fonti del Clitunno
06042 Campello del Clitunno (PG)
Open: winter Tuesday to Sunday
9am-12noon and 3-6pm. Summer
Tuesday to Sunday 9am-12noon
and 4-7pm.

Spoleto
Pinacoteca
Palazzo Comunale
06049 Spoleto (PG)
☎ (0743) 2181 (Comune
switchboard)
Open: Tuesday to Sunday 10am-
1pm, 3-6pm.

Teatro Romano
Via delle Terme
06049 Spoleto (PG)
Open: daily 9am-1.30pm and 3-7pm.

San Gemini
Terme San Gemini
05029 San Gemini Fonte (TR)
☎ (0744) 630035 or 630426
Open: May to September daily
8.30am-12.30pm and 3-7pm.

Tourist Information Offices

ROUTE 10A
Pesaro
Ente Provinciale Turismo
4 Via Mazzolari
61100 Pesaro (PS)
☎ (0721) 30258

Urbino
Ufficio Informazioni
35 Piazza Duca Federico
61029 Urbino (PS)
☎ (0722) 2441

Gubbio
Azienda Autonoma di Soggiorno e
  Turismo
5 Piazza Oderisi
06024 Gubbio (PG)
☎ (075) 9273693

ROUTE 10B
Perugia
Azienda Promozione Turistica
21 Via Mazzini
06100 Perugia (PG)
☎ (075) 25341

Informazione Azienda Turistica
96A Corso Vanucci
06100 Perugia (PG)
☎ (075) 23327

Assisi
Azienda Autonoma di Soggiorno e
  Turismo
12 Piazza del Comune
06081 Assisi (PG)
☎ (075) 812534

ROUTE 10C
Spello
Pro Loco
21 Via Garibaldi
06038 Spello (PG)
☎ (0742) 651221

Bevagna
Pro Loco
Palazzo dei Consoli
Piazza Silvestri
06031 Bevagna (PG)
☎ (0742) 360123

Montefalco
Pro Loco
68 Corso Mameli
06036 Montefalco (PG)
☎ (0742) 79122

Trevi
Pro Loco Comune di Trevi
Piazza Mazzini
06039 Trevi (PG)
☎ (0742) 78528 or 78246

ROUTE 10D
Spoleto
L'Azienda di Promozione Turistica
Piazza della Liberta
06049 Spoleto (PG)
☎ (0743) 220311

San Gemini
Pro Loco
Porta Romana
05029 San Gemini (TR)
☎ (0744) 630130

Todi
Azienda Autonoma di Soggiorno e
  Turismo
38 Piazza del Popolo
06059 Todi (PG)
☎ (075) 883062

Northern Italy: Fact File

Accommodation

Hotels are generally classified on a star system, which ranges from one to five. The prices a hotel charges depends on its classification and on the season, the peak season running from 1 July to 1 September. The prices of *albergo*, *pensione* and *camere* are also determined by the local authorities, and like hotels, should have the tariffs displayed in each room.

Hotel reservations cannot be made through ENIT (Ente Nazionale Italiano per il Turismo) the Italian National Tourist Offices Abroad, although they do hold lists of organisations who can book hotels (normally 4 or 5 star) in all major tourist areas. EPT (Ente Provinciale Turismo), APT (Azienda di Promozione Turistica) or AA (Azienda Autonoma di Soggiorno e Turismo), the tourist offices found in most Italian towns, and the Pro Loco offices in smaller centres, hold comprehensive lists of hotels and *pensione*, and some will actually phone and book rooms for visitors. Most of the larger offices will supply accommodation lists on written request.

Camping

Camping is a major part of the Italian tourist industry and tourist offices hold details of the local sites. Federcampeggio, the Italian Camping Federation, publishes two lists of camp sites which cover the whole country. The first of these is a comprehensive list with details of all the country's sites, but a price is charged. The second is a more abbreviated list which is issued free. Either list may be obtained from:
Centro Internazionale Prenotazioni
Federcampeggio
Casella Postale 23
50041 Calenzano (FI)
☎ (055) 882391

Mountain Refuges

Most of the mountain huts *(rifugi)* are owned by the CAI (Club Alpino Italiano) and are priced according to their standard and the facilities they offer. Those accessible by road may resemble simple hotels, although generally most huts offer cheap overnight accommodation with basic facilities and simple meals for passing walkers. They are only open on a regular basis from early July to mid-September, although they may open at weekends at other times of the year, or if special arrangements are made. In popular areas, such as in the Dolomites, it is wise to book in advance, especially if the refuge lies on one of the more popular hiking routes. In any case always check at the local tourist office that a *rifugi* is open before heading off into the hills. Details about CAI *rifugi* are available from:

Club Alpino Italiano
3 Via Ugo Foscolo
20100 Milano (MI)
☎ (02) 802554 or 8057519

Student Hostels

Student's hostels are available in some of Italy's university towns and cities. Applications should be made to the Caso dello Studente. The places in which they are available are: Bologna, Ferrara, Florence (for university students only), Genoa, Modena, Milan, Parma, Perugia, Pisa, Rome, Siena, Urbino and Venice.

Youth Hostels

The International Youth Hostel Association has over fifty youth hostels in Italy, full details of which can be found in the International Youth Hostel Federation handbook. They are of a high standard and have good facilities. Many have family rooms but these must be booked in advance. It is also important to book in advance for hostels in major centres during busy periods to avoid disappointment. Reservations are made by placing a 30 per cent deposit. Further information is available from:

Associazione Italiana Alberghi per la Gioventu
44 Via Cavour
00184 Roma
☎ (06) 462342

Additional Information

In this section the addresses and opening times of places of interest are arranged chapter by chapter, under the same route headings and order as in the main guide. The addresses of tourist information centres are listed separately. The tourist offices in large towns are usually called Ente Provinciale per il Turismo or Azienda Autonoma di Soggiorno e Turismo, while in smaller places they are generally known as Pro Loco. The quality of service available from these tourist offices may be variable, although the vast majority are very helpful.

Where applicable opening times are given for summer (1 April to 30 September) and winter (1 October to 31 March), as well as holidays. The holidays include Sundays and public holidays, and any other auspicious date. Museum opening times may change slightly from year to year but will be substantially as stated.

Churches are generally open from 7am until around midday when they close for a couple of hours, before re-opening until sunset. Visitors should dress with respect and take care not to interrupt a service. When visiting cathedrals with important art works take a handful of coins to operate lights and phone guides and a good flashlight can be useful.

Climate

Italy's climate is as varied as its geography. In the winter the Alps are cold and dry, while the northern lakes and the coasts generally experience mild weather. Different again is the Po Plain and the area around Venice, which is cold and damp. The average January temperature in Cortina

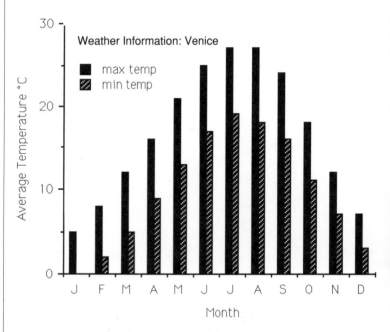

d'Ampezzo is -2.3°C (31.5°F), at Lake Como it is 6.0°C (42.8°F), in Rimini it is 6.7°C (44°F), and in Bologna it is 2.5°C (36.5°F). During the summer many people retreat inland to the mountain resorts in the Alps and Apennines as the lowlands become hot and the coasts humid. The average temperatures for July, the hottest month, are: 15.8°C (60.4°F) in Cortina d'Ampezzo; 23.7°C (74.6°F) at Lake Como; 24.3°C (75.7°F) in Rimini; and 26°C (78.8°F) in Bologna.

Credit Cards

All major credit cards (Access, American Express, Visa etc) are taken at most large restaurants, hotels and shops. Eurocheques and traveller's cheques are also usually accepted. The notable exceptions are filling

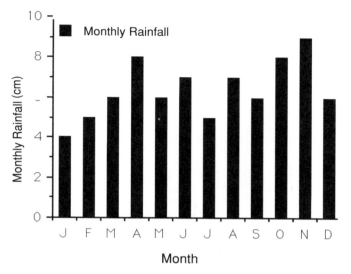

Month

stations, which tend to only accept money or fuel coupons. In the less-frequented parts of Italy it is also useful to have a certain amount of cash on hand as services seen throughout the rest of the country may not exist. Money can be changed at *cambio* offices in major towns, and banks elsewhere. It is normal procedure to show your passport, and all receipts should be kept. Banks are normally open between 8.30am and 12.30pm, and for an hour in the afternoon, between 3pm and 4pm, Monday to Fridays only.

Currency Regulations

The Italian monetary unit is the Lira (plural Lire). No traveller may import or export more than 500,000 Lire in cash, although unlimited amounts of sterling, dollars or traveller's cheques are permitted. It is advisable to check the current situation as the regulations will undoubtedly change after 1992.

Customs Regulations

Normal EEC Customs regulations apply. The Italian age limit for the import of duty-free alcohol and tobacco is 17 (this is largely a technicality as supermarket prices in Italy tend to be lower than duty-free prices for alcohol). Normal personal equipment (cameras, jewellery etc) can be taken into the country, but it is advisable to record all serial numbers and keep receipts for valuable items, to prove that they were not purchased in Italy. Any articles purchased in Italy which exceed the custom's

allowance set by your country are liable for duty.
No visa is required for stays of less than 3 months for holders of passports issued by the EEC, Britain, Ireland, Canada or the United States, but a valid passport is required.

Electricity

The electricity is 220 volts AC, 50 Hertz (cycles per second). Four different types of plug are commonly used — two with two pins and two with three pins in a line. While a two-pin continental adaptor is recommended, purchasing plugs on arrival is easy and inexpensive.

Embassies and Consulates

Foreign Embassies In Italy
UK
80A Via XX Settembre
00187 Roma
☎ (06) 4755441

USA
119A Via Veneto
00187 Roma
☎ (06) 4674

Canada
30 Via Zara
00198 Roma
☎ (06) 8441841

Australia
Via Alessandria 215
Rome
☎ (06) 832721

Foreign Consular Offices In Italy
UK
Palazzo Castelbarco
2 Lungarno Corsini
50123 Firenze (FI)
☎ (055) 212594 or 284133

2 Via XII Ottobre
16121 Genova (GE)
☎ (010) 564833

7 Via San Paolo
20121 Milano (MI)
☎ (02) 803442

60 Corso M. d'Azeglio
10126 Torino (TO)
☎ (011) 687832

1051 Accademia
30100 Venezia (VE)
☎ (041) 27207

USA
38 Lungarno Amerigo Vespucci
50100 Firenze (FI)
☎ (055) 298276

6 Piazza Portello
16100 Genova (GE)
☎ (010) 28274155

32 Piazza Repubblica
20124 Milano (MI)
☎ (02) 6528415

Canada
19 Via Vittor Pisani
20124 Milano (MI)
☎ (02) 652600

Emergency Services

For Fire, Police and Ambulance ☎ 113.
For immediate attention at airports, main railway stations and hospitals, look for the *pronto soccorso*, first aid service.
The Carabinieri are a semi-military police force who take care of civilian disturbances. Their telephone number is posted at the outskirts of every town. The Vigili Urbani take care of everyday problems.

Health Care

British and Irish travellers have a right to claim health services in Italy by virtue of EEC regulations. Form E111, available from the Department of Social Security, should be obtained before leaving Britain. Italian health services are administered by USL (Unita Sanitaria Locale). For minor problems it is advisable to use the extensive private sector as the problem may have resolved itself before you manage to see a doctor in the public health service.
American and Canadian tourists will need to check the validity of their personal health insurance to ensure they are adequately covered.
Drugs that are prescribed by a doctor and dispensed at a pharmacy (*farmacia*), are liable for a minimal local tax, which will not be reimbursed. The *farmacia* always has a list of pharmacies open at night and on Sundays.
Those wishing to walk in lonely mountain areas are advised to purchase *siero anti vipera* before beginning their walk. This is a vaccine to be taken after snakebites and is available over the counter in Italian pharmacies.

Holidays and Festivals

Shops, banks, offices, schools and some museums are closed for the national holidays as below.
New Year's Day
Epiphany (6 January)
Easter Monday
Liberation Day (25 April)
Labour Day (1 May)
Republic Day (2 June)
Assumption *Ferragosto* (15 August)
All Saints Day *Ognissanti* (1 November)
Immaculate Conception (8 December)
Christmas Day (25 December)
St Stephen's Day (26 December)
Some towns also celebrate their patron saints' day with a holiday. The main saints' days are listed below.
St Mark (25 April) Venice
St John the Baptist (24 June) Turin, Genoa, Florence
St Peter (29 June) Rome

St Petronius (4 October) Bologna
St Ambrose (7 December) Milan
In addition carnivals are held during February in the week before Lent, and local festivals in the summer. The following is a list of the major festivals and cultural events that take place in Northern Italy during the year.

February
Major carnivals in Venice, Milan, Verona and Ivrea

March to April
Holy week celebrations in Siena, Assisi, Gubbio and Florence
Easter Sunday — Explosion of the Cart, Florence

May
15 May — Festa dei Ceri, Gubbio
Last Sunday May — Crossbow Palio, Gubbio
May to June — Fiorentino Music Festival, Florence

June
1st week June — Calendimaggio, Assisi
1st Sunday June — Festa dei Navigli, Milan
16 to 17 June — Regatta of San Ranieri, Pisa
24 and 28 June — Gioco del Calcio, Florence
June to July — Festival of Two Worlds, Spoleto

July
2 July — Palio, Siena
16 to 24 July — Festa de'Noantri, Rome
25 July — Joust of the Bear, Pistoia
3rd Sunday July — Feast of the Redeemer, Venice
3rd Sunday July — Umbria Jazz, Perugia and Terni
July to August — Festival of Opera, Ballet and Concerts, Verona

August
2nd Sunday August — Joust of Falcon, Massa Marittima
14 August — Torta dei Fieschi, Lavagna
16 August — Second Palio, Siena
August to September — International Film Festival, Venice

September
European Cinema Festival, Rimini
Biennial Flower Show, Pescia
Music Festival, Turin
3 September — Feast of Santa Rosa, Viterbo
1st Sunday September — Regatta, Venice
1st Sunday September — Joust of Saracens, Arezzo
7 to 8 September — Festa delle Rificolone, Florence
14 September — Holy Cross Procession, Lucca

3rd Sunday September — Palio, Asti

October
1st Sunday October — Palio & Truffle Fair, Alba

November
21 November — Festa della Salute, Venice

Language

Italian is a straightforward language in which words are written as they are pronounced and each letter has only one sound (except for the letters e,o,c and g which have two each).

The basic pronunciation rules are as follows:

c before e or i is pronounced ch (as in cheese) eg. *vicino* (near) veecheeno elsewhere *c* is pronounced as in cat eg. *camera* (bedroom)

ch is pronounced *k* eg. *perche* (why/because) pairkay

e is pronounced either as in *hen* or as the *a* in *day* eg. *ecco* (here) echo or *che* (what) kay

g before *e* and *i* is pronounced *j* eg. *Germania* (Germany) jairmarnia elsewhere *g* is hard eg. *grosso* (big)

gl is pronounced *ly* eg. *aglio* (garlic) alyoe

gn is pronounced *nye* as at the beginning of new eg. *gnomo* (gnome) nye-omo

h is silent eg. *ha* (has) a

sc before *e* and *i* is pronounced *sh* eg. *fascismo* (fascism) fasheezmoe elsewhere *sc* is pronounced *sk* eg. *tasca* (pocket) taska

z and *zz* are pronounced *ts* or *ds (dz)*, although this tends to vary according to the local dialect, eg. *mezza* (medza)

Useful Phrases
Si — Yes (see)
No — No
Per favore or *Per piacere* — Please
Grazie — Thank you (gratseeay)
Prego — Don't mention it (pray-go)
Va Bene — All right (va bayney)
Buongiorno — Good morning (bwon-jorno)
Buona Sera — Good afternoon/Good evening (bwona saira)
Buona Notte — Good night (bwona nottay)
Dov'e? — Where is? (doughve)
Quando? — When? (kwandough)
Che Cosa? — What? (kay koza)
Quanto? — How much? (kwantoe)
Quanto Costa? — How much does it cost? (kwantoe kosta)
Parla Inglese? — Do you speak English? (parla in-glay-say)
Non Capisco — I don't understand (known capee-sko)
Posso Avere? — Can I have? (posso av-ay-ray)
Vorrei — I would like (vorray)
Mi Scusi — Excuse me (me skuzee)

Aperto — Open (a-pair-toe)
Chiuso — Closed (queue-zoe)
Caldo — Hot (cal-doe)
Freddo — Cold (fray-doe)
Grande — Large (gran-day)
Piccolo — Small (pronounced as the instrument)
Buono — Good (bwon-oh)
Cattivo — Bad (ca-teevoe)
Invernale — Winter (in-ver-narlay)
Estate — Summer (e-start-ay)
Festivo — Holiday (fest-ee-voe)

Feriale — Working day (fair-ee-arlay)
Cambio — Currency exchange (cam-bee-oh)

Numbers
Zero — 0
Uno — 1
Due — 2
Tre — 3
Quattro — 4
Cinque — 5
Sei — 6
Sette — 7
Otto — 8
Nove — 9
Dieci — 10
Venti — 20
Trenta — 30
Quaranta — 40
Cinquanta — 50
Sessanta — 60
Settanta — 70
Ottanta — 80
Novanta — 90
Cento — 100
Duecento — 200
Mille — 1,000
Duemila — 2,000
Tremila — 3,000
Un Milione — 1,000,000

Un Miliardo — 1,000,000,000
Primo — First
Secondo — Second
Terzo — Third

In the Hotel
Una camera — A room
Due, Tre camere — Two, Three rooms
Con bagno — With bathroom (cone banyoe)
Con doccia — With shower (cone dot-chee-ah)
Giorni — Days (jor-knee)
Una settimana — A week (oona set-tim-arna)
La colazione — Breakfast (col-lats-ee-oh-nay)
La cena — Evening meal (latchaynah)

Motoring
Accendere i Fari in Galleria — Use Headlights in Tunnel
Tenere la Destra (Sinistra) — Keep Right (Left)

Divieto di Sosta (or *Sosta Vietata*) — No Parking
Avanti — Walk (at pedestrian crossings)
Entrata — Entrance
Uscita — Exit
Lavori in Corso — Roadworks in Progress
Pericolo — Danger
Rallentare — Slow Down
Polizia Stradale — Highway Police
Senso Unico — One Way Street
Divieto di Sorpasso — No Overtaking
Sosta Autorizzato — Parking Allowed (followed by times)
Vicolo Cieco — No Through Road
Zona Pedonale — Pedestrian Zone
Strada Privata — Private Road
Parcheggio — Carpark

In the Restaurant
Il conto — The bill
La lista — The menu
Vino Bianco — White wine
Vino Rosso or *Vino Nero* — Red wine
Vino della casa — House wine, order this by the *litro* or
    Mezzo litro — (litre or half litre)
Servizio compreso — Service charge included
Acqua minerale gassata — Fizzy mineral water
Acqua minerale non gassata — Still mineral water

Sightseeing
Duomo/Cattedrale — Cathedral
Chiesa — Church
Parrochiale — Parish church
Badia — Benedictine monastery
Campanile — Bell-tower
Chiostro — Cloisters
Cripta — Crypt
Tomba — Tomb
Broletto — Town Hall
Comune — Town Council
Loggia — Covered gallery, arcade or balcony
Pinacoteca — Picture gallery
Museo — Museum
Palazzo — Mansion, important building
Bottega — Artist's Studio
Centro Storico — Historic Centre
Castello — Castle
Rocca — Fortress

Maps

Both Lascelles and Touring Club Italiano produce good 1:800,000 scale maps of the entire country. Bartholomew's 1:1,000,000 easy fold map is handy for navigating, and the Michelin map of the same scale is clear and reliable. Touring Club Italiano also produce excellent 1:200,000 scale maps of each region. The 1:50,000 scale maps produced by Kompass Carta Turistica show a good amount of detail and are particularly useful for hikers. Most of the local tourist offices in Italy issue free maps of individual provinces, as well as town plans.

Measurements

The metric system is used in Italy. Conversions are:
1 kilogram (1,000 grams) = 2.2lb
1 litre = $1^3/_4$ pints
4.5 litres = 1 gallon
8km = 5 miles

Police Registration

All tourists must register with the police within 3 days of entering the country. If you stay at a hotel, campsite etc this will be carried out for you.

Post and Telephone Services

Stamps (*francoboli*) are sold at both post offices and tobacconists. Post offices are normally open from: 8.30am to 1.30pm, Monday to Friday; and 8.30am to 12.30pm on Saturdays. Central post offices in larger towns generally offer postal services up until 7 or 8pm. Tobacconists (*tabaccherie*), recognised by the 'T' sign in front of their shop, are normally open from 8.30am to 1pm, and 3.30pm to 8pm, Monday to Saturday.

Public telephones take coins of 100, 200 and 500 Lire, as well as *gettoni* (200 Lire tokens). *Gettoni* are available at tobacconists, bars or news stands, and are sometimes given as change. Some public phones take magnetic phone cards which can be purchased, for 5,000 or 10,000 Lire, at airports, railway stations, public phone offices (SIP) and authorised vendors. Bars often have *telefoni a scatti* which record the number of units for each call; this avoids the need to be continually feeding in small change, but the bar price usually includes a small surcharge. In larger towns, the SIP (Societa Italiana Telefoni), the Italian Telephone Company, provide soundproof booths complete with a meter.

Dial codes from Italy are:
Great Britain 0044
Canada 001
USA 001
Australia 0061

Remember to leave out the first zero of your home country number — eg to dial the Italian Tourist Office in London (071 4081254) from Italy dial 0044 71 4081254.

Photography

All types of film are widely available in Italy, but prices vary and are generally most expensive in popular tourist centres. In almost all museums and churches it is forbidden to use tripods or flash so it is well-worth purchasing a 1000 ASA film when planning to visit indoor sights, although in summer any film faster than 200ASA will make outdoor photography difficult. Some museums, and particularly galleries, forbid photography altogether.

Travel

By Air

Rome and Milan have the main international airports, but Bologna, Genoa, Pisa, Turin and Venice also handle international flights and internal flights run between Ancona, Bergamo, Florence, Rimini and Verona. Alitalia, British Airways, British Caledonian and Aer Lingus are the major airlines flying to Italy from the UK, while either Alitalia, Pan Am or TWA handle most flights from the USA. Most airlines offer discounts to students and those under 26. For information about budget charter flights contact your local travel agents.

By Rail

Italy can be reached by rail from all major European cities. It takes about 24 hours from London to Rome, and the two main routes are: London Victoria-Lille-Basel-Como-Milan-Florence-Rome.

Reduced international tickets, such as Interail cards, are available to those under 26, while in Italy itself a *Carta Verde* can be purchased by young people aged 12 to 26 which gives 30 per cent discount during low season and 20 per cent in high season. Tourists whose normal place of residence is outside Italy may purchase a *biglietto turistico libera circolazione*. This ticket allows unlimited travel on the Italian state rail network, and does not require a supplement for travel on the *Rapido* (see below). Italian National Tourist Offices (see addresses in the Additional Information sections) will provide details of where tickets may be purchased.

In addition regular reductions are available for day returns (maximum distance 50km/31 miles), and 3 day returns (maximum distance 250km/155 miles). Discounts are also offered to families and to parties of between 10 and 20 people. Children under 4, not occupying a seat, travel free, while children under 12 receive a 50 per cent reduction. Those making a round trip of at least 1,000km (620 miles) are also eligible for a special-priced circular ticket. Alternatively, there is a reduced price *chilometrico* ticket, valid for 3,000km (1,860 miles), which can be used by up to 5 people for a maximum of 20 different journeys over a period of 2 months.

The Italian rail system is notoriously difficult and prone to strikes, but it is comprehensive and almost any town can be reached by rail. Visitors are advised to make seat reservations, particularly during August. Italian trains are classified as below:

Super-rapido (Trans Europa Express). Very fast, luxury class only, supplements are payable and seat booking is obligatory.

Rapido. Fast inter-city trains. Some are first class only. Supplement charged (about 30 per cent of standard fare, children pay full supplement). On some trains seat booking is obligatory.

Espresso. Long-distance trains between cities, stopping only at major stations.

Diretto. Trains stopping at most reasonable-sized towns. Look at timetables carefully as there is often little difference between *Espresso* and *Diretto*.

Locale. Stopping at all stations.

A useful but rather expensive French motorail service operates between Boulogne (or Paris) and Milan. It runs twice weekly during the summer and the journey takes 15 hours.

By Road
Coaches and Buses

An extensive, long-distance, express coach system operates between cities within Italy, but also offers links to many of the major European cities. The main route from London passes through Dover, Paris, Mont Blanc, Aosta, Turin, Milan, Venice, Bologna, Florence to Rome.

There is also a good network of local bus services and even the smallest village generally has at least one bus a day to its nearest town. Tickets for buses in towns and cities are sold at main bus stops, tobacconists and news-stands. Some major cities offer a tourist day pass which is valid on all public transport.

Cars

The journey by road from London to Rome is over 1,500km (930 miles). It is best to go over the Alps, as passing through the south of France adds a considerable amount to the journey and the roads are very crowded in summer.

Recommended Routes

1 Boulogne/Calais, Rheims, Lausanne, Great Saint Bernard, Milan, A1 Autostrada.
2 Boulogne, Paris, Bourg en Bresse, Mont Blanc, Milan, A1 Autostrada.
3 Ostende, Munich, Innsbruck, Brenner, Milan, A1 Autostrada.

Fuel

All fuel is comparatively expensive in Italy. Diesel is somewhat cheaper than petrol, and lead-free petrol is offered at a slight discount. The Italian authorities also offer a discount of around 15 per cent on pump prices to all foreign visitors travelling in their own cars. The discount coupons are available from ACI (Automobile Club Italiano) at major border crossings, or from the AA and RAC in the UK. In order to receive the coupons it is necessary to present a passport and vehicle registration document. The coupon booklet also contains five 2,000 Lire *autostrada* tokens (which will just about cover the journey to Milan) and entitles the holder, to call on the free ACI breakdown service, and to free car hire for up to 10 days if their vehicle is off the road and being repaired for more than 12 hours. Two grades of fuel (gasoline) are available: *Benzina, Normale* and *Benzina Super,* and lead free fuel is also widely available. Filling stations usually close for lunch between 12.30pm and 3pm, and many are shut on Sundays. The service stations on motorways, however, are open 24 hours a day.

Driving Restrictions

When in Italy drive on the right hand side of the road. Nearly all Italian motorways are toll-roads with tickets usually dispensed automatically on entry, and payment made on exit. Speed limits on motorways vary, depending on the day of the week and whether it happens to be an important or popular holiday, and on the size of the car in question. The general limits however are 130kph (80mph) on weekdays and 110kph (68mph) at other times. On country roads the speed limit is 90kph (56mph) and in urban areas 50kph (31mph). There are heavy on-the-spot fines for speeding, so visitors should take care to observe the speed restriction signs.

Parking facilities in the larger towns are generally inadequate and it is usually quicker to park well out of the centre and proceed on foot or by public transport than to attempt to find a space in the centre. Check when you park your car you are not in a *zona rimozione* (removal zone) where cars are towed away and are reclaimable at great time and expense, or in a *zona disco,* which means cars are only allowed to park for a limited period and must have a disc (available from filling stations) which shows the hour of arrival in their front window. The authorised parking lots and meters in a town usually charge by the hour, the closer to the centre the higher the tariffs.

Driving Documents and Requirements

All vehicle documents: registration, insurance and driving licence must be carried at all time with on-the-spot penalties for offenders. Visitors should also carry a translation of their driving licence, available from the AA, RAC or Italian State Tourist Authorities. It is compulsory for front seat passengers to wear seatbelts at all times, and children under 5 must be strapped into a child car seat. It is also compulsory to have a nationality plate and a left hand wing mirror, and to carry a red warning triangle.

Mopeds

No driving licence is required for mopeds in Italy and anyone over 14 may use them.

Car Hire

Car hire is available at airports, main stations and in most large towns. The major international firms are represented throughout Italy, supplemented by local firms. Most British and American travel agents selling flights or package holidays to Italy will be able to offer competitive terms for car hire.

Ferries

Ferries operate on the inland lakes of Northern Italy as well as along the coasts. The addresses of the main ferry companies on the lakes are as follows:

Navigazione sul Lago Maggiore
1 Via Baracca
28041 Arona (NO)
☎ (0322) 46651

Navigazione Lago Como
1 Piazza Volta
22100 Como (CO)
☎ (031) 260234

Regione Lombardia Gestione Navigazione Lago d'Iseo
16 Via Nazionale
24062 Costa Volpino (BG)
☎ (035) 971483

Navigazione Lago Garda
Piazza Matteotti
25015 Desenzano (BS)
☎ (030) 9141321

Ferries to the island of Elba are operated from Piombino by the following company:
Torremar
13-14 Piazzale Premuda
57025 Piombino (LI)
☎ (0565) 31100

Ferries to the small islands of Isola Giglio and Isola Giannutri are operated from Porto Santo Stefano by the following companies:
Maregiglio Agenzia Marittima Palombo
Casella Postale 54
58019 Porto Santo Stefano (GR)
☎ (0564) 812920

Toremar
Piazzale Candi
58019 Porto Santo Stefano (GR)
☎ (0564) 814615

Tipping

Service charge of 15 per cent and IVA (VAT) of 19 per cent are included on most restaurant and hotel bills. However, it is normal to give an extra 5 per cent of the bill for satisfactory service. The same is also true for cafés and bars, particularly in the more upmarket places. Remember that in Italy there is also a table charge for sitting in a café which can be quite prohibitive in tourist spots. Cinema and theatre usherettes expect small tips, and porters are generally tipped about 1,000 Lire per suitcase. Other people you might expect to tip are washroom attendants and service station attendants who clean the windscreen. Taxi drivers expect a tip of 10 per cent and tourist guides are normally tipped 1,000 Lire per person.

Tourist Information Centres

Italian State Tourist Offices (ENIT):
UK
1 Princes Street
London W1R 8AY
☎ (071) 408 1254

USA
630 Fifth Avenue
Suite 1565 Rockefeller Centre
New York NY 10111
☎ (212) 245 4961 or 4822

500 North Michigan Avenue
Suite 1046
Chicago IL 60611
☎ (312) 644 0990

360 Post Street
Suite 801
San Francisco CA 94109
☎ (415) 392 6206

Canada
Store 56
Plaza
3 Place Ville Marie
Montreal
Quebec H3B 2E3
☎ (514) 866 7667 or 7668 or 7669

Index

Visitor's Guides
Tour & Explore with MPC Visitor's Guides

Austria
Austria: Tyrol & Vorarlberg

Britain:
Cornwall & Isles of Scilly
Cotswolds
Devon
East Anglia
Guernsey, Alderney and Sark
Hampshire & the Isle of Wight
Denmark
Jersey
Kent
Lake District
Scotland: Lowlands
Somerset, Dorset & Wiltshire
North Wales and Snowdonia
North York Moors, York & Coast
Northumbria
Northern Ireland
Peak District
Sussex
Yorkshire Dales & North Pennines

Crete
Egypt
Finland
Florida

France:
Alps & Jura
Corsica
Dordogne
Loire
Massif Central
Normandy Landing Beaches
Provence & Côte d'Azur

Germany:
Bavaria
Black Forest
Rhine & Mosel
Southern Germany

Iceland

Italy:
Florence & Tuscany
Italian Lakes
Northern Italy
Mauritius, Rodrigues & Reunion
Peru

Spain:
Costa Brava to Costa Blanca
Mallorca, Menorca, Ibiza & Formentera
Northern & Central Spain
Southern Spain & Costa del Sol

Sweden
Switzerland
Tenerife
Turkey
Yugoslavia: The Adriatic Coast

World Traveller
The new larger format Visitor's Guides

Belgium & Luxembourg
Czechoslovakia
France
Holland
Norway
Portugal
USA

A complete catalogue of all our travel guides to over 125 destinations is available on request